ESSAYS ON
KIERKEGAARD

Edited by
JERRY H. GILL

Associate Professor of Philosophy
Florida Presbyterian College
St. Petersburg

Formerly of
Southwestern at Memphis
Memphis, Tennessee

Cover design by JEREMY GILL

Burgess Publishing Company

426 South Sixth Street • Minneapolis, Minn. 55415

Copyright ©1969 by Burgess Publishing Company
All rights reserved

Library of Congress Catalog Card Number 72-88030

Standard Book Number 8087-0724-8

Printed in the United States of America

DEDICATED TO
WILLIAM H. POTEAT

PREFACE

Søren Kierkegaard, an intellectual time-bomb! Although he wrote in the 19th Century, Kierkegaard's ideas did not explode upon the Western intellectual world until the 20th Century. Both the contemporary philosophical and theological scenes have been profoundly affected by this explosion, and chances are that in coming generations thinkers will still be working under the influence of Kieregaardian "fall-out."

Although there have been hundreds of volumes and articles produced on and about Kierkegaard's thought, for a variety of reasons very few have been made accessible to the American undergraduate and graduate student. Sometimes the treatments are too scholarly to be of use, while in other cases a single author's extended account provides only one slant on the vast complexity which is Kierkegaard. In addition, the general inaccessibility of journal articles for classroom use has too often left a professor quite frustrated as to how to introduce students to Kierkegaardian scholarship in a well-rounded and direct fashion.

The present volume is designed to meet precisely this need. It seeks to provide the student of Kierkegaard with a collection of recent articles by reliable scholars, dealing with the major dimensions of Kierkegaard's thought. These selections can be understood by the beginning student and are pertinent to the American philosophical and theological scene. It should go without saying (but just so there will be no mistake, let it be said) that the reading of this volume can in no way be substituted for a firsthand wrestling with Kierkegaard's writings themselves. Robert Bretall's *Kierkegaard Anthology* (Modern Library) is still the best single volume for this purpose. Hopefully, the essays in this present volume will cast a great deal of light on such a firsthand study—and vice versa.

I should like to add a word of appreciation for those who have contributed in a special way to making this book a reality. Two professors, Paul Dietrichson (University of Washington) and William Poteat (Duke University), provided the insight and stimulation for my study of Kierkegaard. Also, I owe a special debt of gratitude to Mr. James Gordon Baker of the Burgess Publishing Company for his friendly perseverance.

i

CONTENTS

PART ONE

THE PHILOSOPHICAL CONTEXT
INTRODUCTION

Any thinker can be understood only in relation to the main themes and problems of his time; thus it is important, in coming to grips with Søren Kierkegaard's thought, to obtain some perspective on how he relates to the philosophical movements which immediately preceded him and to those which stem from him. In a word, it is important to see how Kierkegaard fits into the history of philosophy. While not exhaustive on this subject, the essays comprising the first part of this collection relate SK's thought to certain key persons and issues in the history of philosophy and illuminate the main themes of his thought.

Philosophers often warn against committing the "genetic fallacy" of basing one's understanding and estimation of a thinker's work upon factors pertaining to his life. While this is good general advice, there are thinkers whose work cannot be understood or evaluated apart from an awareness of the events and quality of their lives. SK is one of these thinkers. His life and thought are so inextricably related that it is necessary to begin one's study of him with a consideration of the people who played central roles in the drama that was his life.

The life of Søren Kierkegaard may be viewed as a life of growth through conflict. There seem to have been eight major conflicts in his life, all of which were worked through and resolved. Two of these were personal (with himself and God), two inter-personal (with his father and Regina), two ideological (with the esthetic and the speculative), and two public (with the *Corsair* and the church).

SK's conflict with himself dominated his childhood. The motto "half childsplay/half God in the heart" sums it up: on the one hand he possessed a great imagination and dialectical intelligence, while on the other hand he was attracted to, and made melancholy by, Christianity. He was half happy and intelligent child and half serious and melancholy adult. SK's conflict with his father dominated his youth. The break between them came when SK, who had a growing uneasiness about his father's faith, became aware ("the great earthquake") that his father had had premarital relations with his mother while she was yet a servant girl in his father's household. This break led SK down "the path of perdition" to sins of his own. A reunion between father and son climaxed SK's ethical reform and conversion ("indescribable joy") immediately prior to his father's death.

SK's early manhood was marked by conflict with Regina and the esthetical. He broke off his engagement to Regina, even though he still loved her, because he could not disclose his father's secret to her, and because he felt his oddness would ruin her. He expressed his conversion from "the esthetical way of life" in *Either/Or* and several *Edifying Discourses*. SK reached intellectual maturity by means of his conflict with "the speculative" and with *The Corsair*. He expressed the former in *The Fragments* and *The Postscript*, which are devoted to exposing the fallacy of objectivity and to stressing the necessity of "truth as subjectivity." *The Corsair* ridiculed SK's odd appearance and life, but he was able to absorb and endure this criticism.

SK obtained religious maturity when he resolved his conflict with God. He finally accepted the full forgiveness of God of his sins, and no longer had to make use of "indirect communication" by means of pseudonyms. Instead, he used "direct communication" and the Christian pseudonym "anti-climacus" (cf. *The Point of View*). The final conflict of his life, that with "Christendom," enabled SK to offer himself as a "corrective sacrifice" to offset the evils and limitations of his day. He attacked the church by focusing on Professor Martensen and Bishop Mynster in *The Fatherland* and his own *Instant* (cf. *Attack Upon Christendom*). He became partially paralyzed, and later died in the midst of this attack.

The first essay in Part One (Chapter One) is devoted to correlating the major events of SK's life with the main emphases of his thought. Such a correlation provides an excellent introduction to SK. In addition to providing some genuine insights into SK's thought, this essay—which has never before been available in America—provides numerous factual details and pictures which lead to a deeper appreciation of SK's life. At the conclusion of this introduction, there is a chart (compiled by the editor) which summarizes the relationship between the major events and works in SK's life.

The second essay (Chapter Two) in Part One aims at tracing out the place SK is to be given in the overall development of existentialism as a philosophical position. Although attempts to trace the existentialist motif back to Socrates are perhaps a bit overdrawn, it is true that SK was not the first thinker in the history of philosophy to stress the points which he stressed. In one way or another, Tertullian, Augustine, Luther, Pascal, Nietzsche and Dostoyevski all share in the tradition which finally emerges as existentialism. Each in his own way emphasizes the primary of personal commitment, the limitations of reason, and a deep suspicion concerning human, social institutions (the establishment).

Since SK's time a large number of thinkers have drawn either positive or negative inspiration from him: Barth, Tillich, the Niebuhrs, Sartre, Camus, Marcell, Heidegger, Jaspers, Maritain, Unamuno, W. H. Auden, etc. It is to be borne in mind, of course, that generally speaking those who follow in the wake of SK's efforts, as well as those who preceded him, may be divided into two main groups: religious existentialists and atheistic existentialists. This fact raises another issue which is dealt with in the second essay of Part One, namely, in what sense can one speak of existentialism as a philosophy, since its so-called proponents are so diverse? Moreover, does not the very character of the existentialist stance systematically negate the possibility of treating it as a philosophical position or system? (This is a problem with which Chapter Eight of the present volume wrestles also.)

From a strictly philosophical point of view, the main area of concern in SK's writings is that of epistemology. This concern SK shares with all philosophers working in the shadow of early modern philosophy (17th and 18th centuries). The development of rationalist thought on the continent and empiricist thought in Britain focused almost exclusive attention upon such questions as "What is truth?", "How does one obtain it?", "What are the criteria for recognizing it?" The rationalist and empiricist traditions culminated, and to a large degree were synthesized, in the philosophy of Immanuel Kant. At the heart of Kant's work was a concern for the possibility of religious knowledge, and SK wrote within the context which had been constructed by Kant and his immediate predecessors.

The third essay in Part One (Chapter Three) examines the relation between Kant's response to the empiricist challenge of Hume and SK's efforts to construct a religious epistemology. The thesis is that the relation between the thought of Kant and SK is essentially one of parallelism. Chapter Four is concerned with the relation between SK's work and the rationalist position of Lessing, who had concluded that religious (eternal) truth could not have any relation to factual (historical) truth. Its thesis is that SK was in essential agreement with Lessing.

THE LIFE AND WORKS OF SØREN KIERKEGAARD

PERIODS	DATES	EVENTS	WORKS
Childhood Conflict with self	1813	Born May 5th, at 2 (now 27) Nytorv, Copenhagen. Now a police station.	
	1828	Confirmed (April 20) at 14 by Bishop Mynster	
	1830	Entered University of Copenhagen (Oct.) at 17	
Youth Conflict with father	1830–1834	Studied at University, sister and brother died (Tutored by Martensen)	
	1834	Mother (July) and sister (Dec.) died.	First article (Dec.)
	1835	The great earthquake	
	1837	First met Regina Olsen—taught Latin for 1 yr.	
	1838	"Indescribable joy" entry in Journal (May) Father died (Aug.) (re-union)	Short book (Sept.) Criticism of Hans C. Andersen's novel
Early Manhood Conflict with Regina and conflict with the esthetical	1840	Completed theology examination (cum laude) July Toured Jutland (Aug.) Engaged to Regina (Sept.)	
	1841	Completed M.A. thesis (Sept.) Preached first sermon (Holmens Church) Broke engagement to Regina (Oct.) Visited Berlin (Oct.)	Socratic Irony (dissertation) Sept.
	1842	Returned from Berlin (Mar.)	
	1843	Returned to Berlin (May)	(1) Either/Or (2) Fear & Trembling (3) Repetition (4) Many Edifying Discourses

Period	Year		Works
	1844	Moved from 230 (now 28) Norregade to his first home on Nytorv	(1) Philosophical Fragments (2) The Concept of Dread (3) More Edifying Discourses
Intellectual Maturity Conflict with the speculative and conflict with the *Corsair*	1845	Brief visit to Berlin (May)	Stages on the Road of Life
	1846	Brief visit to Berlin (May) *Corsair* attacked S.K. (Jan.-Oct.) Visited King Christian VIII	(1) Concluding Unscientific P.S. (Feb.) (2) The Present Age (Mar.)
	1847	Regina married to Schlegel (Nov.) S.K. sold 2 Nytorv	(1) Edifying Discourses (Purity of Heart) Mar. (2) Works of Love (Sept.) (3) The Book on Alder (Dec.)
	1848	War and revolution (March-April) S.K. achieved personal adequacy (metamorphosis Journal entry) April	Point of View (published 1859)
Religious Maturity Conflict with God	1849	Returned to Christianity (use of anti-climacus)	(1) More religious discourses (2) Sickness unto Death (July)
	1850	Moved back to Norregade	(1) Training in Christianity (July) (2) More edifying discourses
	1852-1854	Reflected on his "attack" (loading the gun)	Many Journal entries
The Corrective Sacrifice Conflict with the Church	1854	Bishop Mynster died (July) Prof. Martensen named successor	Article against Martensen in *The Fatherland* (Dec.)
	1855	S.K. launched "attack" (Oct. 2) S.K. hospitalized (Oct. 11) S.K. died (Nov. 11) aged 42 S.K. buried (Nov. 18) Huge crowd	(1) Articles in *The Fatherland* (Jan.-May) (2) *The Instant* Published May-Oct.

CHAPTER ONE

SØREN KIERKEGAARD:
THE FATHER OF EXISTENTIALISM

by Peter P. Rohde

Søren Kierkegaard was born in 1813, the year when, as he says himself, 'so many another bad note was put into circulation'; an allusion to the national bankruptcy which followed on six years of hopeless war with Britain as an ally of Napoleon, a partnership that was practically forced upon Denmark when in a sudden attack and the bombardment of Copenhagen in 1807 the British destroyed or captured the considerable Danish fleet. The period following the war and bankruptcy was the poorest in Danish history, and it was these years of poverty which provided the setting for Kierkegaard's life.

He died in 1855, two years before the abolition of the 400-year-old Sound Dues, which had long been the principal source of national revenue; two years before the passage of the law introducing internal freedom of trade and transforming Denmark from a conservative society regulated by guilds into a modern liberal democracy; and two years before the demolition of the fortifications which surrounded the capital, Copenhagen, and which for several hundred years had checked its growth, and the inclusion of new areas under the municipality for factories and working-class housing, whereby the city was converted from a large provincial-like centre into a modern metropolis.

The year 1857 was thus the year, above all others, when the new age burst the fetters of the past and the old society was radically transformed by industrialism. Yet that old society, with its conservative and traditional outlook, the society of the guilds and Absolutism, formed the social background to Kierkegaard's life and work.

In such a setting a man can react in one of two ways: he can acquiesce, or he can rebel. Kierkegaard acquiesced, and turned from the affairs of this world; but it may be worth noting that there was another who chose deliberately to rebel, and whose posthumous fame has been no less remarkable than Kierkegaard's. This was Karl Marx. While Marx and Engels were drafting their political programme, *The Communist Manifesto*, Kierkegaard, at exactly the same time, was writing his religious manifesto, *The Works of Love* (Kaerlighedens Gerninger).

Reprinted with permission from the author, Peter P. Rohde

For all their great differences, the two men have many points of resemblance. They sprang from the same social situation, and both reacted against the prevailing contemporary philosophy, Hegelianism, though in very different ways. Marx wanted to apply it by, as he said, 'turning it upside down'; or rather, turning right side up what Hegel had turned upside down. Kierkegaard aimed at something far more radical: he meant to destroy the entire Hegelian system, on the principle that it is impossible to contain the multiplicity of life in a system. A system of thought is possible, but not one of life. It is this basic idea which, more than any other, inspires Kierkegaard's work, and which has significantly influenced recent philosophy through Existentialism.

Kierkegaard's life was uneventful, but to the ethical and religious personality it is not events which matter. He experiences and is moulded by the few events, and makes an indelible impression by his personality on those he comes in contact with. Those whom Kierke-

■ Søren Kierkegaard at the age of 27, together with his signature, and flanked by his pen, reading glass, and pipe. On the extreme left is his reading-glass case, traditionally held to have been made by Regine Olsen. Though deeply in love with the girl, he broke off their engagement; and the love story left many traces on his works. Regine Olsen afterwards married Johan Frederik Schlegel, Governor of the Danish West Indies, now the American Virgin Islands.

gaard came into special, and vital, contact with were his father, who made him a believer; Regine, the girl to whom he became engaged, and who made him a poet; the writer Meïr Aron Goldschmidt, who occasioned his contempt for the world; and the bishops Mynster and Martensen, whom Kierkegaard saw as the personification of perverted 'Christendom.'

The Father—or Faith

Michael Pedersen Kierkegaard came of poor peasant stock in West Jutland, where poor soil and a bleak climate have engendered a puritan outlook that is apparent in the population even today.

Michael Pedersen had been a shepherd boy. That was when the heath had covered nearly the whole of Jutland and allowed few other occupations but sheep-farming and the associated wool-combing; today the same regions are the centre of a highly developed textile industry. Michael Pedersen's childhood was not very different from that of most Jutland children then, and was poor, drab, and lonely. As a young man he travelled to the capital and settled there as a wool merchant. Luck went with him, and in time he made a considerable fortune. He became a well-known figure, and his house was the meeting-place of some of the city's intellectuals; for though he had received no formal education, he was able, thanks to his keen brain combined with a lively imagination, to debate on equal terms with university men. But behind his passion for debate and philosophy lay the anxieties of a troubled mind. The son had inherited his father's logical mind and imagination, as well as a deep and inveterate melancholy.

'There was a father and a son. Both very intellectually gifted; both witty, especially the father. Everyone who knew and visited their house found it, I think, very entertaining. As a general rule, they would argue and converse like two good wits, not as father and son. On a rare occasion, looking at his son and finding him very concerned, the father quietly confronted him and said: Poor child, you go in silent despair!' So Kierkegaard writes in his journals, where he also asserts that his father had made of his childhood a torment without equal. Why? The father had aimed at bringing the child up as a thinker, a writer, an ethical man, and a Christian. And the child had early come to realize that there was a strange inconsistency between his father's piety and his mental unrest. He says in the journals: 'The worst danger is not when the father is a freethinker, or even when he is a hypocrite. No, the danger is when he is a pious and godfearing man, when the child is deeply and intensely convinced of this, and yet feels that a deep disquiet lies hidden in his soul, to which not even godliness and piety itself could bring peace. The danger is that the situation will lead the child to conclude that God is not, after all, the God of infinite love.'

In short, there is a nagging suspicion which is spoiling the relations between the father and son and disturbing the son's religious peace. To quote the journals: 'A relationship between father and son, where the son finds out everything that lies hidden, and yet dare not credit it. The father is a man of substance, godfearing and stern; only once, when intoxicated, he lets out a few words which give rise to the most dreadful suspicions. Otherwise the son never hears of it, and dare not ask either his father or anyone else.'

What is was that the son in an unguarded moment had found out cannot be known for certain, but we may suppose that it was connected with sex, knowing as we do that the father married his servant a year after the death of his first wife and that this second wife (Søren Kierkegaard's mother) gave birth to a son two months after the wedding.

Certainly, however, the revelation was a mental shock to the son, shaking his former, absolute confidence in his father. More than that, his whole moral outlook was affected, and he plunged desperately into a period of dissipation, in which he completely neglected his theological studies at the University. He had acquired from his father a religiosity, almost of the Old Testament, which he never lost, and in his father's despair he saw a divine punishment, in his wealth and prosperity a curse, in his great age a warning that he would survive all his children—a view which the old man himself had held.

He died, however, in 1838, and the event stimulated the son to pull himself together. He saw that he had been wrong and felt that he owed it to his father to keep his promise and pass his examination, now that he could no longer, as he said, deceive the old man. This he did in the course of the following two years.

Regine—or Authorship

At the same time he became engaged to a sixteen-year-old girl of the Copenhagen upper classes, named Regine Olsen, whom he had known and felt drawn to for a year or more. Scarcely, however, had the engagement taken place when he began to have scruples. To quote the journals: 'On the second day (after the engagement) I saw I had been wrong. Penitent that I was—my *vita ante acta*, my melancholy —that was enough!'

Kierkegaard realized, in short, that he could not overcome his melancholy, and he felt unable to confide in the girl what he believed to be its causes. The figure of his father barred the way; and the tragedy of the family curse was a thing that could not be revealed. He was thrown back upon himself and his solitude, and was incapable of 'realizing the universal'—that is to say, incapable of human relationships, of opening his mind to others, or even of taking Church office, as he had often intended but never did.

■ Peter Christian Kierkegaard, the philosopher's elder brother, photographed in old age, when he bore an unmistakable resemblance to their father, Michael Pedersen Kierkegaard. The portrait gives a better idea of the father's appearance and personality than the rather poor miniature below. The other miniature is of Kierkegaard's mother, née Anne Lund.

Two months later he had made up his mind that he would not be justified in attaching this light-hearted girl to himself, and perhaps making her unhappy by his melancholy. Yet a broken engagement was in those days a serious matter, which could reflect unfavourably on the woman in particular. To save Regine, Kierkegaard therefore decided to take all the blame on himself, and in such a way that it would be apparent to everyone that it was she who had broken off the engagement, and could hardly do otherwise. So for several months he played the part of an irresponsible philanderer, noisily showing off in public and seeking by every means to turn appearances against himself.

In this he succeeded, except in the eyes of Regine, who saw through him and refused to accept the breach. The affair thus became doubly distressing for both of them. When the break was a fact, Kierkegaard wrote in his journals: 'When the bond broke, my feeling was: Either you plunge into wild dissipation, or absolute religiosity —of a sort different from the parson's *mélange.*'

He chose the latter. But at the same time he chose something else: he chose authorship. It was in November 1841 that he broke definitively with Regine. Two weeks later he travelled to Berlin (the only place abroad that he ever saw, and that he visited three times), so as to escape from the scene of these agonizing experiences. And there he began to write. It came over him like a torrent driving him ceaselessly on during the next ten years—the most concentrated period of output ever displayed by a Danish author, and surely one of the most compact in world literature.

The year of his real debut was 1843. Before that he had written only a few occasional pamphlets and his University thesis, *On the Concept of Irony, with Constant Reference to Socrates.* Now, in 1843, he published no fewer than six books, of which the first is the longest he ever wrote. It is significantly entitled *Either/Or* (Enten-Eller); and it leads us straight into the world of Kierkegaard's thought. An 'either/or' confronts us with a choice, and it is Kierkegaard's meaning to force the reader into making a decision. He must decide how he wants to live out his life, instead of simply drifting passively down the river of life. So in *Either/Or* Kierkegaard sets out two ways of life, which he calls the 'aesthetic' and the 'ethical.' To 'aesthetic,' however, he gives a different meaning from the one that we usually give to it; he means the immediate and sensory that is every man's starting point in life. In the first part of his work he shows us a variety of aesthetic lives and types, from the lowest, which is sensory and nothing but sensory, as exemplified in the figure of Don Juan, to the man who has realized the emptiness of a purely aesthetic life, yet who nevertheless clings desperately to it, well knowing that it can lead only to despair.

But why does a life on the aesthetic plane lead only to despair? Because, in Kierkegaard's opinion, man has within him something else, which will not be satisfied by a sensory life. This something else is the eternal. Man, he believes, is made up of diverse and opposing parts. He is, he says, a synthesis of body and spirit, of temporal and eternal, of finite and infinite, of necessity and freedom. It is characteristic of the aesthetic, however, that it overemphasizes one side of the synthesis: the corporeal, the temporal, the finite, and the necessary. Yet the other side is none the less there; and it continually makes itself felt by an anxiety, a 'sympathetic antipathy and an antipathetic sympathy,' which alarms and attracts at the same time. The term which best describes this call of the spirit in the sensory world, Kierkegaard finds, is 'dread' (angst). Thus dread is an indication that man has the eternal within him. Without the eternal there would be no dread. But the man who has felt the dread within, and who yet obstinately persists in an existence in the sensory sphere will end in despair. On these twin concepts, of dread and despair, Kierkegaard wrote two of his most inspired books: The Concept of Dread (Begrebet Angest; 1844) and The Sickness unto Death (Sygdommen til Døden; 1849). These two books are psychological essays, but in Either/Or the same themes are treated in situations of imaginative literature, from the introductory Diapsalmata (aphorisms), in which the alternating moods of the aesthetic man find expression, through examples taken from literature, such as Don Juan, Antigone, and characters from the plays of Scribe, to invented figures like 'the unhappiest' and John the Seducer. Together they form a gallery of characters ranging from the immediately sensory, who in a sense is innocent just because of his immediacy, because, in other words, he does not reflect very much on what he does, to the reflecting seducer, who has thought everything out and really acts in defiance and despair.

But the man who through the call of despair has felt the inadequacy of a life in the aesthetic sphere, and who does not, in defiance and despair, remain in it, is mature enough to choose something else and enter into the ethical sphere. This is indicated by the fact that the eternal has asserted its claims on the man, who not only accepts it but believes in the possibility of realizing the ethical claims in the temporal, in the sensory world. Such a man is the ethicist who writes long letters to a friend who is an aestheticist, in the second part of Either/Or. The ethicist is a fighter and an optimist, who feels that he is fighting for a good cause and has no doubt that he will have the strength to convince his friend and the whole world what is the good. He will not deny life in the aesthetic sphere, but feels sure that it is possible to unite the two points of view in a kind of synthesis. Not without reason, one of the chapters in the second part of Either/Or is confidently headed: 'On the balance between the aesthetic and the ethical in the development of personality.'

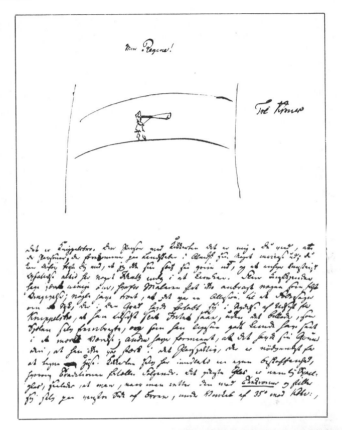

■ Undated letter from Kierkegaard to Regine: 'My Regine! The person with the telescope is me.' The letter must have been written in the early days of the engagement, most likely in September 1840. The portrait of Regine is thought to have been painted at the same time.

That no doubt, is what Kierkegaard himself felt at that time. Having been strongly attracted to the aesthetic in its more refined forms, he doubtless still hoped that it would be possible to find some kind of synthesis between the two worlds. It is true that he himself had abdicated, having renounced Regine and thus the possibility of his ever marrying. But he had neither abandoned his connection with the world altogether, nor the hope that all in one way or another would be for the best.

He was unexpectedly confirmed in this hope one Sunday in the spring of 1843, when, leaving Vor Frue Church in Copenhagen, he chanced to meet Regine, who also came out from church. She nodded to him. That was all; but he was intensely moved. So she was not ill disposed to him; and she did not consider him a cheat! All manner of ideas began to revolve in Kierkegaard's brain, suggesting that perhaps they could come together in some form of spiritual marriage, unsullied by the lusts of the flesh.

But at first he avoided any contact and went off again to Berlin in order to work undisturbed. There he wrote two books, *Fear and Trembling* (Frygt og Baeven) and *The Repetition* (Gentagelsen). Both are in the form, so characteristic of him, which lies mid-way between imaginative literature and philosophy, and in which the ideas he is grappling with are presented in clear essence. The idea he is chiefly concerned with in both is faith, though in very different ways.

In *Fear and Trembling* he again considers the relationship with Regine: a relationship which obsesses him because of an understandable sense of guilt. The chief protagonist in this short book is Abraham, who was ready to sacrifice his own child at God's command. Kierkegaard's father had sacrificed his child—or at any rate its happiness—for God in the same way; and he had been ready to sacrifice Regine for the same reason. In his own case, it had meant that he had sacrificed what was most precious to him in this world: he had renounced.

But Abraham had been restrained at the last moment, and after he had shown absolute obedience to God had been given back his child. And applying this experience to his own personal case, Kierkegaard realized the connection: if Abraham had his son returned to him, while he had to renounce his relations with Regine, it was because Abraham had understood the deepest meaning of absolute obedience to the absolute. That is what we call faith; and in faith lies the conviction that for God all things are possible. It follows that the man who has faith does not need to renounce. The man who renounces proves in doing so that he lacks faith. Or, as Kierkegaard says in the entry in his journals dated May 1843, that is to say, at the time he was working on *Fear and Trembling*: 'If I had had faith I should have kept to Regine.' And he adds: 'Faith, therefore, has hope of this life as well, but only by virtue of the absurd, not because of human reason; otherwise it would be mere worldly wisdom, not faith.' In fact, he now sees that at the time when he believed a marriage to be impossible and renounced it he should have had faith, when he would have been filled with the conviction that for God all things are possible, even, against all reason, the ability to make an impossible marriage possible; and in that belief he should have remained true to Regine. This idea he sets down philosophically in what he terms 'the double movement of infinity,' which consists in first breaking with finiteness but being then enabled, through religion, to recover it. Thus it is possible to make life in this world compatible with life in God after all. Renunciation brings man into a negative relationship with the world, but faith brings him back into a positive relationship with it.

This whole chain of reasoning can be said to have been suggested by the nod which Regine allowed herself when she happened to meet her former fiance one Sunday morning as they were both leaving church. The consequence, as he saw it, was the renewed possibility of achieving a marriage, in one way or another, and in one form or another; a consequence, be it noted, of the absurd, by which he means by virtue of a logic outside the reach of human comprehension and therefore, to human eyes, absurd or paradoxical.

The paradoxical aspect of religion may also entail that religion, in certain situations, can conflict with ethical demands and so appear immoral. God's commandment to Abraham to sacrifice Isaac was requiring him to act like a murderer; and when Kierkegaard was obliged to break with Regine this was contrary to the ordinary view of ethics. These are the problems Kierkegaard discusses in *Fear and Trembling*, in the chapter which carries the rather involved heading: 'Is there a teleological suspension of the ethical; that is to say, are there situations in which a man can be forced to disregard ethical demands for a higher authority?' Kierkegaard answers this question in the affirmative; and it is in just this that the paradoxical character of religion is made plain, since it can lead to demands which, from the point of view of ordinary ethics, are unethical.

We should remember, however, that it is a question of a suspension, not an abolition, of the ethical, and suspension is temporary. So he says: 'What is suspended is not lost, but is preserved in the higher function that is its *telos*, its purpose.' The ethical thus asserts itself as the basis of human life, lifting it out of the aesthetic sphere and bringing it into harmony with the claims of the universal, which in turn are a reflection of the religious claims.

But then comes the question of why some people are placed in such a situation by God that they have to act in a way which must bring them—if only temporarily—into conflict with ethics. And who are they? They are the people who, whether by a judgment of God or by guilt, have got outside the universal, the ethical. That guilt puts a man outside the ethical is self-evident, guilt being by definition a breach with the universal or ethical. The judgment of God is another matter, for it signifies that there are men whom God has chosen for a special mission, and who cannot, therefore, be measured by the same yardstick as others.

The man who puts himself by guilt outside the universal—as indeed all men do—can bring himself back within the claims of ethics only by virtue of the absurd; in other words, by the faith that for God all things are possible. But he cannot achieve this without first learning to renounce. For, rightly considered, guilt consists in clinging to this world and setting it above the kingdom of God; that is to say, by committing oneself absolutely to the relative and relatively to the absolute. Hence it is an essential requirement that one should first learn to renounce and be willing to abjure the things of this world; and then, since for God nothing is impossible, it is possible that by virtue of faith in God's omnipotence, which can accomplish what, to the human mind, is impossible and therefore absurd, one will recover a positive relationship to this world. Faith in the absurd, in other words, is the same as the double movement of infinity.

The Repetition is in every sense an extension of *Fear and Trembling*. The concept of repetition is, of course, nothing else but the double movement of infinity, by virtue of which one repeats, or recovers, the world, after first making the negative movement renunciation. Yet the two books are not alike. *The Repetition* treats faith psychologically. It is, as its sub-title says, 'an essay in experimental psychology.' As so often in Kierkegaard, we see things through the eyes of an observer, and this observer is a man interested in the problems but not personally involved: a cool, rather ironic, occasionally somewhat cynical philosopher of life who is uncommited to religion, let alone Christianity.

Such a man is the pseudonymous character, Constantine Constantius, who tells the story. The young man who experiences a love affair resembles Kierkegaard to a hair. And the love affair resembles, to a hair, the one that he suffered.

The book's present form is not, however, the original one, and we do not know for certain how the first version ended. From a few hints in the journals, we may conjecture that it ended with the suicide of the young man in love, probably because he felt unable to honour the claims of a relationship initiated by himself. Thus where Kierkegaard broke off and went away, his *alter ego* commited suicide. These are two different ways of solving the conflict: the conflict which consists in neither person being capable of making the double movement of infinity.

In its present form, however, the book has quite another ending, and for a good reason, one which is connected with Kierkegaard's own experience. We must remember that the new phase in his production had been set in motion by the little encounter outside the church,

■ There are perhaps only four authentic portraits of the retiring Søren Kierkegaard, who all the more often had to submit to being caricatured beyond recognition. This woodcut after a sketch by an unknown artist is thought to be a good likeness. It dates from a period, probably about 1840, when Kierkegaard did his hair in a 'cockscomb' in French fashion.

when Regine had nodded to him, filling his mind with ideas which both alarmed him and made him deepen his concept of faith and visualize it in the double movement of infinity, while maintaining its intangibility in the form of paradox. When can a smile and a nod have had so many consequences?

But returning to Copenhagen from Berlin, with two manuscripts ready for the press, Kierkegaard was staggered to learn that Regine had become engaged. She was engaged to the young man, Fritz Schlegel, who had been paying her his attentions before Kierkegaard had come into her life, and with whom she had become reconciled. To Kierkegaard this meant that all he had envisaged after that fateful nod, all the dreams he had dreamt of some spiritual marriage between them, or at least mutual loyalty, married or unmarried, and the whole system of thought which had crystallized like a pearl in the mussel-shell of the smile had proved vain and futile. His world seemed to crumble and turn to dust at his feet. He would make a laughing-stock of himself if he were now to publish his new book, in which the hero commits suicide from disappointed love—because his own loved one had become engaged to another, as the ending of *The Repetition* would of course be maliciously misinterpreted. He promptly tore up the last seven or eight pages of his manuscript (it may even have been set up in type) and at top speed wrote a new conclusion, in which we learn that the girl has married another, and in which the hero, instead of taking his life, triumphantly exclaims: 'I am myself again; here I have the repetition; I understand all, and life seems finer to me now than ever ... I am myself again; the machinery has been started up. Cut are the meshes I was ensnared in; broken is the spell that had bewitched me, so that I could not return to myself ... It is over; my skiff is afloat. The next minute I shall be back where my soul hankered, where ideas surge with elemental fury ... where a man ventures his life every moment, every moment loses it and regains it. I belong to the idea. When it beckons me, I follow it; and when it makes an appointment I wait days and nights; there none calls me to dinner, there none waits with supper. When the idea calls I leave everything; or rather, I have nothing to leave; I betray no-one, I grieve no-one by being true; my spirit is not grieved by having to grieve another. When I return home, no-one reads in my look; no-one questions my appearance; no-one demands of my manner an explanation, which I cannot even give anyone, of whether I am blissfully happy or deep in misery, whether I have gained life or lost it. The cup of intoxication is handed back to me again. Already I breathe in its fragrance; already I sense its effervescent music. But first a libation for her who saved my soul, which lay in the solitude of despair: praise be to womanly magnanimity! Long live the flight of thought; long live danger in the service of the idea; long live the hardship of combat; long live the jubilation of victory; long live the dance in the whirl of the infinite; long live the wave that hides me in the abyss; long live the wave that hurls me up above the stars.'

This ecstatic outburst which Kierkegaard substitutes for the tragic ending was meant as his reply to criticism. He would be no ludicrous, pitiful fool. On the other hand, the world might gain the impression, if it liked, that Regine's engagement came as a relief to him. The reality, his true reactions to the news, can be gleaned from his journals, where, after first hearing the news, he fumes with rage and scorn for the girl who had once cried 'It will be my death!' and who yet lived happily on, two years later, in the arms of another man.

Nevertheless in the young man's ecstatic outburst there is more truth, more of Kierkegaard's own inmost being, than he was aware of when he set down these words. For what the young man says, that he can now feel free of all human interests and can therefore devote himself unreservedly to the idea, *i.e.*, to his philosophical and artistic work: that was precisely the impulse which, deepest down, forced the break with Regine, as he was later to realize. The break and its final consummation in Regine's engagement, shattering every dream of a marriage of the spirit, had floated his skiff; except that it was no skiff, but a mighty liner, which now headed, under full sail, for the ocean of philosophy and literature.

The next few years, indeed, were to witness his most intense period of production and the most brilliant successes of his creative art.

Writer and Thinker

Fear and Trembling and *The Repetition* appeared together in October 1843. In the same way, in June 1844, with only four days between them, Kierkegaard published the two books *Philosophical Scraps; or a Scrap of Philosophy* (Philosofiske Smuler eller en Smule Filosofi), 'by Johannes Climacus, edited by S. Kierkegaard,' and *The Concept of Dread*, 'A simple-psychological-demonstrative reflection regarding the dogmatic problem of original sin, by Vigilius Haufniensis.'

The many pseudonyms can seem like an affectation but indicate a deliberate strategy, by which Kierkegaard aims to avoid teaching or preaching; nor can the opinions expressed in his books always be definitely ascribed to him. When a work like *Philosophical Scraps* is described as 'edited by S. Kierkegaard,' we may be sure that it is to a special degree an expression of his own thoughts; but only in those cases where he is shown, not as editor, but as author of the work in question, can the opinions in it be ascribed to him with certainty. This applies, on the whole, to only the many collections of sermons which he published between the literary and philosophical works.

Philosophical Scraps is an attempt to elucidate Christianity. It is, in other words, a work of dogmatics, though, to be sure, a work of an altogether undogmatic character. Perhaps it would be more correct to say that it is an attempt to present Christianity as it should be if it is to have any meaning. Here Kierkegaard's ideas on the paradox, as prepared in *Fear and Trembling*, come to full flower, because Christ's incarnation is itself a paradox; partly because it means the appearance of the infinite in time, which no human mind can compass, and partly because God, as guiltless, must be absolutely different from man, whose destiny is to be in falsehood, since he is in sin.

The Concept of Dread is concerned with sexuality, taken as the constituent element in the concept of original sin. This extraordinarily penetrating work, perhaps the first work of depth-psychology in existence, is based on the previously mentioned concept of man as a synthesis of soul and body, temporal and eternal, freedom and necessity; and dread is the feeling which grips and dominates the man whose synthesis is threatened by the fact that one aspect of it—the body, the temporal, and the necessary—is gaining control. Dread is thus a warning voice, though it can be, as well, a temptation to new sin; for, as Kierkegaard says, in words which anticipate Freud's view in *Das Ich und das Es*, and in *Über das Schuldgefühl*, 'Man is not conscious of guilt because he sins, but sins because he is conscious of guilt.'

The man who, through the voice of dread, has realized the inadequacy of the aesthetic, sensory sphere has reached the maturity to choose something else and enter the ethical sphere. This is marked by the assertion of its claims by the eternal. But as was the case in the

■ When things went against the awkward philosopher in the
capital—and that was often—he would go walking in Grib
Forest in North Zealand. 'There is,' he says in the manuscript
of 'Stages on Life's Way,' 'a place in Grib Forest called Otteveis-
krogen, found only by one who seeks worthily, for no map
shows it. The name itself seems, indeed, contradictory; for how
can a meeting-point of eight paths form a nook (kog), how can
the public and frequented be reconciled with the solitary and
concealed...?' Here is the forester's cottage where the eight
paths meet, not far from the point where—in Viking fashion—
a tumulus has been raised in memory of Soren Kierkegaard.

aesthetic sphere, so in the ethical: we must distinguish between different stages. At its lowest stage man still believes that he can, alone, meet the requirements of eternity in the world of time. At its highest stage, the ethical man has discovered how little he can achieve by his own endeavours. The man who has realized this has become mature enough to cross over from the ethical to the religious sphere, which is based on this very recognition of the inadequacy of human endeavour.

This idea, which had been implicit in all the previous publications from *Either/Or* onward, dominates the next major work, *Stages on Life's Way* (Stadier paa Livets Vej; 1845), a voluminous book and perhaps Kierkegaard's most mature artistic achievement. In a way it reiterates the idea of *Either/Or*, just as the title is a variation on that of the début book; but with the vital difference that in the new work the religious stage is separated into a special stage, as a logical consequence of the ideas embodied in the former works exposing the impotence of human ethics.

Stages on Life's Way, a work of art and perhaps the maturest expression of Kierkegaard's ideas, is a major work in Danish literature. Before seeing it through the press, however, he was already at work on yet another great book, this time a work of philosophy, and nothing less than a reckoning with the predominant contemporary school of philosophy, Hegelianism, which he feared and opposed with all his energy, because it represented a backward step towards paganism and saw the whole development of the world as a manifestation of a necessary logical—or as they said then, dialectical—process, with Christianity an inferior part. Had Hegel's system been anti-Christian it would not have given such great offence to Kierkegaard; but just because it accepted Christianity and incorporated it in the system it was dangerous, and in the great work with the singular title *Concluding Unscientific Postscript to the Philosophical Scraps* (Afsluttende uvidenskabelig Efterskrift til de filosofiske Smuler), of 1846, he settles accounts with Hegel's doctrine or system. It is probably the wittiest philosophical work ever written. In the first place, Kierkegaard attacks Hegel's tendency to systematize the whole of existence, declaring that a system of existence cannot be constructed since existence is incomplete and constantly developing. Likewise, he attacks Hegel's confusion of two things which are entirely unconnected: namely, logic and existence. Hegel had endeavoured to introduce mobility into logic; Kierkegaard demonstrates the mistake of trying to mix the categories into a single hotch-potch. Hegel thought he had created the objective theory of knowledge; Kierkegaard, sharply opposing this, put forward the thesis that subjectivity is truth, or—to quote his own definition of what is truth—'the objective uncertainty, maintained possession of the most passionate fervour, is the truth, the highest truth, for one existing.' To which he adds: 'But the given definition of

truth is a paraphrase of faith.' Kierkegaard deduces one further consequence of his definition of truth: 'When subjectivity, intense fervour
(inderlighed), is the truth, then truth objectively fixed is paradox.'

The threads are thus brought together in this, the most systematic, work of the great system-hater. It is certainly no system; but
those who have the jaws to bite on this vast work, and the teeth to
crush its tough nuts, will there find Kierkegaard's ideas in their most
consistent and coherent form.

Goldschmidt—or the Clash with the World

Having completed this long series of philosophical-literary
works, Kierkegaard had intended to give up writing and seek a coun-
try living. But that was not to be. He was by this time an established
and acclaimed author, and among his warmest admirers was Meïr
Aron Goldschmidt, a young writer who, at the age of 21, had started
to publish a political journal, *Corsaren* (The Corsair), which from a
liberal standpoint attacked the Autocracy, conservatism, the censor-
ship, and anything which smacked of reaction. He went in for derisive
satire, and few escaped his acid pen. One of the few was Kierkegaard,
whose genius Goldschmidt fully appreciated. Kierkegaard, for his
part, tended to regard *Corsaren* as a muck-raker, and in the end he
wrote a newspaper article, expressing his distaste at being praised in
a paper of this kind and demanding to be abused instead. Kierkegaard's purpose with this letter was to confront Goldschmidt, whose
talent he in his turn appreciated (and of whom he entertained certain
hopes), with a choice, an 'either/or': either to reveal himself as the
scoundrel he might be, or to think again and abandon his scurrilous
journalistic methods, instead of continuing with an ambiguous
'both/and': acting like an ethical individual and yet at the same time
employing disreputable methods.

Goldschmidt's reply was immediate. It is true there was no abuse,
but in several issues of the paper he ridiculed Kierkegaard's person in
text and caricature. The method of caricature is nowadays a common
feature of even the most respectable newspapers, but in those days it
was novel, and seemed to contemporaries the last word in meanness.
Kierkegaard was deeply stung. He saw himself made a general laughing-stock, and it had a tremendous effect on him, fanning the aristo-
cratic intellectual contempt for the common man that had always
lurked within him. His scorn for the masses now flared up. The majority is always wrong, he says in his journals: 'Truth is always in a minority; and the minority is always stronger than the majority, because
the minority consists of those who do have an opinion, while the
strength of the majority is illusory, being formed by those who have
no opinion.' ... 'Nobody will be that exhausting thing, the individual.
But everywhere they are at your service with the lying substitute, a
number. Let us unite; then we shall be strong. This is humanity's

■ The author Meïr Aron Goldschmidt, who tormented Kierkegaard in his satirical paper 'Corsaren' (The Corsair). He was
particularly fond of depicting him in various ridiculous situations—in squabbles with persons named, mustering his rather
decrepit troops, giving away his books (because nobody would
buy them), and even 'training his girl,' by riding on her back.
At a time when such methods were unusual, Kierkegaard was
not unnaturally shocked, and he regarded the publication as
scurrilous. His latent misanthropy broke out in psychopathic
self-assertion. 'A genius in a small town,' he said of himself and
the mob rule of Copenhagen.

deepest demoralization.' From there it is not far to Dr. Stockmann's
'The compact majority is always wrong!' in Ibsen's *An Enemy of the
People*.

In particular, his scorn and irony are directed at the clergy, who
make themselves comfortable in secular society and follow the majority. They, more than any, he sees as traitors to their calling, and gradually the idea ripens in his mind that the way ahead can be pointed
only by the man who is ready to lay down his life in martyrdom. With
this realization comes the next question: What of himself in this connexion? Is he the man called upon to sacrifice his life? Has he been
given a special mission by God? During this period a presentiment
forms in his mind that perhaps God has chosen him to speak to his contemporaries direct, to speak with authority as the Apostles had done.

This idea matured only gradually and against many doubts and
scruples. For who *can* speak with authority? Who *can* presume to pro-
claim a message? Of course, only the man who can personally live by

the commandments. But no man can in the case of the Christian commandment, for no man is free from sin. For this reason in all his previous works he had deliberately avoided any form of gospel. He had never tried to convert people to Christianity; his whole endeavour hitherto had been to show his contemporaries what Christianity was —or should be, if it was to have any meaning. His writings had been characterized from beginning to end by the 'either/or' on which he had based his first book. You can be a Christian, or you can not be; it is your own affair, and only you can decide. But you shall not have the excuse for shirking the choice that you did not know what Christianity was—what it was all about!

That had been the background to Kierkegaard's authorship up to now. It had not been preaching, not an appeal, only a demonstration. It had explained what Christianity was. And to emphasize that he wrote without authority he had published his works under various pseudonyms. None of these can be directly identified with Kierkegaard himself. He had been aiming at the work of 'midwifery' which Socrates had claimed. He had wanted to help people to choose by making it clear what the choice was about; but nobody could choose for them. At the moment of choosing, a man is alone with himself and his responsibility.

For the precise reason that he had so strongly insisted that he did not preach a message, and that he spoke without authority, the idea of personally coming forward with a message must have seemed to him a break with everything he had done before. No wonder he hesitated and felt uncertain, and that some event was needed to make him venture the plunge into direct testimony.

■ 'The whole world turns on S. K.' (Klaestrup).

Mynster/Martensen—or the Clash with the Church

The event which set things in train was the death of Bishop Mynster. Mynster had been Bishop of Zealand and Primate of the Church of Denmark for twenty years. He had been a great influence on old Michael Pedersen Kierkegaard, and partly in deference to his father the son had continued to respect the great prelate. Mynster was, first and foremost, a man of wide culture and a man of the world. There is no reason to doubt his personal piety, but it was inseparable from his general culture, which drew its strength as much from the Classics and Goethe as from the Gospels. In Søren Kierkegaard, as the years pass, we find a growing criticism of the ageing bishop, whose form of Christianity seemed to him an adulteration. 'Bishop Mynster's service to Christianity, really, is that by his considerable personality, his culture, his prominent position in fashionable circles, he developed the fashion, or solemn convention, that Christianity was something no person of culture could do without. To an eternal and Christian view, however, this is a rather ambiguous service. For surely Christianity is much too great to be patronized. And in his earnestness there is something of a mixture—so touched, so deeply moved, he is at the thought of its past glories, and yet, when it comes to the point, so sensitive about being ever so slightly belittled himself ... And yet I love Bishop Mynster, and it is my one desire to do all that I can to enhance his reputation; for I have admired him, and, as a man, admire him still. And whenever I can do something to his advantage, I think of my father, whom I think it pleases.'

That was what Kierkegaard wrote in his journals in 1848. Later the tone grew sharper: 'In the splendid Palace Chapel an imposing Court preacher, the chosen of the cultivated public, steps forward before a chosen circle of the fashionable and cultivated public and preaches emotionally on the text of the Apostle: "God chose the mean and despised"—and yet nobody laughs!'

Mynster, for his part, did not care for Kierkegaard and kept him at a distance, rightly suspecting him as a dangerous rebel. But in spite of the latent conflict between the two, Kierkegaard continued to show deep respect for Mynster while the bishop lived. He thought that he owed this to his father's memory.

But in 1854 Mynster died and was succeeded by Martensen, a man of some standing. His *Christian Dogmatics* enjoyed a European reputation, and he had made studies of Christian mysticism, exemplified especially in Jacob Böhme, who had opened up new vistas. But he, too, was an orthodox Hegelian, with the self-imposed task of confuting the subjectivity of Romantic morals by means of 'theoretical knowledge of objectivity, of the absolute form of the State and religion,

science and art.' Thus his theological writing became markedly speculative in its character, culminating in the dogmatics which system-
atized the Christian world of ideas down to the order of precedence
among the angels.

For this man Kierkegaard could have no sympathy at all; and
when, in his memorial sermon on Bishop Mynster, he went so far as to
call him 'a witness to the truth,' thereby promoting the admired and
idolized Mynster, in a way, to the ranks of the martyrs, Kierkegaard
could contain himself no longer. This struck him as blasphemy, and as
a distortion of every Christian value. There had to be a protest now!

It was the starting point of the final phase of his authorship, in
which Kierkegaard abandoned his pseudonymity and in a series of
pamphlets addressed the general public direct, in order to open its
eyes to the falsification of Christianity that was being carried out by
the clergy in Christianity's name. The attacks culminated in the publication of the little journal called *Øjeblikket* (The Instant), which appeared in nine issues. The tenth was ready for publication when he
collapsed in the street and had to be taken to hospital, where he died
shortly afterwards, shattered by the great internal strain imposed by
his recent activities.

The last years of his life thus marked an intense outburst of production, in which his work to some extent acquired a new content, and
to a great extent a new form. In his desire to find an audience he
abandoned his former exclusive form to become broad, popular, even
demagogic, and his style came to resemble the journalism he had
despised.

As regards content, the last publications added nothing new, but
they were new in that it was Kierkegaard himself who spoke, and not
his pseudonyms.

This is bound up with the aim he had set himself. He spoke in his
own name, not in order to rebuke the Church and the clergy for not
fulfilling the strict demands of Christianity (for he was well aware
that neither they nor he could do that), but because, while they failed,
they refused to *admit* that they neither could nor would conform to the
demands, preferring to live in domestic comfort and prosperity and
worldly culture, while trying to make themselves and the world believe that this was the meaning of Christianity.

The Father of Existential Thought

Kierkegaard's attack on established Christianity had wide reper-
cussions and left a permanent mark on the Church of Denmark, which
has become less institutional, perhaps, than any other Church in the
world. Yet it is not the assault on the Church we chiefly consider when
seeking the reasons for Kierkegaard's influence today. Clearly, whatever justification there might have been for his attack on established
Christianity, the attack was somewhat over-wrought, governed, as it

■ The dignified father of the Church, Bishop J. P. Mynster, with
whom Søren Kierkegaard conducted a religious-philosophical
feud that profoundly affected the sensitive philosopher.

was, by an extreme hankering for individualism, asceticism, and renunciation. The last entries in his journals, written a few days before his breakdown, begin with these words: 'The purpose of this life
is—to be carried to the highest degree of weariness of life.'

His life had led him from the silent renunciation enforced by his
engagement to Regine to a consistent denial of every affirmative concept of life, after the clash with Goldschmidt had intensified his pes-
simistic view of man in general and the Church had made him despair
of the possibility of getting even the clergy to live by the Christian
doctrine. But this renunciation of the world only gradually gained a
hold in his writing, and does not affect that part of his work which
was written before he launched his attack.

■ Søren Kierkegaard walking in Copenhagen with a friend; from
a later painting.

What has focused interest on Kierkegaard and given him increas-
ing world importance is something entirely different: namely, his
struggle against philosophical systematization, with its belief that it
is possible to solve the riddles of existence speculatively. He demanded absolutely that theories must be realized in existence, and
he believed it was just this that the contemporary philosophers omitted to do: 'Most systematicians stand in the same relation to their
systems as a man who builds a great palace and lives in a barn adjoin-
ing it: they do not live in the great systematic structure, yet in moral
things that must always be a vital objection. Morally, a man's ideas
must be the building he lives in—or else there is something wrong.'
    Of course it was chiefly Hegel—the systematician *par excellence*
—he had to attack. He admired Hegel's intellectual capacity, but
maintained that with his system he could give nobody the key to existence: 'If Hegel had written his *Logic*, and in the preface had said it

was only an intellectual exercise, indeed one in which at many points he had shirked things, he might have been the greatest thinker that ever lived. Now he is only comical.'

Hegel, in fact, had never grasped the simple point that it is not possible to understand existence intellectually: 'It is quite true what philosophy says—that life must be understood backwards. Which thesis, the more we reflect on it, leads us precisely to the conclusion that life in time is never properly understandable, for the very reason that at no point can I find complete repose in which to take up the position —backwards.'

This understanding of the limited range of the intellectual powers and their incompetence to deal with the great and ultimate questions has come increasingly to influence the philosophy of our time. This has split off into a purely scientific research, with limited objectives, and a philosophy of life which discusses the ultimate problems of existence, but which lays no claim to the name of science in the strict sense of that word. It has found its most characteristic formulation in Existentialism, which has permeated the philosophy of Germany and France and is spreading to the English-speaking world, and which also has enthusiastic adherents in Italy and Spain. Kierkegaard is the father of all Existentialist thinkers. He was the first in modern times who strove consciously to think existentially; that is to say, in the full awareness that we understand backwards but live forward-looking, and that when we direct our attention to the problems of existence we must do so, therefore, not dispassionately and objectively, but with the application of our whole personality.

Curiously enough, Denmark had, at the same time, another outstanding religious figure who thought existentially—the cleric and poet, N. F. S. Grundtvig. The two men differed immensely in almost everything, and indeed are the two poles of Danish culture in the nineteenth century. Kierkegaard was the supreme individualist, bent all times on isolating the individual with his responsibility. Grundtvig came to emphasize fellowship, and so proved a major force in Danish culture, the great inspirer both of the folk high schools and of the agricultural cooperative movement. But in one respect they agree: both were opponents of systematic philosophy and speculation. Both opposed the idea that all the antitheses of existence could be made to vanish into a higher philosophic synthesis, depriving life of its tensions, and the Christian view of existence as a struggle between good and evil of its meaning.

The two men, each in his way, have been of great importance; but internationally Kierkegaard has the advantage, because Grundtvig principally expressed his ideas in poetry, a poetry which, in its individual idiom and its obscure symbolism, is untranslatable, whereas Kierkegaard employed a crystal-clear dialectic which can very well be transplanted to other languages—even though much is lost because at the same time he was a great stylist, with a rare sense of rhythm. Still, enough will remain, and his meaning can never be in doubt: using the subtlest weapons of logic and philosophy, he achieved the feat of demonstrating the impotence of logic and philosophy in face of the supreme problems of existence.

■ Kierkegaard's seal.

CHAPTER TWO

KIERKEGAARD AND THE PROBLEM OF EXISTENTIAL PHILOSOPHY

by Louis Mackey

I. Thought and Being.

On the philosophical side the starting point of Kierkegaard's thinking is a reply to Hegel. If it is the characteristic right of mind to know the truth, Hegel reasons, then "everything we know both of outward and inward nature, in one word, the objective world, is in its own self the same as it is in thought. . . ." To think or reflect is to bring out the truth of the object. But this act of thought is my act, so that "the real nature is a *product* of *my* mind, in its character of thinking subject—generated by me in my simple universality, self-collected and removed from extraneous influences. . . ."[1] Followed to its end, this inference leads Hegel to the conclusion that the necessary self-development of the concept *(Begriff)* is identical with the objective structure of reality. What is (ultimately) real is also (ultimately) rational.

Kierkegaard never doubted that the object of thought is real. The idea that thinking could be about nothing is unintelligible. "That the content of my thought *is* in the conceptual sense needs no proof, or needs no argument to prove it, since it is proved by my thinking it" *(Postscript* 282; SV VII 306).[2] There is a problem, however, concerning the relationship of being "in the conceptual sense" to being in whatever other senses it may have. Being is not of a piece, but is inwardly differentiated by its own modalities (cf. *Postscript* 268n; *Fragments* 32-33,60). The problem of the relation of thought and being cannot be understood unless we are aware of the various meanings of "being," and similarly, of the meaning of "thought."

Suppose, for example, the assertion is made that "truth is the conformity of being and thought." Let "being" be taken to mean the abstracted or prototypical *form* of being, being as the most universal genus. Then the assertion of the conformity of being and thought is tautologous. Being generically understood is, as Hegel was aware, the emptiest of concepts. As the being of all things it characterizes everything and distinguishes nothing. Since it also characterizes thought, it is analytically true to say that thought conforms to being. For all

Reprinted with permission from Louis Mackey and THE REVIEW OF METAPHYSICS, March and June 1956.

that is said thereby is that thought *is;* the sense in which it "is" is not specified. Thus the being of truth in this instance is no more than the abstract form of truth itself. Thought conforms to (generic) being, therefore the truth is; *i.e.*, it conforms to (generic) being. The being here affirmed is the bare bones of reality, the distillation of pure is-ness. But such is-ness is only the presupposition of inquiry, and if it is made the result of an inquiry into the nature of truth, then it is certain that the investigation never actually got under way (cf. *Postscript* 170).

It is therefore necessary to ask what legitimate meaning can be given to Hegel's assertion of the identity of being and thought. Kierkegaard's answer is that the assertion is correct if it is understood as a tautology. Thought and being are identical if both are taken in an ideal sense. Thought in the ideal sense is the Objective Idea, the system of all possible concepts standing in formally necessary interrelationships. Being in the ideal sense is the modality of Essence, the system of all possible essential kinds standing in formally necessary interrelationships. Regarded in this way, thought and being are indeed identical, different names for the same thing. Formal logic coincides with formal ontology.

Being and thought are identical in the case of Ideas and Essences, because being in the case of Essences *means* thought objectified, and thought in the case of Ideas *means* the structures of being. This identity is abstract and formal; the Ideas and the Essences *are*, and are one and the same, but they do not *exist*. The essence of man, man in general, is not an individual existing man. The formal structures of being are modally different from their concretion in time and space. Similarly, the system of objective ideas with their necessary relationships is not an actual process of inference carried out by an existing thinker. The logos of being, "objective reason," differs modally from the subjective activity of reasoning (cf. *Postscript* 112).

To affirm the identity of thought and being in the only legitimate sense is to abstract from existence—as Kierkegaard says, to desert existence for another continent (ideality). The affirmation of this identity says nothing about the being of the individual—and certainly philosophical wisdom ought to throw some light on the concrete—nor about the nature of his thinking—and certainly, whatever objective thought may be, it is a concrete individual who philosophizes with the aid of his concrete processes of thinking (cf. *Postscript* 293-95).

Of course Hegel does not mean the identity of thought and being in a purely abstract and formal sense. He is concerned to offer an explanation of actuality as well as ideality. What he means to say is that thought and being in their full concrete self-development include the moment of actuality—the existence of the thinker and his thought. For the idea by its own nature passes over into its other and returns to itself, incorporating both itself and the other in a higher synthesis.

The principle of contradiction applies only at the level of finite reflection, where the idea has not yet come into its own. At the higher level of the absolute idea all finite contradictions are mediated.

At this higher level, Kierkegaard agrees, contradictions are indeed mediated, so that "it is objectively in order to annul the difference between good and evil, together with the principle of contradiction, and therewith also the infinite difference between the true and the false" (*Postscript* 181).

But contradictory relationships, formally considered, are not the same as concrete relationships of negation and mutual exclusion. The relationship by which truth excludes falsehood is not the same as the act by which a man disciplines his thinking to avoid error. The formal opposition of good and evil is not the same as the act of will by which a man affirms the good and renounces the evil.

As a matter of fact, formal contradiction or opposition is not radical negation or exclusion at all. In logic, for example, a self-contradictory proposition, whatever its peculiarities, stands on the same level of being with other propositions. Like other propositions, it can be a premise from which conclusions (all conclusions) are validly deduced, and it can itself be the conclusion of a valid argument. Or in "value theory," good and evil, true and false, as "values," are of equal and correlative status. They are both equally real in the sense in which ideas can be real, as essences. They do not, in their being as essences, exclude each other from being as essences.

Far from excluding each other, essential contradictories and opposites require each other. In so far as they *necessarily* contradict or oppose each other, they require each other to oppose or contradict. He who thinks the good and the true must also necessarily think their opposites. There is therefore at this level of being (idea or essence) not only no contradiction, there is the necessary reconciliation of all oppositions into a formal unity. Mediation expresses the necessity with which opposites are thought together.

But is this the case in actual existence? A man must think both good and evil in the same thought, but can he become both good and evil at once? He must think truth and falsehood together, but can he pursue and achieve both at once? And can the real exclusions operative in existence be reconciled with the synthesis of ideas in a still higher synthesis (cf. *Postscript* 357 ff.)? These are the questions which Kierkegaard puts to the Hegelian concept of mediation. Recognizing that mediation is a necessity at the level of essence, he denies that it operates so as to reconcile essence with existence and thereby even generate existence out of essence.

In order to understand his position we must say something more about existence and thinking as opposed to being and thought.

Existence or actuality *(Tilvaerelse, Virkelighed)* differs radically from essence or possibility *(Vaesen, Mulighed)*. The being of essence is to be eternally and necessarily self-identical. Essence is what it is immutably (cf. *Fragments* 61). Necessarily identical with itself and related by a strict formal necessity to other essences, an essence is nevertheless only a possibility in relation to existence. No essence need be "instanced" or "illustrated" (whatever these terms may mean) by particulars, but every essence may be (cf. *Postscript* 282 ff.).

Actuality, on the other hand, is that being which is the result of a process of becoming *(Tilblivelse, Vorden)*. It is not changeless, since it is the product of a change. Actuality is that being which has come to be.

Since it has come to be, actuality is by its very being spatial and temporal. As spatial and temporal, actuality is differentiated into a plurality of particularities, as opposed to the universality of every essence.

The change of becoming, by which actualities come to be, is contingent. Kierkegaard supports his position by a consideration of the nature of necessity.[3] Whatever exists necessarily cannot come into being. If it is necessary, it "already" is, there is no "time" at which it is not. Necessary being cannot suffer change. For this reason everything that comes into being proves by doing so that it is not necessary.

Necessity cannot be comprehended in terms of possibility and actuality.[4] What *is* necessarily simply *is;* it is neither possible (for then it might not be) nor is it actual (for then it came to be and is not necessary). Nothing exists or comes to be with necessity. It an actuality were necessary before it came to be, then it would have *been* and could not have come to be. If it were necessary after it came to be, then it has always *been* and could not have come to be. Necessary being is always and completely self-identical. Necessity is in fact the formula for the eternal self-sameness of essence as such.

Since all becoming takes place contingently, the impetus of every process of actualization is not a logical (essential) ground, but a contingently operating cause. The original *terminus a quo* of all contingent causes (the Prime Mover) must also be a contingently working cause. Otherwise the whole process of becoming is no longer contingent, but necessary; that is, nothing comes to be. If, for example, God is understood as a being from whom the world proceeds as a necessary emanation, then the world exists necessarily, the contingency implied in becoming is illusory, as is becoming itself, and nothing really happens in the world. The fact that things happen implies that they happen contingently.

All thinking that is done by human beings is infected by the particularity, the mutability, and the contingency of spatio-temporal existence. It will therefore differ from objective thought as existence differs from essential being.

All thought is necessarily abstract; to think is to conceptualize, and a conception is the subjective correlate of an essence or objective idea. But when thought is regarded objectively, as a system of conceptual interrelationships, and not as the activity of an existing thinker, abstract thinking becomes "pure thought." Pure thought is therefore predicated of a fictitious objective subject, consciousness *überhaupt*, the pure cognitive subject-in-general. Pure thought is "thought without a thinker." It "ignores everything except the thought, and only the thought is, and is in its own medium" (*Postscript* 296). Pure thought is the identity of the essence of mind with the essence of being.

When a concrete thinker thinks abstractly, therefore, thought is in a medium foreign to itself. In time and space, related concretely to a particular individual as his activity, thinking becomes something other than pure thought. Any man who thinks must be transparent in his thinking to this existential transformation of thought. "He who exists is constantly in becoming; the actual subjective thinker constantly reproduces his existence in his thinking and places all his thought in becoming" (*Postscript* 79; SV VII 74).

Thinking is affected in two interrelated ways by existing. All actual thinking, as opposed to pure thought, is intermittent and uncertain.

Thinking is intermittent. Pure thought is absolutely continuous in the eternity and unity of the idea. It never starts or stops, but simply is. Since it is in the mode of essence, it is not something that "goes on" at all, but a *status* of concepts and relations. The existing thinker, however, thinks "before and after" (*Postscript* 293). His thinking begins and ends, begins and ends again, indefinitely throughout his life. Time sunders the unity of pure thought, spreading it out discursively and successively. At no point does thinking achieve identity with thought itself. If, says Kierkegaard, a dancer announced that he could leap higher than any dancer before him, we should all admire him. But if he said he could fly continuously, he would be laughed at. Leaping after all is the accomplishment of a man, an earthly being who in his intermittent leaping is still bound by the law of gravity. But flying is the privilege of winged creatures and if kept up continuously would imply an emancipation from earthly limitations (cf. *Postscript* 112-13). So also a thinker may be capable of spectacular flights of abstraction, and he deserves our admiration, provided he comes back down to earth again. But for an existing thinker to think pure thought presumes a freedom from the conditions of existence that is impossible as long as he exists.

As it breaks up the continuity of pure thought, so existence transforms the formal necessity of logical relationships into the contingent connections of actual inference. Formal logic itself is not thinking, but an object of thought, something that can be thought about. As the necessary structure of essential relationships, it is something all thinking looks to and tries to reproduce in itself. But when a logical argument is reproduced in the thinking of an existing being, and thereby translated into a temporal process, it loses its certainty and its finality. For all process is by nature contingent.

It is obvious enough that thinking gains in certainty as it moves farther and farther away from the concrete, deals with more and more abstract features of actuality. The act of abstraction possible intermittently to a thinker is a movement within existence away from existence toward essence. Mathematical and logical inferences possess a high degree of certainty, whereas the reasoning of an historian about history must be hemmed in on all sides by doubts and conditions.

Inferences like p, therefore p; or $p \supset q$, p, therefore q, are less likely to be vitiated by contingency than any concrete inference I may make. They deal with barren abstractions. Yet in two ways they are contingent. First, since even such reasoning is process, q does not follow in inference from $p \supset q$ and p as it does in formal argument. There is no guarantee that in time the p of the second premise and the q of the conclusion have not become something different from the p and q of the implicative premise, or that the relation of implication between p and q has not itself changed. Formally of course they cannot change, yet (secondly) such inferences are never made for their own sake—p and q are only "dummy letters"—but are always form for some concrete content, where the contingency of the inference increases with the concrete complexity of the content.

Objectively viewed, logic as a system of formal relations holds dominion over all thinking. It is the ideal prototype of certainty at which all thinking aims. But it cannot incorporate movement, and by its very perfection is separated from both the actual object of thought and the actual process of thinking. Thus subjectively viewed, formal logic is all hypothesis; the thinker is never certain if logical relations apply or can be applied to this particular problem. The objectivity and the uncertainty of logic taken together constitute "the unity and the contradiction in which it is negatively related to existence" (*Postscript* 100; SV VII 98).

The existence of the thinker is a synthesis of being and thinking in the mode of temporal actuality. The thinking of the existing being is a synthesis of the certainty of thought and the uncertainty of becoming. The uncertainty in existence is about the possibility of valid thought. The uncertainty in thought is about its own adequacy to comprehend actuality. Hence the "negative relationship" of thought and existence; actual thinking, though it has a structure analogous to that of formal argument, is not itself logic and lacks the necessity of logic, and formal logic does not exist, is not actual thinking.

Time therefore establishes a complex set of distinctions between thought and being, and within thought and being themselves. Thought as the objective idea is different modally from the actual process of thinking. The existence of the thinker is different modally from the realm of essence in which the pure ego has its being. Formal logic differs modally from the existence of the thinking subject. The subject's thinking differs modally from essential being. And the individual's activity of thinking differs from his existence, if only because it is one of many activities of the same subject.

Suppose that now the proposal is made to reconcile the disparity of thought and being by an act of mediation. But mediation itself is not an activity, but the necessary coherence of opposites and contradictories in the mode of essence. Mediation synthesizes conceptual oppositions. But the manifold opposition of thought and being just defined is not an opposition within ideality, but between ideality and actuality. Mediation is an "activity," that is, a *status*, of pure thought (or pure being, which is the same thing). To employ mediation to reconcile pure thought (= pure being) with existence and actual thinking would be to allow mediation to be judge and litigant in its own case (cf. *Postscript* 336 ff.).

"I can abstract from myself; but the fact that I abstract from myself means that I also exist" (*Postscript* 296; SV VII 321). The act of abstraction is an activity which requires time. No activity is possible in the eternity of abstraction itself. I am other and more than thought *when* I am thinking and precisely *because* I can think. If I were in my own thinking to attempt a mediation of thought and existence, I would by that very fact testify to their continued difference.

To summarize: the relation of thought and being, in the sense of the objective idea and the realm of essence, is a simple identity. But the relation of actual thinking and actual existence to essential being and the objective idea is a problem. It is a problem which cannot be solved in terms of objective ideas and essences, since as Kierkegaard perceives, it does not even arise at this level (cf. *Postscript* 267-70, 273-74). The problem of the relationship between two distinct modes of being cannot even be formulated, much less settled, by a thinking which operates solely in terms of one of the modes involved. Kierkegaard's metaphysical opposition to Hegel is just this, that he "explained" existence in terms of pure thought—the dialectic of mediation and reconciliation—when the real problem lay elsewhere. The Hegelian explanation of existence is in reality a suppression of existence, and his answer to the problem of the relation of thought and being is a pseudo-answer to a pseudo-problem. The real question for the philosopher is not, How is the eternal truth to be understood by eternal beings? but, How is the eternal truth to be apprehended temporally by one who exists in time? (cf. *Postscript* 172).

A paradox now arises. Pure thought and essential being differ radically from actual thinking and actual existence, and yet I who exist also think and my thinking has a considerable claim to objective validity. This paradox involves Kierkegaard in both a conclusion and a problem. The conclusion, that a systematic "philosophy of existence" is impossible, leads in its turn to the problem.

If existence is conceived systematically, if it is viewed as a member in full standing of a definitive system of ontological categories, then it is conceived, says Kierkegaard, "as abrogated" *(som ophaevet)*. Existence is movement in time. There is no finality in existence, at least not until the world comes to an end. To be sure, if relations among actualities were necessary relations (in a determinist world), then existence would be in every important respect finished from the moment of its inception. But all becoming is contingent, and change follows change with never more than momentary rest.

To have a definitive ontology means exactly that everything *is* finished, that being has once and for all been reckoned with and impounded in a network of concepts. A system is the concludedness of all essential kinds in a unity of formally necessary relationships. To have a system is to be a determinist with a vengeance. To think that being is reducible to a systematic ontology is to deny outright the reality of time, happening, and contingency (*Postcript* 107-13; *Fragments* 62-64).

If then existence, which is the very opposite of system, is nevertheless "thought" systematically, it can only mean that it is not thought as *existing* but as "revoked into the eternal," translated into the "essence of existence." Existence cannot be the subject matter of an ontological system. It cannot be, as Kierkegaard would say, taken care of in paragraph 14. The presence of such a discussion in a systematic philosophy demonstrates either (a) that the philosophy is self-refuting, if existence is rightly understood, or (b) that it is not existence which is discussed, but the "essence of existence," which is a roughshod way to override existence, inasmuch as existence in its concreteness is not an essence but a mode of being (cf. *Postscript* 111; *Fragments* 60).

But now comes the problem mentioned above: is not this conclusion also self-destructive? After all one *does* think about existence. Kierkegaard wrote a good many volumes about it, and presumably did not think he was talking nonsense. He was of course aware of the problem and dealt with it in his own way.

The problem can be formulated in this way: if existence is really unthinkable, what happens when an existing individual thinks? Can his thinking have objective validity and still sustain a significant relationship to existence? Or do the existential and the intellectual cancel each other, so that his existence becomes an everlasting succession of chaos upon chaos, and his thinking a bombination in the void?

With respect to the possibility of an existential philosophy, we may ask: can a man philosophize so as to give expression to the fact that it is an existing individual who thinks and that his existence is the object of his thought—without allowing his philosophy to become confession? If this is not possible, there can be no existential philosophy, for confessional self-knowledge is only the raw material from which philosophical wisdom has yet to be extracted. And if what is thus extracted is only a *tour de force* of pure thought, then philosophy had better abandon its ancient claim to practise the love of wisdom. A wisdom that throws no light on man's existence is a sorry wisdom indeed, a vanity of vanities, and the *caput mortuum* of the whole philosophical enterprise.

The possibility of an existential philosophy will be our concern in what follows.

II. The Subjective Thinker.

Kierkegaard distinguished between pure thought—the objective idea, thought without a thinker—and abstract thought, which for all its abstractness is the activity of a finite thinker and so bears a definite relationship to his existence (cf. *Postscript* 278). This relationship Kierkegaard specifies in three equivalent ways: abstract thought is an act of conceptualization, an act of abstraction, and a translation *ab esse ad posse.*

All thinking operates in terms of universal concepts. As Hegel demonstrated, even the "This," the "Here," and the "Now," the evocations of particularity, become universals as soon as they are thought.[5] The most elementary articulation of experience—and it is doubtful if a human being ever has any wholly inarticulated experience—is a conceptual reconstruction of that experience.

Now as the activity of an existing human being, the activity of conceptualizing is as concrete as any act he can perform. Subjectively considered there is nothing on the face of it that would distinguish conceptualization from any other activity as regards its concreteness. But there is no doubt that objectively something happens to an item of experience when it is thought. To think something is precisely to abstract from, to draw away from *(abstrahere),* its concreteness. Actuality is spatio-temporal, particular, fluctuating, and contingent. But when an actuality is thought, it is fixed in a relatively static concept, universal in intent, and necessarily implicated with other concepts in logical relations. Since the activity of thinking is itself the act of a man, this fixation is of course momentary and uncertain and wavering, but it is a decided movement in the direction of objectivity and the objective idea. All thinking is a movement within existence away from existence, toward the outer borders of existence (*Postscript* 103-05).

But to abstract is not only to abstract *from* existence, but also to abstract *something* from existence. What is thus drawn away and conceptualized by thinking is some universal aspect or aspects of actuality. These universal aspects, comprehended in a concept, stand related to existence as *possibility* to actuality. Greenness, dogness, manhood, circularity, etc., are all characteristics that may (or may not) be illustrated in various actual contexts. To call them abstract possibilities is not to deny their reality, but their reality is to *be* concepts, to *be* possibilities (cf. *Postscript* 292). Thinking therefore "consists in translating the real into the possible" (*Postscript* 280).

There is obviously a mystery here, the mystery of the double participation of thinking in essence (the realm of possibility) and existence. How is it that abstract thinking stands related both to that ideal object at which it aims and to the existence of which it as an activity is itself a part? What is the meaning of an act of abstraction that takes place in existence? This is not, so Kierkegaard believes, a mystery soluble by thought. As in the former case of the relation between the ideal and the actual, to "solve" this mystery by thinking is *ipso facto* to produce a false solution. "Actuality [*Virkelighed*] is an *inter-esse* between the moments of that hypothetical unity of thought and being which abstract thought presupposes.... Actuality or existence [*Tilvaerelse*] is the dialectical moment in a trilogy, whose beginning and whose end cannot be for the existing individual, since *qua* existing individual he is himself in the dialectical moment" (*Postscript* 279; SV VII 302).

Existence in time combines thinking and being in a way that does not really synthesize the two but presents the individual with an unresolved tension. Insofar as by thinking the existing individual apprehends the *essence* of things, he is in his existence apparently related to essential being. But insofar as by existing in time he is constantly expressing his disparity from essential being, that apparent relationship is, equally apparently, always being negated. Likewise, insofar as his thinking is not wholly objectified as pure thought, the individual appears in his thinking to sustain a constant relation to actuality. And yet his thinking itself is an act of abstracting *from* actuality. Existence separates thought and being at the same time that it relates them.

Abstract thinking cannot overcome this disunity in existence. It cannot "close the trilogy." For one thing the abstract thought by which the problem is supposed to be solved is the act of an existing individual, and its own inner unity is in question. It is in fact itself the problem. And on the other side, although it is a concrete act, abstract thinking is a tension away from concreteness in the direction of abstract essentiality. "Abstract thought considers both possibility [*Mulighed*] and actuality, but its concept of actuality is a false rendering [*Gjengivelse*], since the medium within which the concept is thought is not actuality, but possibility. Abstract thought can get hold of actuality only by nullifying [*ophaeve*] it, and this nullification of actuality consists in transforming it into possibility" (*Postscript* 279; SV VII 302).

Abstract thought works in concepts which comprehend essences. Now it would appear that essence is present indifferently in the mode of possibility and in the mode of actuality. There is apparently no difference *in essence* between an actual X and a possible X. Suppose then that abstract thought can be said to comprehend the essence of actualities. But the mode of being in which essence is when it is in actuality is not itself thinkable as an essence. Thus abstract thought in its inevitable preoccupation with essence cannot comprehend actuality in the mode of its actuality. To think a thing is to apprehend it as in the mode of possibility.

In a word, abstract thought itself can never define the relationship in which it stands to existence. Its relation to actuality can never be clarified by its own conceptual formulations, since every such formulation expresses a possibility without reference to its relation to actuality. "All that is said about actuality in the language of abstraction and within the sphere of abstract thought, is really said within the sphere of the possible. In the language of actuality: all abstraction is related to actuality as a possibility; but not to an actuality included within abstraction and possibility" (*Postscript* 279; SV VII 302).

So we still have not a result but a problem, not the solution of a difficulty, but the confession of its insolubility at the level of thought. Kierkegaard therefore turns from his discussion of thought to a consideration of the nature of *action*.

If the content of thought, he says, were actuality instead of possibility, there could be no possible contrast between thought and action. Thought and action would be the same, and the most perfect conception of an action would be or contain or immediately entail that action. But thought is always a translation *ab esse ad posse*, whereas all action (even in the most general sense of becoming) is a transition *a posse ad esse*. In the case of the voluntary action of human beings, action occurs when the individual, having thought the action as a possibility, puts an end to the possibility *as such* and actualizes it. Action in this case is a decision to identify oneself with the content of his thought, to "exist in it," to bring the essential content into existence. Between the possible action (the conceived action) and the actual action (the decision) there is no difference in essential content, but there is a crucial difference in mode of being. There is a profoundly significant difference, certainly, between conceiving the good and doing the good, between thinking about honesty and actually being honest. In opposition to the disinterestedness of abstract thought, action involves an *interest* not in ideas or essences for their own sake but in actualizing them. That very disinterestedness which is the mark of the objectivity of thought must be sacrificed in action to the subjectivity of the individual's concern to realize possibilities in his concrete existence (cf. *Postscript* 302 ff.). Action becomes personal and ethical while thought remains impersonal and morally neutral.

Several interesting consequences follow from this analysis. The eternal, which it is the goal of thought to think, is related to action as futurity (cf. *Postscript* 271-72). That which is eternally possible in itself is for becoming that which is or may be coming to be. For the acting individual, the eternal is not an object for contemplation, but a demand for a decision. Possibilities which are given to thought to view in their ceaseless contemporaneity are presented to the individual concerned with existence to be resolutely actualized or (in the case of possibilities of evil) rejected. A possibility which is continuously present and available to thought may be lost forever by a failure of active resolution. Opportunity lingers always about the doorway of thought; what is not thought today can always be thought tomorrow or next year; there is no hurry and no loss by default. But for action opportunity may knock only once, and a possibility (for good, for example) not seized when it presents itself may be irrevocably missed.

The demand for decision and resolution in action also explains why, although the principle of contradiction may well be a vanishing factor for thought as thought approaches objectivity, there is still an either/or in existence. Contradictory possibilities which can and must be contemplated together cannot be actualized together. To endow one possibility with existence in the moment of decision is to reject with equal decisiveness its opposite. To "synthesize" or "mediate" genuine oppositions in action is at best to compromise and at worst, by wavering, to lose the moment of opportunity altogether (cf. *Postscript* 270-72).

The consideration of action by itself serves only to accentuate the disparity between thought and existence. What is true for thought is not true for action: for thought the correlativity of opposites, for action the mutual exclusiveness of opposites; for thought the abiding presence of the eternal essence, for action the fleeting present of the moment of decision; for thought the retreat to possibility, for action the advance toward future actuality.

Yet it is in action and its relation to thought that the possibility of an existential philosophy first comes to light. It is in the *tension* between the drive of action toward existence and the drift of thought toward essence that philosophy has its being.

Kierkegaard's main attack is centered on the problem of truth. He accepts the view that truth consists in a correspondence between thought and the being which is its object. But he is careful to note that the character of the "being" intended makes a critical difference to the nature and availability of truth. We saw above that if thought and being are taken to mean the objective idea and essence respectively, the truth of their correspondence is nothing more than abstract identity. We saw also that this "truth" is never the property of any existing thinker and that it does not illumine his own being. Truth so defined *is* but does not *exist*. It is easy to see why concern for truth at this level tends to dissolve correspondence in coherence.

If thought and being are defined as empirical thinking and being, the case is different. Here truth means the truth of the natural, social, and historical sciences. But it is equally true at this level that truth is not a reality. For the knowing subject and the object of his knowing are always contingently coming to be and passing away, so that empirical knowledge is varying and unconsummated. Truth is here an ideal, a desideratum, something pursued but never possessed. The best results of scientific cognition are problematic (cf. *Postscript* 169-70).[6]

Both the above definitions—rationalistic and empiricistic—focus on the objective aspect of truth. Truth is that property of our knowledge by which it most faithfully and with the least admixture of subjectivity represents its *object*. The ideal of objectivity is the point at which the knowing subject's interference in the fidelity of cognitive representation becomes a negligible constant or a calculable variant. Thinking strives to immolate itself in pure transparence to its object. Yet no such transparency is possible for finite beings, and to try to calculate one's own interference in the objectivity of his knowledge entails an infinite regress.

The ideal of objective truth

has no relation to the existing subjectivity; and while we are always confronted with the difficult question of how the existing subjectivity slips into this objectivity, where subjectivity is the pure abstract subjectivity [the negligible or calculable cognitive subject *überhaupt*] (which again is an objective determination and does not denote any existing man), it is certain that the existing subjectivity more and more evaporates. (*Postscript* 112)

The ideal of objective truth is impossible to achieve and deceptive to pursue. Truth only *can* exist in and by the individual's apprehension of it. Truth may well *be* in general, but it can only be understood in particular. Each individual man is something more and something less than consciousness-in-general, and each individual man must freely and originally appropriate whatever truth can truly be said to exist for him. "To believe an ideality on the word of another is like laughing at a joke because someone has said that it was funny, not because one has understood it" (*Postscript* 289). To accept a philosophy because of the ponderous authority of the philosopher or because there are no discoverable flaws in his logic is in the one case a prostitution of a man's freedom and in the other a mere formal acceptance of something that has not been wrought in the material of his own being—and is therefore not true for him who accepts it.

This is the ground for Kierkegaard's insistence that a decision is necessary between the objective and the subjective pursuit of truth. To attend only to the objective side, the *what*, of truth is by minimizing one's appropriation to arrive perhaps at something vast in extent and formally certain—which is not true for the subject. To attend to the manner of one's appropriation, the *how*, of truth is to lose in objectivity, not to know so much or so accurately—but at any rate to have made the little one does know intimately and exhaustively his own (cf. *Postscript* 171). For the existing individual, therefore, *subjectivity is truth* (*Postscript* 169-224, 306).

We must go slowly and be careful, even at the cost of repeating ourselves. This is the point at which Kierkegaard is most often misunderstood and reduced to an absurdity he did not intend. "Subjectivity is truth" needs to be cautiously interpreted in the light of its whole context. "Subjectivity" for Kierkegaard does not mean the angularity that attaches to every man, the quirks of temperament to which we are all subject and have to do our best to live with. Nor does it mean the capriciousness of wish and will that intermittently inclines us to one or another folly (*Postscript* 116-17). To call this kind of subjectivity truth, and to speak in this sense of the "subjective thinker," would be the most blatant self-contradiction and would make nonsense out of truth and thinking both.[7]

"Subjectivity" refers rather to the process by which the individual appropriates what he thinks, and so brings the truth into existence. It is neither thoughtless, like private eccentricity, nor impersonal, like objective knowledge (cf. *Postscript* 147-62, 178, 178n, 180-83). The "subjective thinker," in Kierkegaard's words, has a "double reflection" (*Postscript* 68). In so far as he thinks, he abstracts from existence and works for objectivity. But the more objective and abstract his thinking becomes, the more tenuous are its ties with existence and the existing thinker. He becomes increasingly conscious of his own irrelevance to the object of his thought. "What good would it do me," Kierkegaard wrote, "if truth stood before me, cold and naked, not caring whether I recognized her or not, and producing in me a shudder of fear rather than a trusting devotion?"[8]

The subjective thinker realizes that truth must be independent of his own particularity in order to be *true*. "All wisdom of life," says Kierkegaard, "is abstraction" (*Postscript* 381n.). But he is also aware of the other proposition: that truth must be integrated with his own being in order to *exist*. "Only the truth which edifies is truth for you" (*Either/Or* II, 294). That which edifies is that which "builds up" *(opbygge)*. Only when the truth builds a man up, only when it becomes *constitutive of his personal existence*, does the truth really exist. When a man thinks, he thinks the possible, but he must at the same time, in accord with the structure of action discussed above, be always translating the possibilities he thinks into actuality. The existing thinker can abstract from himself and his existence only momentarily, and even then he exists and must re-acquire the consciousness of his existence in relation to the abstraction he contemplates (cf. *Postscript* 67, 170).

Hence the "double reflection"—the reflection of thinking away from the self toward objectivity, possibility, and the second reflection of action toward the subject and his actuality. These two aspects of the one process of subjective thinking cannot be separated. If they are, there is nothing left but abstract possibility on the one side and an unexamined life on the other. Nor can the appropriation—to be understood in the literal sense of "making one's own"—be postponed until thought has finished its work (cf. *Postscript* 101-06). It is impossible for a man to *think* about the good until he formulates his ethical system and then and then only (perhaps when he is fifty) begin to make moral decisions. From antiquity, Kierkegaard observes, skeptics have been disquieted by the uncertainty of knowledge and at the same time have recommended an easy compliance with local customs in regard to moral conduct—revealing thereby the distractedness of their thinking.[9] A man exists while he thinks, and a thinking that is not brought into engagement with his existence is simply fatuous.

For whatever other purposes objectivity may be desirable in itself (and Kierkegaard never denies that there are such purposes, in the sciences, for example), it is of all things not the *ne plus ultra* of philosophical wisdom. A philosophy that is to be relevant to existence must be *made* relevant to existence by the philosopher in the very activity of philosophizing. By his double reflection he gives evidence of his presence in that tension of thought and action where, it was said above, philosophy has its being.

It is not the end of all intelligibility, therefore, when Kierkegaard defines truth as "an objective uncertainty held fast in an appropriation process of the most passionate inwardness" (*Postscript* 182)— provided, that is, we understand what he means by "objective uncertainty" and "passionate inwardness."

The goal of thinking is objective truth. But when the thinking is that of an existing human being, objective truth is brought into a paradoxical relationship with existence. This is the same paradox we noted earlier: what is eternally (essentially) true and certain, when it is apprehended by an individual thinking and living in time, loses its certainty. Every objectivity is also an uncertainty from the standpoint of existence (*Postscript* 183).

Yet it is existence which must be, in Kierkegaard's words, "interpenetrated" by thought. Existence demands action, and action means decision and commitment. But no man acts when he acts uncertainly, almost decides, just about commits himself, very nearly comes to the point of doing something, etc. Every genuine action commits the actor to more than thought can warrant and with more assurance than thought can provide. A man acts by embracing an objective uncertainty with inward concern for its actualization. He does not by acting efface the objective uncertainty of, let us say, the ideal to which he devotes himself. But in the full consciousness of its uncertainty he *nevertheless* acts, and what is objectively uncertain (perhaps his ideal is an illusion) is *subjectively* assured of realization in his own existence. Because by his active appropriation he brings truth into existence, he can give it in his own *decisions* the certainty it lacks in his *thought* (*Postscript* 304-05, 304n.).

This is what it means to appropriate an objective uncertainty with passionate inwardness. Kierkegaard calls passion "the interest in existing," defined by the intersection of thought and existence (*Postscript* 313; 276-78). When a man envisions his possibilities for action in all their uncertainty and still has the moral concern to go ahead and act, then he has acted with passion. Only an examined life is worth living. But without passion, the examined life easily ceases to be life at all and slips into an indefinite parenthesis of reflection. Thought and action must be held together in existence by passion. When it is said, therefore, that truth is subjectivity, emotional or volitional chaos is not being set in the place of objective thinking. What is meant is that truth is not a matter of thinking alone, but exists only in the "existential dialectic"—the double reflection—in the dialectical tension of thought and action *within* the subject himself (cf. *Postscript* 79n.). Objectivity is not banished from thought, but its limitations and inadequacies are existentially clarified, and its relation to actuality is made fast in the act of personal appropriation.

The "passionate appropriation of objective uncertainty" is an intensely personal kind of truth, yet it is not without witness in the history of philosophy. Kierkegaard was understandably fond of recurring to Socrates in this connection:

> In the principle that subjectivity, inwardness, is the truth, there is comprehended the Socratic wisdom, whose everlasting merit it was to have become aware of the essential significance of existence, of the fact that the knower is an existing individual. For this reason Socrates was in the truth by virtue of his ignorance.... The Socratic ignorance gives expression to the objective uncertainty attaching to the truth, while his inwardness in existing is the truth. (*Postscript* 183)

Another example, not cited by Kierkegaard, is found in Kant's treatment of moral freedom. Kant is aware of nothing so much as of the "objective uncertainty" of freedom. Time and again he renounces the possibility of a theoretical proof of freedom. But time and again he also recalls the practical necessity for freedom. Without freedom there is no morality and no selfhood. If there is no freedom, it is impossible for me to be a man. The Kantian demand for freedom is the demand of the whole practical side of man for room to exist in. And while the theoretical knowledge of freedom is left forever pending, the moral man goes on to prove his freedom to himself at least by practising it. The formality and occasional obtuseness of Kant's manner should not blind us to the existential passion with which he embraces the objective uncertainty of moral freedom.

Once the possibility of subjective *thinking* is made clear, however, we have still not shown how existential *philosophy* is possible. Philosophical thinking must be communicable, but the individual and personal character of subjective truth raises definite problems in this direction. We have touched in our discussion upon three meanings of thought in Kierkegaard: pure thought, objective (abstractive) thinking, and subjective (appropriative) thinking. We need to sketch the different meanings of communication corresponding to these different modes of thought.

At the level of pure thought there is no communication at all. The only "mind" at this level is the pure ego, and the only "thought" is the objective idea identical with essence. The pure ego is a simple unity to which the objective idea is eternally present. Ideas do not pass from one subject to another, for there is only one subject and no possibility of movement. There is no activity here, no existing beings, no concrete thinking or teaching or learning—and no communication (*Postscript* 68n.).

Objective thinking takes place in existence, where the activity of communication is possible. But the more objective the thinking becomes, the more direct and straightforward is the form of communication. We noticed above how objective knowledge aims at the reduction of personal appropriation to a minimum. To the extent that this reduction is successful, the communication of objective knowledge tends to become a simple exchange of ideas at a purely intellectual level, its appropriation a formal assent to correct propositions. Indeed, so long as its objectivity is unimpaired, objective knowledge is quite indifferent to the way it is apprehended. The results that cost a researcher a lifetime of experimentation can be appropriated in half an hour by a student. And they are just as true, just as much knowledge for the latter as for the former. That is in fact why the researcher spent his life acquiring the results, so that others could pick them up as a matter of course. It is a success for objective knowledge when its apprehension has become a triviality.

At its maximum the communication of objective knowledge approaches a negation of communication. Its goal is the sharing of cognitive subjects in a common intentionality, or the possession by them of formally identical intentionalities of a common essence. But all cognitive subjects, simply qua cognitive, are themselves formally identical. The difference between subjects that is essential to a genuine activity of communicating is suppressed by abstraction—so that there is no more that one man can communicate to the other, because they have nothing that is not already in common. The end of objective communication (which of course is never reached as long as men continue to be men) is the silence of eternity, the mute identity of pure thought and pure being in the pure ego. As thinking gets more objective, concrete subjects lose their concreteness and melt together, so that (if it actually could achieve its end) objective thinking would be "aware only of itself and . . . not in the strict sense of the word a form of communication at all" (*Postscript* 70).

But what of the communication of subjective truth? Here the problem is how a particular existing thinker transmits his personal appropriation of the truth—the only truth that exists for him—to another such existing thinker. We saw that the subjective thinker is one who stands always in the dialectic of the double reflection—one who thinks and also embodies his thinking. "In thinking he thinks the universal; but as existing in this thought and as assimilating it in his inwardness, he becomes more and more subjectively isolated" (*Postscript* 68). By his appropriation of what he thinks, the subjective thinker makes it uniquely his own and apparently not negotiable. Objective truth, because it belongs to no one in particular, is shared by all indifferently. Subjective truth, bound up as it is with the individuality of the thinker, constitutive of his being as this particular person, does not seem to be shareable at all.

Obviously a man cannot communicate his existential appropriation of his thought. No man can or may hand over his being to another; no man can or may be for another man what each man can and must be for himself—namely, himself. But if the thinker translates his personal truth back into eternal verities, then it ceases to be the particular existing truth he desired to communicate. It reverts to abstraction, and the purpose of existential communication is not the transmission of abstractions. It would appear that subjective thinking gets caught in the toils of subjectivity and winds up, like pure thought itself, mute and unutterable.

Nevertheless it is Kierkegaard's contention that the existential thinker can and does communicate. But he communicates indirectly, in a form that is appropriate to the form of his thinking itself. Just as the existing individual manages to combine thinking and action, so his communication must combine the intelligibility of objective thought with the urgency of the demand for action.

All communication between men *must* operate in the medium of ideas and concepts—in the realm of possibilities. That truth which the individual has brought into existence by transforming it from possibility to actuality must, if it is to be communicated, be reconstituted as possibility. But, and this is the crucial point, it must not be presented as an object for contemplation alone, but in such a *way* that it recommends itself to the recipient of the communication as a possibility *for him*. As subjective truth depends for its being on the *manner* of its apprehension, so an indirect communication depends for its effectiveness on the *manner* in which it communicates its content.

Truth communicated as possibility must be such as to compel the recipient to face the problem of actualizing it (cf. *Postscript* 282-307 passim, 320-21).

That this is a necessity in the case of subjective truth is easily seen from the side of the recipient. Obviously I have not understood the communication of a subjective thinker until I have appropriated for myself that truth which he offered to me as a possibility. If I become an admirer, an oath-taking disciple, or a critical connoisseur of his thought, then I have missed the whole point and there is no truth *in me.* "Whatever is great in the sphere of the universally human must therefore not be communicated as a subject for admiration, but as an ethical *requirement.* . . . A communication in the form of the possible operates in terms of the ideal man . . . whose relationship to every individual man is that of a requirement" (*Postscript* 320-21).

Lest it be thought that this is didacticism, it should be noted that the "ethical requirement" is not that the recipient model his conduct on a certain set of rules, as opposed to some other. A philosophy is not a moral code. To make it such, and in this way, would be false both to the uncertainty of human knowledge and to the right and duty of the recipient to realize the truth for himself. The requirement imposed by indirect communication is simply that the recipient exist as a man, that he create his own truth out of his own life, experience, and knowledge, of which this particular communication is one part. The truthful reception of an indirect communication is neither submission to precept nor the compilation of a *Festschrift,* but a re-examination and re-appropriation of one's own truth in the light of what is communicated.

It is easy enough to see the need for such communication. But how it is done is another matter. Kierkegaard argues that the indirect communication must be doubly reflected, by analogy to the double reflection of the subjective thinker. By a first reflection the author of the communication conceives his content as a possibility and gives it expression in language. The articulation of an idea is inseparable from understanding it qua idea. But by a second reflection, the form of his communication must express his existential relation to what he communicates, the manner in which he understands himself in terms of it, the mode in which he has appropriated it himself.

This in turn signals the recipient that he must not understand the communication directly, as a system of ideas to be read off for their objective content alone, but that he is required to remake his own existence in the context of this new communication. This is not to identify understanding with acceptance. The recipient may very well understand the communication in such a way as to reject it. But he has at any rate not understood it until he has explored in the passion of his own inwardness its significance for his existence.

The concrete mechanisms by which such a communication is effected are many. Kierkegaard himself makes use of a great variety of methods: mystifying language, irony and humor, pseudonyms, story-telling, apparent frivolity, etc. But none of these particular *methods* is essential to the *form* of indirect communication. The method of straightforward argument can be the vehicle for an indirect communication as well as any other, as it is, for example, in large sections of the *Postscript* and *The Concept of Dread.*

Indirect communication, therefore, may be characterized formally apart from an extended discussion of particular methods, which may be as manifold as the imaginations of their authors. One way Kierkegaard characterizes it is to say that an indirect communication is a communication "without results" (cf. *Postscript* 121-25, 216-17). A direct communication communicates "results" in the form of concepts and propositions. A scientist publishes a paper when he has experimentally verified a solution to one of the problems of his science. What the subjective thinker communicates, however, is not an objective result, but a demand for inward understanding. He *offers* problems instead of *solving* problems.

Kierkegaard (to take him as exemplifying his own theory) regarded it as his task to "create difficulties" in the way of existence, since everyone else was busy making life easy—disastrously easy —by handing out pat answers to existential questions (*Postscript* 165-67). The acuity of his dialectical reasoning and the apparent dogmatism of some of his statements may be confusing at first, but careful reading of Kierkegaard reveals (as I hope will be even clearer at the end of this discussion) that he never answers any of the existential questions he puts. His dialectic and his energetic affirmation are all for the sake of elaborating the problems themselves. How could a man answer problems in the sphere of thought when the problems are the sort that (on his own insistence) only arise in existence? The power of Kierkegaard's argument and the forcefulness of his assertions, plus the complete absence of "results," were calculated to make the reader aware of such problems and oblige him to wring out his own solution of them.

Of course this is not the whole of what is communicated by the subjective thinker. There is a dialectic here. Even if his communication were nothing but a series of questions, it would be something of a "result" to have formulated the questions. Short of gibberish, there is no way of avoiding the presence of objective content in what one says. Nor is it desirable to do so, inasmuch as some objective content and some direct understanding of it must be present in any communication. Kierkegaard for example intends that his propositions be understood like any other propositions, that his arguments be followed like any other arguments, and so forth. But the point is that it is not only the objective meaning of propositions and arguments that is being communicated. The meaning is the objective *means* by which a further truth is conveyed. But the perception of this truth requires the recipient to go beyond understanding the objective meaning, to the appropriation of this meaning-content in "passionate inwardness."

As for the subjective thinker there is no way to escape the dialectic of thought and his existence in his thinking itself, so in indirect communication there is no way out of the analogous dialectical situation. That is what makes the communication indirect. That is why (in Kierkegaard's second characterization of it) the practice of indirect communication is an *art*. It is the "deceptive" nature of art to relate the artist and his audience by setting a distance between them (aesthetic distance). Every work of art means more than it says. It must be "doubly reflected," its immediate form and content must be related by the viewer (or hearer or reader) to himself and his own vision of life, before he can understand what the artist is communicating. What the artist does through the medium of sensuous form the existential philosopher does through the medium of propositions and arguments (cf. *Postscript* 67-74).

If, therefore, a human being can sustain a meaningful relation to existence in his thinking, and if he can communicate his thinking in a way that does not violate its existential character, then an existential philosophy is a real possibility. To demonstrate this *possibility* on Kierkegaard's terms was the whole object of this section of our discussion. But we have actually said little about the concrete *character* of existential philosophy. This is the object of our concluding section.

III. Existential Philosophy.

From the preceding discussion we can now infer the following characteristics of existential philosophy.

1. The difficulty in existential thinking, Kierkegaard says, is "to interpenetrate one's existence with consciousness, at one and the same time eternal and as if far removed from existence and yet also present in existence and in the process of becoming . . ." We have seen, in our discussion of the dialectic of thought and its appropriation, how this is effected, how "existence itself combines thinking with existing, in so far as the thinker exists" (*Postscript* 273, 274).

The importance of the *dialectical* nature of existential thinking cannot be over-emphasized. In addition to intellectual acuity, the existential thinker requires, Kierkegaard says, imagination, feeling, and passion. Especially passion, without which he cannot think existence while existing (*Postscript* 312-13). It is in and by passion that a man truly apprehends what Kierkegaard calls the "qualitative disjunction"—the fact that he is both a thinker and therefore abstracting from existence, and at the same time existing and concerned to understand his existence.

Now this qualitative disjunction is undoubtedly itself a structural characteristic of human existence. Kierkegaard did not regard existence as structureless and unintelligible. Unless we affirm the presence of the form of Man in each individual man, he says, we are reduced on the side of understanding to the desperate silence of skepticism and on the side of action to the desperate opportunism of the Sophists (*Fragments* 30). The difficulty with thinking existence is not that it has no intelligible structure, but that concrete existence is *more* than its structure (*Postscript* 295). A thinker may very well apprehend and express abstractly this structure of existence, the qualitative disjunction. He may speak correctly and at length about the essence of existence—but he is not for that reason an existential philosopher. For he has not understood existence existentially. He has not lived in the qualitative disjunction and there appropriated the truth of existence with passion. To speak correctly about existence and to philosophize existentially are two different things.

Not every "philosophy of existence," therefore, is necessarily a case of existential philosophy. For it is possible to philosophize unexistentially about existence. On the other hand, many philosophers who do not explicitly discuss the same concepts or share the same "results" as the *Existenz* philosophers have nevertheless philosophized in the existential manner. Kant and Socrates, mentioned above, are but two examples, to whom many more could be added from the history of human thought. For if it is anything at all, existential philosophy as Kierkegaard defines it is not the name for a set of doctrines or a group of like-minded men who write about *Existenz*, *Angst*, *Verzweiflung*, etc.—it is neither a system nor a school, but the name for a *way* of wrestling with those problems of the meaning of man's existence that have concerned every major thinker.

The job of the existential philosopher, as opposed to the "philosopher of existence," is to "understand *himself* in his existence" (*Postscript* 314). The distinction of thinking and existence cannot be only the *object of* his thinking, it must first and foremost be *present in* his thinking. His thinking must be not only transparent to its object (the aim of objective knowledge), it must also be transparent to itself. Here again it is the subjective factor, the *how*, that makes existential thinking existential. If a philosopher forgets this, his thought loses reality, and his truth does not exist.

The difference between objective and existential thinking Kierkegaard expresses in yet another way:

> While abstract thought seeks to understand the concrete abstractly, the subjective thinker has conversely to understand the abstract concretely. Abstract thought turns away from concrete men to consider men in general; the subjective thinker seeks to understand the abstract determination of being human in terms of this particular existing human being.... Every human being must be assumed in essential possession of what es-

sentially belongs to being a man. The task of the subjective thinker is to transform himself into an instrument that clearly and definitely expresses in existence whatever is essentially human. *(Postscript* 315, 318)

In so far as it gives utterance to what is "essentially" human, existential philosophy will possess the objectivity and the universality necessary to intelligible discourse. By its very objectivity and universality it reveals its relevance to all men and not just to the philosopher. But the "essence of man" as communicated by the existential philosopher will not have finality; it will not take the form of a definitive ontology of existence. For it is the universal objective structure of human existence *as understood* in his existence by a particular human being. And if this structure is to be understood by other men, they must in turn make their own individual appropriations of it.

The truth of human existence is never captured once for all, *ordine geometrico demonstrata,* so that philosophers may eventually retire to the untroubled enjoyment of their inheritance. There is a profound certainty attaching to the individual's living understanding of his existence. But this certainty is not a place where we can individually or as a group remain. It is a place at which we must, as individuals and each individual many times, repeatedly arrive.

2. Existential philosophy, in its communication as well as in its appropriation, is a work of freedom. Kierkegaard writes that "... just as the subjective existing thinker has made himself free through the reduplication given his reflection"—his appropriation of the truth of existence—"so the secret of all communication consists precisely in emancipating the recipient..." *(Postscript* 69).

When he appropriates the truth with passion and makes it a constituent of his being, the thinker "makes himself free." The act of subjective understanding, because it is a decision and a commitment, is also the ethical act of self-determination. When he translates a possibility of thought into the actuality of his personal existence, when he understands the truth by living in it, a man gains both understanding (as a thinker) and authentic individuality (as a man). And the achievement of individuality through one's action is the concrete exercise of freedom. Freedom as the possibility of such action (the essence of freedom) is the abstract condition of individuality. The attainment of individuality by the passionate inward actualization of the truth is the existential consummation of freedom (cf. *The Concept of Dread,* passim).

The existential philosopher's communication, therefore, must be faithful to the freedom of its recipient, "lest through being too extraordinarily communicative he should succeed in transforming a learner's existence into something different from what a human existence in general has any right to be" *(Postscript* 78).

The nature of existential truth demands that it be apprehended by every individual in the privacy of his own freedom. It is neither

communicated nor apprehended "directly," but by the detour of translation, from actuality to possibility on the part of the communicator,
and from possibility to actuality on the part of the recipient. Existential truth cannot and must not retain an impersonal self-identity
in the process of communication, or it ceases to be existential, and the
recipient of it is defrauded at once of the truth and of his freedom. It
is the meaning of existential truth that it makes men free. When a
thinker "succeeds" in communicating it directly, he succeeds only in
enslaving the recipient to an illusion.

The simple intellectual relationship of man to man that is possible and even desirable in the sciences and in disciplines like mathematics and formal logic is out of place in existential philosophy. Here
the intellectual situation is complicated by the presence of a moral
factor, so that the legitimate desire to communicate must not transform itself into the desire to communicate at any cost, to think for another man so as to reduce him to a state of dependence. Whatever he
may owe him in an intellectual sense, no man can or dare be in debt
to another for that truth which can only exist in so far as he himself
brings it into being. Every act of communication, by which a thinker
advances with the truth he has earned in the exercise of his freedom,
must be accompanied by an act of withdrawal that leaves the recipient room for the necessary exercise of *his* freedom. Too great a concern for recognition, too much eagerness to make disciples, is a sign
that a thinker has ceased to think and communicate existentially—
just as, we saw above, too much willingness to admire and to take
oaths on the word of another is a self-deception on the part of the recipient.

It is understandable that Kierkegaard regarded Socrates as the
greatest of all teachers and the prototype of indirect communication
(cf. *Fragments*, Ch. I). In the Socratic dialogues of Plato, Socrates'
interlocutors never come to the acceptance of a doctrine. Problems are
raised, examined, and left unsolved. But in the course of the dialectic
the interlocutors are purged of their "double ignorance"; they come to
a genuine awareness of what they do not know—that awareness
which Socrates remarked made him the wisest man in Athens. If on
the basis of this honest apprehension of ignorance they go on to positive enlightenment, they do so themselves by giving birth to the truth
out of their own souls. This is the existential validity of the doctrine
of recollection and the maieutic method: that knowledge comes not
from the teacher but from the learner, and that the teacher, by dialectically removing the obstacles in its way, is only the occasion of
the truth and not its cause.

The communication of existential philosophy is true to the dialectic of personal and impersonal factors in the relation of teacher
and learner. There is an important respect in which the personal
reality of the teacher is not of interest to the learner, and vice versa

(cf. *Postscript* 289). It is ideas and not personalities that they share. But the teacher and the learner are both interested in *themselves* personally, and only when they are so concerned does the exchange of ideas become a process of education. The teacher is concerned with his reality as a teacher, and the learner with his reality as a learner. But their relationship is destroyed if the teacher tries to learn for the learner and if the learner desires to take over the truth ready-made from the teacher.

The master and his disciple may have all their ideas in common and never communicate. Teacher and learner may disagree at every point and yet communicate. For they reason together, but they appropriate alone. Disagreement is in fact of greater educational value than agreement; we learn more from those we argue with than from those we can always say "Yes" to or who always say "Yes" to us. It is with difficulty that the disciple breaks with the master, but it is only in the breaking-away that the process of learning is fulfilled in truth.

An existential philosophy is the work of the creative individual, isolated in his freedom, and is only communicated across that gulf which their freedom cuts between men. Every reappropriation of it is a re-creation, an original apprehension of the eternal essential truth by a free but finite spirit. It is no more to be desired than it is likely to happen, that philosophers should gradually, by the accumulated results of generations of thinkers, come into the millenium of perfect agreement and take their rest. Presumably the ideal of medical research would be the cessation of medical research in an era of perfect health. But the ideal of existential philosophizing is the re-creation of truth anew in every individual as long as men continue to exist.

3. Kierkegaard himself expressed briefly his own ideal of existential philosophy, and we might well conclude by taking note of it. He writes, "While the Hegelian System goes on and becomes an existential philosophy in sheer distraction of mind, and what is more, is finished—without having an ethics (where existence properly belongs), the more simple philosophy which is propounded by an existing individual for existing individuals, will more especially emphasize the ethical" (*Postscript* 110).

Philosophy is not made for God or for pure egos to contemplate, but for men to live by. It is a work of man, made for the benefit of men. Even its concern for Being is from the standpoint and for the sake of human beings, not from the standpoint of Being and certainly not for the sake of Being—which, if it needs anything, can scarcely need our philosophy. All talk about reality is not an essence-eye view of essence, but a man's view of reality and his place in it.

But the life of man is the area of ethical inquiry, where "ethical" is taken in the largest sense. "The stamp of the ethical is what every existing individual has the right to expect of all that calls itself wisdom" (*Postscript* 274). The ethical man, confronting the eternal in the form of futurity, in the ceaseless tension to actualize his possibilities, is therefore engaged in what Kierkegaard calls a "persistent striving" to realize the truth of his existence.

> As soon as it is remembered that philosophizing does not consist in addressing fantastic beings in fantastic language, but that those to whom the philosopher addresses himself are human beings; so that we have not to determine fantastically *in abstracto* whether striving is something lower than the systematic finality or *vice versa*, but that the question is what existing beings, in so far as they are existing, must be content with: then persistent striving will be the only thing that does not contain a disillusionment. (*Postscript* 110)

The reason for philosophizing existentially is not the ideal superiority of such a way of thinking. The ideal of persistent striving for the truth is not "morally better" than the ideal of absolute truth. It is a question of what is relevant to the situation of a man. A persistent striving for the truth of one's own being is *ontologically* superior just in so far as it is the only kind of philosophizing that is faithful to the nature of man's existence. "If a man occupied himself, all his life through, solely with logic, he would nevertheless not become logic; he must therefore himself exist in different categories" (*Postscript* 86). Whatever else a man may think about—that he may think about many things there is no doubt—it is certain that existential thinking is necessary if he is to understand himself. For the purpose of understanding himself and his existence—for the purpose of acquiring wisdom—a persistent striving for the truth is the only means at hand.

> In the ethical sense . . . the persistent striving represents the consciousness of being an existing individual; the constant learning is the expression for the incessant realization, in no moment complete as long as the subject is in existence; the subject is aware of this fact, and hence is not deceived. But Greek philosophy always had a relation to ethics. Hence it was not imagined that the principle of being always a learner was a great discovery, or the enthusiastic enterprise of a particular distinguished individual, for it was neither more nor less than the realization that a human being is an existing individual which it is no great merit to be aware of, but which it is thoughtless to forget. (*Postscript* 110-11)

Kierkegaard continually reverenced the Greek thinkers whose philosophy was their life and whose life expressed their philosophy. For every cut he takes at Hegel there is a sentence in praise of the Greeks. He rejoiced in Socrates' actually "dying away from the world" in accord with his belief, as opposed to the professor who, though he accepts the Socratic doctrine of immortality, lives quite comfortably in the world and has never entertained the slightest thought of dying away from it. Likewise, he respected the Stoics with their calm withdrawal, the Epicureans' unbridled joy in life, and even the puppy-dog antics and vulgarity of a cynic like Diogenes. This, for all its naivete, is philosophy, and not the manufacture of books and talk. "In Greece, philosophizing was a mode of action, and the philosopher was there-fore an existing individual. He may not have possessed a great amount of knowledge, but what he did know he knew to some profit, because he busied himself early and late with the same thing" (*Post-script* 295).

What Kierkegaard wanted was not the end of philosophical thinking, but a restitution of thought to its place in intimate conjunc-tion with action. Philosophy, he thought, must be an inseparable union of the intellectual and the ethical, if it is to be the activity of a man and not of a disembodied mind. His ideal of philosophy as a per-sistent striving (ethical) after truth (intellectual) is no more than a translation of the ancient ideal of philosophy as the love (ethical) of wisdom (intellectual). The irony and the tragedy of Hegel is that he too attempted the construction of an existential philosophy, but fell prey to an overweening intellectualism and wound up spinning out a system that was neither pure enough to be logic nor convincing enough to explain existence. Respecting Hegel as a man who essayed great things and failed (*Postscript* 100n.), Kierkegaard aimed to re-store philosophy in its pristine meaning to men, by restoring human-ity in the full concreteness of existence to philosophy.

FOOTNOTES

1. *The Logic of Hegel*, tr. W. Wallace, p. 44.
2. References to the English translations of Kierkegaard's works are given in parentheses in the text. In the case of direct quotations, where I have sometimes al-tered the translation, reference is also given to volume and page numbers of the second edition of the *Samlede Vaerker*.
3. The following is an abstract of *Fragments* 60-62.
4. Cf. Wallace, op. cit., p. 267.
5. *The Phenomenology of Mind*, tr. J. B. Baillie, pp. 149-60.
6. Probability, on Kierkegaard's analysis, is not an approach to certainty, but an uneraseable question mark over all empirical knowledge. Probability and certainty, he argues, are qualitatively different. Certainty is not the highest point on a continuous scale of quantitatively graded probabilities. Probability does not pass over into cer-tainty by degrees. The series, $1/2 + 1/4 + 1/8 + 1/16 \ldots$, in a sense approaches but does not reach 1. But in another sense, since between any finite member of the series and 1 there is an infinite number of other members, the series never really approaches 1. Analogously, no degree of probability, regardless how high, actually approaches certainty. The highest probability is still uncertain, and the most probable hypothesis, if it is not so close to certainty as to be absolutely certain, remains absolutely uncertain. But a probability which cannot be graded higher or lower as it approaches more or less closely to an absolute standard cannot be measured at all. The concept of probability vaporizes itself unless it is given a stipulative definition within postulated limits. The inevitable arbitrariness of such limits confirms and heightens the problematic charac-ter of all scientific knowledge (cf. *Postscript* 25-31; *Fragments* 76).
7. Relevant also at this point is Kierkegaard's insistence that thinking cannot be-gin "immediately with the immediate." To do so would be to think by accident, or by a circumstantial or temperamental coincidence that is, not to think at all. For thinking is always a deliberate conscious activity. Cf. *Postscript* 102.
8. *The Journals of Søren Kierkegaard*, tr. Alexander Dru, No. 22, p. 15.
9. *Ibid.*, No. 426.

CHAPTER THREE

KANT, KIERKEGAARD, AND RELIGIOUS KNOWLEDGE

by Jerry H. Gill

The contemporary scene in the field of philosophy is characterized by intellectual segregation. The empiricists and existentialists stand over against one another, with only a few thinkers attempting to integrate the two. In spite of this ideological bifurcation, there is an essential unity which underlies the entire contemporary scene, and which often goes unnoticed. No matter how divergent and opposed these two major movements are, they are both agreed that a qualitative distinction must be made between the two main areas of human experience and reality. This distinction is variously expressed as one of science or morality, fact or value, cognitivity or non-sense, and knowledge or mystery. The empiricists maintain that only that aspect of reality and experience which can be conceptualized and confirmed is of real significance. The existentialists maintain that only that aspect of reality and experience which deals with human emotions and values is of real significance. In short, both movements agree on the dichotomy between fact and value, or knowledge and mystery, but each focuses on a different aspect of this dichotomy.

This divided-but-united situation is reflected in the contemporary discussion surrounding the question of religious knowledge. Confessionally-oriented theologians (following the Barthian tradition) and existentially oriented theologians (following the Bultmannian tradition) both work under the assumption that religious awareness and faith are not related to conceptual cognitivity in an essential way. Although there are signs of renewed interest in religious cognitivity among "analytic theologians," the most popular position is still the one based upon the work of Søren Kierkegaard. The "infinite qualitative distinction" between knowledge and faith which pervades Kierkegaard's thought continues to dominate the contemporary scene. Moreover, a case can be made for the position that Kierkegaard's distinction between knowledge and faith is closely related to a similar distinction in the philosophy of Immanuel Kant. In the following discussion I will summarize the positions of these two thinkers with an eye to exemplifying this similarity.

Reprinted with permission from PHILOSOPHY AND PHENOMENOLOGICAL RESEARCH, Vol. XXVII, 2, December 1967.

I

Kant inherited his philosophical problems from his intellectual ancestors. Having been thoroughly schooled in, and convinced of, the rationalistic views of Leibnitz and Wolff, Kant was rudely awakened from his "dogmatic slumber" by the profundity and precision of David Hume's thinking.[1] Hume had put an end to the high hopes of both the continental rationalists and the British empiricists. The former sought, and claimed to have found, an epistemological foundation for all knowledge and reality in the necessary conclusions deducible from self-evident truths. The latter sought, and claimed to have found, such a foundation in the probable conclusions "inducible" from sense impressions. Hume followed the empiricist approach more thoroughly than his predecessors and was able to demonstrate that neither deduction nor induction can provide an adequate foundation for knowledge. Deduction, with its "self-evident" premises, turned out to be definitional (analytic) and empty of factual content, while induction proved to be based upon the unjustified assumption that the future will be like the past. Thus Hume had eliminated the possibility of factual truth claims in mathematics, science and metaphysics.

Kant was convinced of the validity of Hume's reasoning, but at the same time he was aware that mathematical, scientific, and metaphysical knowledge form a vital part of the human situation, and seem to be quite well established. The question which serves as the focal point of Kant's philosophy is: "How are mathematical, scientific and metaphysical knowledge possible?"[2] In other words, since such knowledge is a reality, what must be the case in order to account for its existence? The answer which he worked out not only serves as a synthesis of rationalism and empiricism, but represents a profound epistemological revolution which Kant himself likened to Copernicus' astronomical revolution.[3]

Kant's epistemology, set forth in his *Critique of Pure Reason*, is based on the belief that knowledge is composed of two aspects, namely content and form. With the empiricists he maintains that the content of knowledge is supplied by sensory experience, but in harmony with rationalism he maintains that the form (or structure) of knowledge is supplied by the mind. Kant asserted that the mind plays an active part in the knowing experience by imposing upon the data of sensation certain fixed "categories." Thus what is known is sensory experience after it has been "filtered through," or organized by, the built-in categories of the understanding. Both of these elements are necessary, but neither is sufficient, for knowledge to take place.

> But, though all our knowledge begins with experience, it by no means follows that all arises out of experience. For, on the contrary, it is quite possible that our empirical knowledge is a compound of that which we receive through impressions, and that which the faculty of cognition supplies from itself (sensuous impressions giving merely the occasion), an

addition which we cannot distinguish from the original element given by sense, till long practice has made us attentive to, and skilful in separating it.[4]

Although no sensations of these categories are possible, we do possess "ideas" of them. The concepts of space, time and causation[5] are perhaps the most crucial and will have to suffice as examples in this brief discussion. Concepts such as these are common and essential in ordinary and theoretic understanding, and yet they have no content of their own, *i.e.*, they cannot be perceived. Rather, according to Kant, they are the very framework by means of which objects can be experienced and understood. Moreover, because of their all-pervasive, categorical nature, these concepts can be said to yield necessary (a priori) and factual (synthetic) knowledge.[6] All human experience and knowledge must be characterized by space, time, causation, etc., since these comprise the very nature of the human mind. Thus statements involving these concepts are both necessarily true and factually significant.

This necessary-factual, or *a priori-synthetic*, knowledge provides an answer, according to Kant, to the crucial question, "how is knowledge possible?" Mathematical and scientific knowledge find their basis and justification in the categories of the understanding, since the latter are the necessary conditions of human thought. Geometry, which is dependent upon the category of space, and arithmetic, which is dependent upon the category of time (sequence), yield a knowledge which is necessary, but *not* empty of factual content. In like manner, science, which is dependent upon the category of causation as the basis of inductive inference, yields a knowledge which guarantees that future experiences will follow a causal pattern similar to that of past experiences. Kant was convinced that *a priori-synthetic* knowledge, based on the categories of the understanding, provides a thorough and final answer to the problems raised by Hume.

To put the whole matter another way, Hume had maintained that (1) all statements that are known to be true apart from experience (a priori) are also analytic (definitional), (2) all statements that have factual content (synthetic) are only known to be true on the basis of experience (a posteriori), therefore (3) all significant statements are either a priori-analytic or a posteriori-synthetic, and finally (4) since a priori-analytic statements make no factual claims and a posteriori-synthetic statements unjustifiably assume causal inference, knowledge claims are without justification. Kant, on the other hand, replied that since the categories of the understanding are necessary to explain the fact of human knowledge, and since these categories yield concepts which are both necessary and factually significant, there must exist a priori-synthetic statements which provide a sound basis for knowledge claims.

One example of an a priori-synthetic statement is all that can be given in this brief survey of Kant's thought. This example is one of Kant's favorites.[7] The mathematical proposition $7+5=12$ is both necessarily true and factually significant, since its truth can be determined apart from experience (a priori), but it actually says something about the world of experience (synthetic). It is not analytic, since 12 is not part of one's mental conception when one thinks or says $7+5$ and it is not a posteriori, since its truth is not dependent upon the experience of actually counting objects. $7+5=12$ is a priori-synthetic because it is based upon the mental category of sequence (time). The serious logical shortcomings of Kant's understanding of mathematics will have to be overlooked in this exposition.

Kant's account of metaphysics does not conclude with the same positive results as his account of mathematics and science. Since both mathematics and science are attempts to conceptualize about the world of sensory experience (phenomena), their use of the categories of the understanding is quite appropriate. The results of the application of these categories to the phenomenal world are reliable because the phenomenal world actually derives its reality from the categories in the first place. Metaphysics, however, is traditionally defined as the study of reality as it really is (noumena), apart from the limitations of sensory experience—the study of reality in and of itself (ding an sich). In such an endeavor, it is clear that the application of the categories of the mind would be completely inappropriate, since these phenomenal categories would distort one's understanding of the noumena in the same way that dark green sunglasses distort one's perception of color. But if these categories of the understanding, which comprise the human intellect, cannot be used in metaphysics, what categories can be used? Clearly none, for these are the only mental categories man has at his disposal—man's knowledge is limited by the nature of his intellect. Thus Kant concludes that metaphysics, as it has traditionally been conceived, is strictly impossible.

> All conceptions, therefore, and with them all principles, however high the degree of their *a priori* possibility, relate to empirical intuitions, that is, data towards a possible experience. Without this they possess no objective validity, but are mere play of imagination or of understanding with images or notion.[8]

Kant devotes a good deal of space to a discussion of the mistakes and confusions which result from the abortive attempt to transcend the categories of the understanding by conceptualizing about the noumenal world.[9] Instead of transcending the categories, one actually ends up applying them to themselves, which in turn results in either empty abstractions or anthropomorphic hypostatizations. The history of philosophy is replete with examples of both. Kant mentions three such mistakes, and classifies them as "The Psychological Idea," "The

Cosmological Idea," and "The Theological Idea."[10] The first is a result of applying the category of "substance" to the noumena in order
to obtain the concept of a soul, or self. The second is a result of applying the category of "causation" to the noumena in order to construct a
concept of the world. The third results from applying the category of
"possibility" to the noumena by way of constructing a concept of God.
It is on the basis of the inapplicability of the categories of the
mind of the noumenal world that Kant develops his profound criticisms of the traditional arguments for God's existence. The ontological and causal arguments are inpotent because they attempt to arrive
at conclusions about reality beyond the phenomenal world by means
of the categories of phenomenal knowledge and experience. Thus they
become pure abstractions, empty of factual (existential in the logical
sense) content. There are, of course, other logical reasons which Kant
offers in criticism of such arguments, but this is not the place to review them. Kant states his conclusion thus:

> Now I maintain that all attempts of reason to establish a theology by the
> aid of speculation alone are fruitless, that the principles of reason as ap-
> plied to nature do not conduct us to any theological truths, and conse-
> quently, that a rational theology can have no existence, unless it is
> founded upon the laws of morality. For all synthetical principles of the
> understanding are valid only as *immanent* in experience; while the cogni-
> tion of a Supreme Being necessitates their being employed transcenden-
> tally, and of this the understanding is quite incapable.[11]

Traditional metaphysics is, then, impossible. Nevertheless, Kant
realized that thinkers will continually be tempted to apply their reasoning powers beyond their limits, and that the "metaphysical urge"
is here to stay. To cope with these two facts, Kant offered two sugges-
tions. First, he wrote a shortened and simplified version of his epistemological analysis entitled, *Prolegomena To Any Future Metaphysics*,
in which he advised thinkers not to bother themselves with traditional
metaphysics, since it is a strict, logical impossibility. Second, he pro-
posed that the term 'metaphysics' be "recoined" so as to refer to the
analysis of the nature and limitations of human thought—following
Kant's own example!

> Critique, therefore, and critique alone contains in itself the whole well-
> proved and well-tested plan, and even all the means, required to estab-
> lish metaphysics as a science; by other ways and means it is impos-
> sible.[12]

Kant's account of morality is set forth in his *Critique of Practical
Reason*. The type of reasoning employed in matters of ethics is not
speculative (with conceptual understanding as its goal), but rather it
is practical (with moral action as its goal).[13] Although this type of
reasoning is not subject to conceptual categories, it is subject to the
categorical imperative of duty. Each and every man is confronted

with the imperative, "Do your duty," and whether a particular decision is moral or immoral is determined solely on the basis of whether or not it was made in response to this call of duty. For Kant, an imperative to do one's duty necessarily implies the freedom to be able to do one's duty. It was upon this foundation of personal freedom that Kant built his entire system of moral and educational excellence.

The line that Kant drew between pure (speculative) and practical (moral) reason was clear and impassable. There were at least two important reasons for drawing the line in this way. First, it enabled Kant to isolate and thus delimit the nature and limitations of speculative reason. Second, it enabled Kant to establish moral philosophy and action on an independent and autonomous basis. Others had suggested similar distinctions before him, but none had worked out the dichotomy between fact and value so thoroughly. Here is the cornerstone of nearly all of contemporary philosophy. "The theoretical use of reason was concerned with objects of the cognitive faculty..... It is quite different with the practical use of reason. In this, reason is concerned with the grounds of determination of the will."[14]

Kant's account of religion, unsurprisingly, fits smoothly into the epistemological and moral dichotomy outlined in the foregoing discussion. Traditionally, religion had found its basis in the realm of knowledge, and more particularly in the field of metaphysics. The claims of religion were construed as knowledge claims about ultimate (noumenal) reality. This approach not only led to insoluble conflicts between interpretations,[15] but it left religion open to the criticisms of logic and science. By delineating the phenomenal limits of knowledge claims, Kant rendered this view of religion entirely sterile. The end of metaphysics meant the end of religious speculation and/or theology. But far from considering himself the enemy of religion, Kant conceived of himself as its chief benefactor. By making a thorough and clear distinction between speculative reason and practical reason, he had provided religion with a basis in the moral realm, which not only removed it out of range of intellectual criticism, but allowed it to focus on its primary business as well. Religion's main concerns are, according to Kant, obeying God and serving mankind, and these have to do with morality, not knowledge.

Although his critiques make some mention of this conclusion,[16] Kant worked out its implications most thoroughly in his *Religion Within the Limits of Reason Alone*. Herein he makes a distinction between a reasoned and a revealed religion. The former is based on practical reason and is primarily concerned with morality, while the latter is based on historical facts and is primarily concerned with doctrines and practices. Moreover, only the former can be universal, since it is based on the moral imperative which every man experiences, while the latter is based on special information which is limited to a few. One of the main concerns of Kant's *Religion* is to develop the relationship between his moral religion within the limits of practical reason and the Christian religion set forth in the Scripture. He maintained that when men

> fulfil their duties to men (themselves and others) they are, by these very acts, performing God's commands and are therefore in all their actions and abstentions, so far as these concern morality, perpetually in the service of God, and that it is absolutely impossible to serve God more directly in any other way (since they can affect and have an influence upon earthly beings alone, and not upon God).[17]

One final point remains to be discussed in this survey of Kant's thought. Once having separated knowledge and morality, and having identified religion with the latter, Kant allowed himself to conjecture concerning the implications of his view of religion. It has already been mentioned that he was convinced that the imperative nature of moral duty implies individual freedom. In addition, Kant maintained that the moral imperative of duty implies personal immortality and the existence of God.[18] Since man is faced with the moral imperative to become a person who does his duty, in short a virtuous person, it is only reasonable (from a practical standpoint) to "postulate" the continuation of life after death and the existence of an eternal, all good God. The former (immortality) is necessary to allow sufficient time to achieve the desired virtue, and the latter (God) is necessary to serve as the ground and standard of the desired virtue. Beginning with the experiential fact of moral responsibility, Kant reasoned to opportunity (immortality) and justice (God). If a man is to be held responsible, he must be provided with the opportunity of achievement, and there must be a source and standard of achievement.

> On the other hand, a requirement of pure *practical* reason is based on a *duty*, that of making something (the *summum bonum*) the object of my will so as to promote it with all my powers; in which case I must suppose its possibility and, consequently, also the conditions necessary thereto, namely, God, freedom, and immortality ... but the subjective effect of this law, namely, the mental *disposition* conformed to it and made necessary by it, to promote the practically possible *summum bonum*, this presupposes at least that the latter is *possible*, for it would be practically impossible to strive after the object of a conception which at bottom was empty and had no object.[19]

This is Kant's famous "moral argument" for the reality of God and immortality. The terms "imply," "necessitate," "argument" are used in a qualified sense. In no sense can these considerations be considered as rational demonstration. Nonetheless, they are practical implications of the moral life which establish the reality of religion in the only way it can, and needs to be established. It is in this way that Kant claimed to have "abolished knowledge in order to make room for belief."[20]

II

Kierkegaard inherited his philosophical problems from Hegel. Contrary to what might have been expected, Kant's philosophy did not put an end to traditional metaphysics. In almost no time at all philosophers were maintaining that the elements and categories of human understanding actually reflect the structure and nature of the noumenal world. Thus the analysis, or critique, of human speculative reason which Kant had championed was turned into the key which unlocked the secrets of reality. The systematic philosophy of Hegel represents the climax of this new path into metaphysics. Hegel's "Absolute Idealism" unites the nature and structure of the mind (Idealism) with the nature and structure of transcendent reality (the Absolute). The originality, profundity, and comprehensiveness of Hegel's philosophy made it the most influential ideology of the nineteenth century. It even effected a marriage between philosophy and Christian theology!

In his *Philosophical Fragments*, Kierkegaard analyzes the epistemology of idealism, contrasting it to that of New Testament Christianity. He concludes that the marriage between the two is a mistake and must be annulled. It is my contention that in his attempt to overcome the Hegelian identification between idealistic philosophy and Christian theology, Kierkegaard relied upon an epistemological position essentially similar to that of Kant. That is to say, he espoused an absolute dichotomy between knowledge and faith, and assigned religion to the realm of feelings and morality. Before embarking upon a summary of his reasonings in the *Fragments*, this quote from his *Journal* will be offered as initial substantiation of the above claim:

> But such a scientific method becomes especially dangerous and pernicious when it would encroach also upon the sphere of spirit. Let it deal with plants and animals and stars in that way; but to deal with the human spirit in that way is blasphemy, which only weakens ethical and religious passion. Even the act of eating is more reasonable than speculating with a microscope upon the functions of digestion.... A dreadful sophistry spreads microscopically and telescopically into tomes, and yet in the last resort produces nothing, qualitatively understood, though it does, to be sure, cheat men out of the simple, profound and passionate wonder which gives impetus to the ethical.... *The only thing certain is the ethical-religious.*[21]

In the first chapter of *Philosophical Fragments* Kierkegaard sets forth the idealist epistemology and contrasts it to that of New Testament Christianity. Classical idealism maintains that knowledge is obtained by rational, introspective dialectic. Plato's doctrine of "recollection," Descartes' concept of "intuition," and Hegel's doctrine of "the truth as the whole" all exemplify this approach. The presupposition which underlies such doctrines is that knowledge is a matter of the learner becoming aware of that which is already within him.[22] In

other words, there is an essential unity between the knower and ultimate reality, which enables the mind of the former to reflect the latter
—even though this unity is very often hidden behind the vicissitudes
of sensory experience.

The logical corollary of the foregoing position is that time, history, and individual existence must be viewed as nonessential and
irrelevant to truth and knowledge. All such factors become mere accidental "occasions" for the reflecting of eternal truth.[23] To put it
differently, the original relationship between the mind and reality is
said to be one of harmony and continuity, with particulars simply
serving to disclose this unity to the knower.

Over against this view Kierkegaard sets an alternative view
which maintains that time, history and individual existence are essential in coming to the knowledge of truth. Although he introduces
this view as a tentative "thought project," Kierkegaard takes this to
to be the epistemological position of New Testament Christianity. The
underlying presupposition of this approach is that knowledge is a
unique achievement which actually effects something in the learner
which was not there previously. The particular temporal experiences
of the existing individual thus become extremely important as decisive media of knowledge.[24] In this position the original relation between the mind and reality is one of discontinuity, with particulars
serving to bridge the gap between the two. In this dichotomy between
the mind and reality one can see marked similarities to Kant's epistemology.

Kierkegaard spends a good deal of time in the latter part of chapter one and in chapter two developing some of the theological implications of the epistemological picture outlined above. He maintains that
in the view which places real value on the particulars of time and individuality, not only is the learner originally without knowledge, he
is without the basic condition or ability to receive knowledge as well.
Thus, unless someone (God Himself) supplies him with the condition
(faith) whereby he can receive the truth, the learner will always remain without knowledge. To put it philosophically, the egocentric
predicament will consign the learner to skepticism. Moreover, the
teacher (God) must provide this condition by descending to the level
of the learner, and not by insisting that the learner ascend to the level
of the teacher. All of this renders the specific relationship between
the learner and the teacher (the Moment, when knowledge is obtained) extremely significant and decisive.

The idea that the mind of the knowing subject can ever transcend
the egocentric predicament, and move from ignorance of reality to
knowledge of it, presents itself as a paradox which can not be grasped
by reason. Put theologically, the paradox is that God (as teacher)
would descend to the level of the learner in order to provide him with
the faith which enables him to know the truth.[25] Either man has

knowledge or he does not. If he has it, as in classical idealism, then all he needs is reminding. If he does not have it, as in New Testament Christianity, then it would seem illogical to conceive of his ever obtaining it because he would not recognize it when confronted with it. And yet, Christianity maintains that knowledge can be obtained. This is the "Absolute Paradox" delineated in chapter three of the *Fragments* and summarized in chapter four:

> Unless the God grants the condition which makes it possible to understand this, how is it to be supposed that the learner will be able to discover it! But that the God himself gives this condition has been shown above to be a consequence of the *Moment*, and it has also been shown that the Moment is the Paradox, and that without it we are unable to advance, but return to Socrates.[26]

Kierkegaard maintains that reason must reject such a paradox as meaningless, for it is unable to grasp something that thought can not think. Although a good deal of ink has been used to distinguish between paradox and contradiction in order to protect Kierkegaard from being labelled an irrationalist, the opening pages of chapter three of the *Fragments* make it clear that Kierkegaard uses 'paradox' as a synonym for 'rational contradiction.' One simply cannot, according to Kierkegaard, expect pure, speculative reason to perform beyond its inherent limitations. By means of human reason there is no way to obtain knowledge of reality, nor to break out of the limitations of the egocentric predicament. The attempt to apply reason to ultimate reality only ends in contradiction.[27]

The parallels to Kant's views concerning the limitations and antinomies of speculative reason are obvious. Furthermore, Kierkegaard, like Kant, devotes a good deal of space to criticism of the traditional proofs of God's existence.[28] He argues that deductive proofs are circular and irrelevant to questions of existence, while inductive arguments do not yield proof because the evidence is never all in. Thus, with Kant, Kierkegaard concludes that a strict, rational knowledge of reality, including God, is absolutely impossible.

In the "Appendix" to chapter three, Kierkegaard asserts that the only way out of this skeptical situation (the way made possible by Christianity) is for reason to admit its limitations and set itself aside in order to make room for faith. Only an active, passionate faith can embrace and accept the paradox. This does not mean that the learner "understands" the paradox, but only that he, by reason, understands that it is a paradox, and accepts it as such by faith. Thus, it is only by means of a "leap" that the knower is able to transcend the egocentric predicament. He can not know *how* he has obtained knowledge, but he can know *that* he has obtained it. He can not understand it, but he can experience it.

> We do not ask that he understand the Paradox but only understand that this is the Paradox. How this takes place we have already shown. It

comes to pass when the Reason and the Paradox encounter one another happily in the Moment, when the Reason sets itself aside and the Paradox bestows itself. The third entity in which this union is realized (for it is not realized in the Reason, since it is set aside: nor in the Paradox, which bestows itself—hence it is realized *in* something) is that happy passion to which we will now assign a name, though it is not the name that so much matters. We shall call this passion: *Faith.*[29]

Although Kierkegaard does not connect such faith directly with morality, as does Kant, he does connect it with the realm of feelings and existential experience in a way which makes it similar to Kant's act of "postulating" God and immortality on the basis of the moral imperative.

In chapters four and five, and in the Interlude between them, Kierkegaard raises the question concerning the nature of religious faith. In the case of the disciple who was contemporaneous with the historical Christ (chapter four), it is clear that his faith was not dependent upon a knowledge of the historical circumstances concerning Jesus. Nor was it dependent upon the disciple's knowledge of Jesus' teachings. Both of these only served as "occasions for self-understanding."[30] Faith is not a form of knowledge at all, since "no knowledge can have for its object the absurdity that the Eternal is the historical."[31] In like fashion, faith is not an act of the will, since such an act presupposes the ability to grasp the truth—and man does not have this ability. In fact, faith itself is this ability (or condition) to grasp the truth, and it must be given by God.

Faith is, then, neither knowledge nor an act, but a miraculous gift of God which enables the disciple to accept the paradox that "knowledge" of God (reality) is possible. I have put quotation marks around the term 'knowledge' because Kierkegaard uses it in an ambiguous manner. On the one hand, he appears to maintain that cognitive (propositional) knowledge of God is impossible, and on the other hand he seems to maintain that experiential knowledge of God is possible. Space will not permit further discussion of this important point. Suffice it to say that for myself I do not think Kierkegaard is sufficiently clear in his use of the term 'knowledge.' At any rate, it is clear that he wants an "absolute, qualitative distinction" drawn between 'knowledge' in the scientific and/or philosophical sense and 'faith' in the religious sense.

The same conclusions are said to hold for the disciple who was not contemporaneous with the historical Jesus. If faith were dependent upon the knowledge of historical facts, all "secondhand" disciples down through the ages would be at a decided disadvantage—and, indeed, could not be said to have faith at all![32] Thus it is that religious faith must be defined as completely independent of all forms of human knowledge. That God revealed Himself in history can be received by faith alone.

The historical fact for a contemporary is that the God has *come into existence;* for the member of a later generation the historical fact is that the God has been present through *having come into existence.* Herein precisely lies the contradiction. No one can become immediately contemporary with this historical fact, as has been shown in the preceding; it is the object of Faith, since it concerns coming into existence. No question is here raised as to the true content of this; the question is if one will give assent to the God's having come into existence, by which the God's eternal essence is inflected in the dialectical determination of coming into existence.[33]

In the final pages of the *Fragments,* Kierkegaard sets forth one of the most important implications of the above account of faith. It must be noted, in passing, that there is a definite sense in which this implication undercuts Kierkegaard's original distinction between classical idealism, in which the particular is irrelevant, and New Testament Christianity in which the particular is of decisive importance! Kierkegaard reasons that since faith is independent of any and all forms of knowledge about the historical Jesus, such knowledge only serves as an "occasion" (his term) for confronting the individual with the paradoxical claim that God has made Himself knowable to mankind. In the same way, the testimony of other believers only serves as a pointer to the ultimate reality which is to be accepted by faith. For this reason, the reliability of the particular witness is essentially unimportant. The following quotation clearly states Kierkegaard's rather perplexing point:

If the fact spoken of were a simple historical fact, the accuracy of the historical sources would be of great importance. Here this is not the case, for Faith cannot be distilled from even the nicest accuracy of detail. The historical fact that the God has been in human form is the essence of the matter; the rest of the historical detail is not even as important as if we had to do with a human being instead of with the God. Jurists say that a capital crime submerges all lesser crimes, and so it is with Faith. Its absurdity makes all petty difficulties vanish. Inconsistencies which would otherwise be disconcerting do not count for anything here; they make no difference whatsoever. But it does make a difference on the contrary, if someone by petty calculation should try to auction off faith to the highest bidder; it makes so much difference as to prevent him from ever becoming a believer. If the contemporary generation had left nothing behind them but these words: 'We have believed that in such and such a year the God appeared among us in the humble figure of a servant, that he lived and taught in our community, and finally died,' it would be more than enough. The contemporary generation would have done all that was necessary; for this little advertisement, this *nota bene* on a page of universal history, would be sufficient to afford an occasion for a successor, and the most voluminous account can in all eternity do nothing more.[34]

Having laid out the philosophical skeleton of his position in the *Fragments,* Kierkegaard proceeded to "clothe" it with religious significance in the *Concluding Unscientific Postscript.*[35] This work delineates the dichotomy between objective knowledge and subjective faith even more forcefully than does the *Fragments*. In fact, the *Postscript* is divided into two books, the first of which is concerned with "the objective problem concerning the truth of Christianity," and the second of which is concerned with "the subjective problem concerning the truth of Christianity." Only the first book and the first part of the second book are integral to our present considerations.

After stating the problem in terms of the possibility of basing one's eternal happiness upon a particular historical fact,[36] Kierkegaard proceeds to examine the relevance of historical knowledge to Christian faith. Although the attempt to establish the truth of Christianity on objective historical facts takes various forms—such as scriptural reliability, ecclesiastical authority and/or longevity— the results are always negative. The reason for this is not that the objective truth of such arguments cannot be established, but rather that even if it could be established, this would not have the slightest effect upon the status of one's faith. Nor would the inability to establish such arguments have any effect on faith. In fact, such concern with objective proof is a clear indication of the loss of faith!

> Here is the crux of the matter, and I come back to the case of the learned theology. For whose sake is it that the proof is sought? Faith does not need it; aye, it must even regard the proof as its enemy. But when faith begins to feel embarrassed and ashamed, like a young woman for whom her love is no longer sufficient, but who secretly feels ashamed of her lover and must therefore have it established that there is something remarkable about him—when faith thus begins to lose its passion, when faith begins to cease to be faith, then a proof becomes necessary so as to command respect from the side of unbelief. And as for the rhetorical stupidities that have been prepetrated by clergymen in connection with this matter, through a confusion of the categories—alas, let us not speak of them.[37]

Note here the phrase "confusion of categories." Such concepts clearly point up the Kantian-like dichotomy which Kierkegaard posits between knowledge and faith.

Next, Kierkegaard briefly examines the relevance of objective, speculative reason to Christian faith. Here, too, the conclusion is negative. Philosophical speculation is fine in its place, but one must never allow it to be confused with religious faith. "Christianity does not lend itself to objective observation, precisely because it proposes to intensify subjectivity to the utmost; and when the subject has thus put himself in the right attitude, he cannot attach his eternal happiness to speculative philosophy."[38]

In part one of Book Two, Kierkegaard discusses the relation between knowledge and faith in connection with the philosophy of Lessing. First, Lessing was supposed to have maintained, and Kierkegaard expresses some doubt about his actual beliefs, that since there is an absolute distinction between eternal truth and factual knowledge, the former could never be dependent upon the latter.[39] The eternal truth can only be known by a "leap" out of the realm of factual knowledge. Now, although Kierkegaard thinks that Lessing confuses the issue of contemporaneity, he admires him for having seen the basic disjunction between these two realms.

> I refer to the fact that he religiously shut himself up within the isolation of his own subjectivity; that he did not permit himself to be deceived into becoming world-historic and systematic with respect to the religious, but understood and knew how to hold fast to the understanding that the religious concerned Lessing, and Lessing alone, just as it concerns every other human being in the same manner; understood that he had infinitely to do with God, and nothing, nothing to do with any man directly.[40]

Second, Lessing also said that "if God held all truth in His right hand, and in His left hand held the lifelong pursuit of it, he would choose the left hand."[41] Kierkegaard takes this to be a distinction between the way of speculative, religious knowledge and existential, religious faith. He enters into a lengthy polemic against the concern for a "system" of thought in connection with Christianity. In addition, Kierkegaard uses this distinction as the springboard for his detailed explanation of the nature and quality of the subjective mode of existence which he presents in the remainder of the *Postscript*. Indeed, Lessing's distinction could be said to be the banner under which Kierkegaard's "knight of faith" does battle!

> The existing individual who concentrates all his attention upon the circumstance that he is an existing individual, will welcome these words of Lessing about a persistent striving, as a beautiful saying. To be sure, it did not indeed win for its author an immortal fame, because it is very simple; but every thoughtful individual must needs confirm its truth.[42]

By way of summary, it can be said that Kierkegaard distinguishes between reason and faith, not in order to call attention to two forms of knowledge, but in order to set faith, as an experience and a commitment, over against all forms of knowledge. He is not opting for subjectivity in matters of objective knowledge, but he is opting for subjectivity in matters of modes of existence. Nevertheless, he clearly maintains that such existential subjectivity—adequacy of life—is in no way dependent upon epistemological considerations. In Kierkegaard's approach, the realms of knowledge and faith are entirely separate. It should be noted that I have given him the benefit of the doubt in stating that he does not offer "subjective knowledge" as a substitute for objective knowledge in matters of religion. He is often interpreted in just this way, and there are certainly a number of passages wherein he seems to be doing just that. I take it that the interpretation I have given is the more plausible of the two.

That this position is essentially Kantian should be fairly clear by now. The basic distinction between objectivity and subjectivity (knowledge and faith), the limitations of the former and the priority of the latter, and the association of religion with feelings and morality all suggest an epistemological pattern which is essentially parallel to that of Kant. Of course, this is not to suggest that there are no differences between the approaches of Kant and Kierkegaard. The most obvious difference is that in the face of the impossibility of religious knowledge, Kant merely "posits" the existence of God and immortality in a tentative fashion, while Kierkegaard "leaps" beyond and accepts the paradox that knowledge of God is nonetheless possible, in a decisive fashion. This is a difference in their responses to the epistemological situation, and not in their analysis of the nature of that situation. It could be maintained that both are inconsistent; Kant because he smuggles God in after exiling Him, and Kierkegaard because he actually takes back with one hand the decisive quality of the particular which he had offered with the other.

REFERENCES

1. Hume, David. *An Enquiry Concerning Human Understanding*, Sections II-VII.

2. Kant, Immanuel. *Prolegomena to any Future Metaphysics* (New York: The Liberal Arts Press, 1951), p. 27.

3. Kant, Immanuel. *The Critique of Pure Reason*. Translated by J. M. D. Meiklejohn, Vol. 42 of *The Great Books of the Western World* (Chicago, Encyclopedia Britannica, Inc., 1952), p. 7, 8. (Preface to the second edition).

4. *Ibid.*, p. 14 (Introduction, Sec. I).

5. *Ibid.*, pp. 24-33 (Trans. Doc. of Ele., Part I, Secs. I and II).

6. *Ibid.*, pp. 14-20 (Intro., Secs. I-VI), pp. 38-59 (Trans. Log., Div. I, Book I).

7. *Ibid.*, p. 18 (Intro., Sec. V).

8. *Ibid.*, p. 94 (Trans. Doc. of Faculty of Judgment, chap. III).

9. *Ibid.*, pp. 177-189 (Trans. Doc. of Ele., Book II, chaps. I-III).

10. *Op. Cit., Prolegomena*, pp. 80-98 (Sections 45-56).

11. *Op. Cit., Pure Reason*, p. 191 (Trans. Doc. of Ele., Book II, chap. III).

12. *Op. Cit., Prolegomena*, p. 114 (solution).

13. Kant, Immanuel. *The Critique of Practical Reason*. Translated by T. K. Abbott, Vol. 42 of *The Great Books of the Western World* (Chicago, Encyclopedia Britannica, Inc., 1952), p. 292 (preface).

14. *Ibid.*, p. 296 (Intro.).

15. Referred to by Kant as "Antinomies."

16. *Op. Cit.*, cf. *Pure Reason*, p. 190 (Trans. Doc. of Ele., Book II, chap. III, Sec. VII); and *Practical Reason*, pp. 346, 7 (Part I, Book II, chap. II, Sec. V).

17. Kant, Immanuel. *Religion Within the Limits of Reason Alone*. Translated by T. M. Greene and H. H. Hudson (New York: Harper and Row, 1960), p. 94.

18. *Op. Cit., Pure Reason*, p. 190 (Trans. Doc. of Ele., Book II, chap. III, Sec. VII).

19. *Op. Cit., Practical Reason*, p. 353 (Book II, chap. II, Sec. VIII).

20. *Op. Cit., Pure Reason*, p. 10 (Preface to the second edition).

21. Volume VII (1846), A, 186. Quoted from Walter Lowrie's Introduction to the *Concluding Unscientific Postscript*, p. xv.

22. Kierkegaard, Søren. *Philosophical Fragments* (Princeton University Press, 1962), translated by David F. Swenson, p. 11.

23. *Ibid.*, pp. 13 ff.

24. *Ibid.*, pp. 16 ff.

25. *Ibid.*, p. 46.

26. *Ibid.*, p. 72.

27. *Ibid.*, p. 59.

28. *Ibid.*, pp. ff. and p. 118.
29. *Ibid.*, p. 72.
30. *Ibid.*, p. 75.
31. *Ibid.*, p. 76.
32. *Ibid.*, p. 126.
33. *Ibid.*, p. 108.
34. *Ibid.*, p. 130.
35. Kierkegaard, Søren. *Concluding Unscientific Postscript* (Princeton: Princeton University Press, 1941), translated by David F. Swenson.
36. *Ibid.*, pp. 18-20 (introduction).
37. *Ibid.*, p. 31.
38. *Ibid.*, p. 55.
39. *Ibid.*, pp. 86 ff.
40. *Ibid.*, p. 61.
41. *Ibid.*, pp. 97 ff.
42. *Ibid.*, p. 109.

CHAPTER FOUR

LESSING'S PROBLEM
AND KIERKEGAARD'S ANSWER

by Richard Campbell

Accidental truths of history can never become the proof of necessary truths of reason.

It is a tribute to the perspicacity of Lessing and Kierkegaard that their way of investigating the problem of the role of historical investigation in the task of theological construction has set the tone of subsequent discussion. The centrality of their problem in our time is shown up by the way Diem depicts Lessing's question and Kierkegaard's answer as the starting-point of the contemporary theological debate.[1] Diem's analysis here is penetrating, even if it only shows up the need for that starting-point to be critically examined.

In this article, after an examination of Kierkegaard's general position, what I wish to suggest is (1) that the problem as Lessing has posed it is insoluble, and thus Kierkegaard's paradoxical solution is no solution; (2) that nevertheless, despite his clear dependence on Lessing, Kierkegaard has restated the problem in the only way which shows any promise for a Christian theology; and (3) that the pursuit of this solution requires that faith be not sealed off from 'natural inquiry,' and consequently, a serious grappling with ordinary historical problems is unavoidable in Christian theology—which is the opposite conclusion to that which Kierkegaard himself drew (and which is widely accepted at the present time).

There does seem some truth in saying that any large-scale endeavour to work through a comprehensive programme of thought produces the radical critic who proclaims, after the manner of a prophet, that the programme is wrong-headed and misconceived, and who himself works through the programme for just one reason—to show, once and for all, that the only thing to do is to abandon an impossible investigation. Søren Kierkegaard was such a critic.

It is well to state in general the thesis to end all theological theses which Kierkegaard is putting forward. It is this: the theological task has been taken as concerned with the problem What is Christianity? Yet this is a fruitless question—a question which, because it is objective and philosophical in form, is open to anyone and everyone. But

Reprinted with permission from Richard Campbell and THE SCOTTISH JOURNAL OF THEOLOGY, March 1966.

therein lies its fatal weakness. Being open to anyone and everyone, it is, as such, personally relevant to no one. For the question which, as such, is personally relevant is not What is Christianity? but How can I become a Christian? To put it otherwise, Kierkegaard is not intent on denying that there may not be a proper question as to what are the essential doctrines of Christianity. But he is insisting that the crucially important matters are not dealt with in answering this question, but rather in meeting the problem of how this objective content can be personally appropriated and become effective for me. This second question, the question which is *my* problem, is the real theological problem. And seeing this means seeing that the traditional theological concern has met its end. Its methods are all wrong, and no amount of refashioning of method can right the deficiency, because its driving question is irrelevant.

I do not propose to examine this thesis in the broad way I have stated it. My purpose is to examine in detail Kierkegaard's own programmatic instance of this thesis as he argues for the irrelevance of historical method for the 'real' theological problem. This narrower issue is the one increasingly emerging as the watershed of theological thinking in recent years.

In this regard, the central question to which Kierkegaard addresses himself is given on the title-page of the *Philosophical Fragments* of John Climacus: 'Is an historical point of departure possible for an eternal consciousness; how can such a point of departure have any other than a mere historical interest; is it possible to base an eternal happiness upon historical knowledge?' As he himself demonstrates in the *Postscript*, this question has been taken over from Lessing, and we must accordingly take up the matter with the latter in due course. For the moment we will follow Kierkegaard's development of his own answer.

The title question makes it clear that what Kierkegaard (and Lessing) are after is what can be called 'eternal truth' or 'eternal happiness.' And in the *Fragments* John Climacus presents the paradoxical results which arise from the issue, which he thinks is the *philosophical* issue, of how Truth in this sense can be learned, that is, of how that which is eternal can be realised in the life of individuals in time. This question was the Socratic question, raised especially in the *Meno*. The paradox of learning for Socrates is: 'For what a man knows he cannot seek, since he knows it, and what he does not know he cannot seek, since he does not even know what to seek.'[2]

The Socratic solution is the doctrine of Recollection, with its corollary in the doctrine of the pre-existence of the soul. Socrates' own role as a teacher was to be a midwife.[3] Now when this doctrine is brought to the overall question behind our inquiry, 'from the standpoint of the Socratic thought ever point of departure in time is *eo ipso* accidental, an occasion, a vanishing moment.'[4] The occasion on which I learnt the Truth can only concern me historically (or perhaps 'poetically').

This foil against which he can develop his own distinctive doctrines was provided Kierkegaard by his early study of Socrates, and for the *Fragments* the discussion of the Socratic paradox is very important, integral to the argument. It provides the major alternative to Climacus' own 'experiment in thought.' The experiment he wishes to put forward is to ask what it would be like if God Himself appeared as teacher. Yet he is aware that really it can count as no more than 'a poetic essay,' for all it arrives at is paradoxical, an 'absolute paradox' which can only be called 'a metaphysical whim,' offensive to thought, an 'acoustic illusion.' As Diem has pointed out[5] these expressions are by no means to be regarded as witticisms of no material significance. Climacus' 'experiment' is not meant as something which can be adopted by the reader as a doctrine holding together the philosophic pursuit after Truth and the claims of Christian revelation. Indeed, he thinks such a synthesis—and in his time Hegel was the living monument to such a synthesis—is totally misconceived. This is the meaning of Climacus' motto: 'Better well hung than ill wed.' The bad marriage is inevitable when such a synthesis is attempted, and it is a synthesis which he thinks can only work on some variation of the Socratic paradox.

What Kierkegaard seems to want to get out of this is what I called his thesis to end all theses, viz. the alternative to the Hegelian synthesis is the cessation of the attempt to explore the theological question in the traditional way. Climacus, then, is not teaching a new doctrine, or a sophistication of an old doctrine. What he has to say in his 'poetic essay' is in principle not teachable, viz. a philosophy; its conclusions are paradoxical, nonsense, and thus wholly negative.[6] This analysis of Kierkegaard's argument is offered in defence of my initial characterisation of his programme. It should be clear that this general thesis stands or falls with the issue of the status of historical investigation, as a crucial instance of that thesis.

Opposed in this manner to the Socratic thought, Climacus suggests that there is the alternative that the moment in time *has* a decisive significance. How far it is possible on this presupposition to acquire a knowledge of the Truth is how his overriding question, Lessing's question, suggests the experiment.

I take it that the details of the argument in the *Fragments* are reasonably well known. Climacus contends that if the moment is to have significance, the learner 'must be destitute of the Truth up to the very moment of his learning it.'[7] He is in a state of Error, not even properly describable as a seeker after the Truth. For the learner to acquire the Truth, the Teacher must bring it to him, along with the condition necessary for understanding it, which means that the Teacher would have to be God. This being so, the state of Error must have been due to the learner's own guilt; it is a bondage from which he cannot free himself. Thus, for the moment to have significance, and this is the guiding presupposition of the whole inquiry, the Teacher must be more than a Teacher; He must be a Saviour, who Himself constitutes an Atonement 'taking away the wrath impending upon that of which the learner has made himself guilty.'[8] Such a Teacher cannot ever be forgotten; He is not the occasion for learning the Truth, like the Socratic teacher; He is Judge.

In this scheme, the learner is not so much a learner as a disciple, who from the Saviour-Teacher-Judge is given a new state; he becomes a new creature by a change that is best called conversion. The transition is in fact a new birth. In this way, the sort of question Kierkegaard is prepared to allow can now be asked: Is this hypothesis thinkable? And to this Climacus makes a play upon the notion of birth. To the born birth is quite thinkable—to the unborn the question does not arise.[9]

From this, Climacus argues that if God does so teach, it will be because of His great love for those in Error, a love not satisfied by elevating the learners, but by His coming to them.[10] Descending to their level, He appears in the form of a servant, suffering all things, and being at last forsaken in death, absolutely like the humblest.

This is called the Absolute Paradox at which Reason can only stand appalled. Not only is God absolutely unlike sinful man, but further, this absolute unlikeness is done away in absolute likeness.[11] This Paradox is said to offend the Reason, which holds aloof from it, keeping to the probable, and declaring the Paradox absurd. Yet in this Reason is in fact learning from the Paradox itself, since it is Paradox, *quia absurdum.*

Here, then, is the experiment in thought. It is clear that what Kierkegaard is positing under the guise of this 'experiment' is an interpretation of Christian categories in terms of the personal 'existence' of the Christian. At the very end of the *Fragments,* Climacus comes out into the open to own that he has really been exploring the essential claim of Christianity.[12] He has been, in fact, engaged upon a conceptual analysis of the claims of Christian revelation apart from their historical setting. Not at any stage has he sought to renounce or radically to reinterpret these claims; rather he presupposes their substantial truth. As Diem well sees, 'he by no means rejects dogmatic work, but himself makes use of the Church's elaboration of doctrine. ... He himself realises that his own special task does not consist in dogmatic work and can even say somewhat surprisingly: "Doctrine, as normally expounded, is on the whole correct. I am not disputing about that. My sole concern is how far it can be effective."'[13]

With his identification of Christianity with his 'experiment,' which ended in Absolute Paradox, Climacus is saying that the heart of Christianity is incurably paradoxical, and thus can only be appropriated by a sheer leap of faith. God's appearance as the news of the day does not give occasion for something else; it is itself the beginning of eternity. The news of the day, this is the historical point of departure for the contemporary disciple, and in this he is not really different from the disciple at second hand. To both the historical phenomenon of Jesus is a point of departure. But this historical phenomenon 'refuses to be reduced to a moment of merely occasional significance, but proposes to interest him in another sense than the merely historical, presenting itself to him as a condition for his eternal happiness.'[14]

That this should be so is the heart of the Paradox, and he alleges that no amount of historical filling-in can make it less so. Only as we understand this argument can we appreciate the oft-quoted lines about the few words, the *nota bene* on a page of universal history, which, had the contemporary generation left them, would be more than enough.[15]

Now this argument only holds if it be true that questions of historical enquiry are irrelevant to theological assertions. In saying that 'these words ... would be more than enough' Kierkegaard is gratefully following Lessing. Further, he takes Lessing's words about the leap required to make the transition from historical trustworthiness to eternal happiness in great seriousness, even if Lessing himself was using 'a bit of cunning.' Kierkegaard's understanding of the Paradox is indeed a construct out of the way Lessing posed his problem—it is Lessing who is the forerunner of the 'experiment in thought,' and we have reached the point at which we must leave Kierkegaard in order to examine the validity of the problem which the experiment seeks to answer.

Lessing's position is complex, and I shall only touch upon certain aspects of it—those which are relevant to Kierkegaard, and through him to much modern theology.[16] The line in Lessing's thought bearing upon our discussion is the one which shows itself in his refusal to accept the sort of historical apologetic which the Church in his time was wont to make. It was he who published the 'Fragments' of Reimarus to challenge this historical apologetic, a programme Lessing considered to be altogether disastrous.

His reaction at first sight seems perverse: 'The more insistently one man wanted to prove Christianity to me, the more doubtful I became. The more wilfully and triumphantly another sought to trample it completely underfoot the more inclined I felt to upholding it, in my heart at least.'[17] When we seek to penetrate behind this sort of defiance, we find that his real objection is to *proof*, the method apologists thought they were producing. This method would reply to historical criticism with historical defence, it being assumed that questions of history were vitally relevant to faith. This method Lessing called 'a theological innovation,' and he accused Goeze, the Lutheran opponent of Reimarus' 'Fragments,' of being guilty of this innovation. His reaction to it was violent, crying shame on those who 'want to hang the whole of eternity on a spider's thread,' dragging down the edifice of faith into the mire.[18]

The reason why Lessing in this way rejects any historical proof of Christianity is that he takes it that there must be a certainty, a reliability, in a proof upon which eternal happiness is made to depend which is missing from a 'proof' of history. His argument is complex, but we must try to sort it out.

'Fulfilled prophecies, which I myself experience, are one thing; fulfilled prophecies, of which I know only from history that others say they have experienced them are another. Miracles, which I see with my own eyes, and which I have had opportunity to verify for myself, are one thing; miracles, of which I know only from history that others say they have seen them and verified them, are another.'[19] At first sight it would seem that Lessing is here drawing a distinction between immediate knowledge and historical knowledge. This is a logical distinction, and on the basis of it Lessing would seem to be claiming that in religion somehow an event pregnant with eternal meaning must have happened to *me* before I can understand or believe it. And at bottom Lessing is wanting to say something rather like this. But it is also clear that this logical point about historical knowledge in general is not his main point here. The Proof of the Spirit and of Power is open to the Christian religion *so long as there continue* fulfilled prophecies and miracles. So long as those who follow Christ have still the power to do miraculous things, and these miracles have been seen and experienced, then who would deny to recognise this proof? This position which he allows, he says, is the position of Origen.

From this it can be seen that his point is much narrower. It is that fulfilled prophecies and miracles only constitute proofs provided there exists in the present an analogy to the asserted events. 'But I am no longer in Origen's position; I live in the eighteenth century, in which miracles no longer happen.... To quote Origen and to cite his words that "the proof of power is so called because of the astonishing miracles which have happened to confirm the teaching of Christ" is of little use if one keeps from one's readers what Origen says immediately thereafter. For the readers will also turn up Origen and find with surprise that he argues for the truth of the miracles which happened with the foundation of Christianity ἐκ πολλῶν μὲν thus, from the narrative of the evangelists; chiefly and particularly, however, he argues their truth on the basis of miracles which were still happening.'[20] What this amounts to is an assertion that many New Testament events do not satisfy the criteria of a reliable historical assertion, as he understands them. On *historical* grounds they are inadmissible.

The puzzling thing, however, is that he goes on to say quite explicitly that this is *not* what he means: 'Who will deny (not I) that the
reports of these miracles and prophecies are as reliable as historical
truths can ever be?'[21] This curious blindness to the force of his earlier
argument can only be explained by the fact that Lessing has now
shifted ground, and is working with quite another distinction. His
point now is that no historical truth, no matter how well it is substantiated, can have any more than a problematic certainty attached
to it. 'But if they (these historical truths) are only as reliable as this,
why are they treated as infinitely more reliable? . . . Something quite
different and much greater is founded upon them than it is legitimate
to found upon truths historically proved.'[22] Now we have moved to the
centre of Lessing's problem, phrased in the way Kierkegaard approved, and which is still so influential. We should take careful note,
in passing, that in arriving at this central problem from a consideration of the historicity of miracle stories, Lessing has shifted ground,
and that the two issues (of the historicity of a particular account on
the one hand, and of the role such a historical assertion, once well
substantiated, can play on the other) are quite distinct. To reject a
particular account on the grounds of its failure to satisfy the criteria
of reliable historical assertions does nothing to settle the problem of
the role such an account could have played, if it had been found satisfactory, in a theological scheme. The invalidity of the transition from
a scepticism about certain allegedly historical events to conclusions
about what it is legitimate to found upon truths historically proved
was not seen by Lessing, nor, I fear, by most moderns who discuss
these problems.

Howbeit, from what Lessing has already said (so we can try to fill
in the gaps in his argument) it follows that there is a difference between *historical proof* and what can be *demonstrated*, where demonstration means logically deduced from self-evident premises. So then,
Lessing is making another logical distinction, this time between the
a posteriori 'proof' which can be adduced in support of an historical
assertion, and the *a priori* 'demonstration' of 'eternal truths.' In view
of his acceptance of historical proof, this must be the meaning of the
key terms in the next step in his argument—'if no historical truth can
be demonstrated, then nothing can be demonstrated by means of historical truths.'[23] That this is the structure of the argument, and
further that it rests upon a *logical* distinction of *category* between
historical assertion and eternal truth can be seen from his famous
conclusion, viz. that to take such an historical truth and with it 'to
jump . . . to a quite different class of truths, and to demand of me that
I should form all my metaphysical and moral ideas accordingly; to
expect me to alter all my fundamental ideas of the nature of the God-
head because I cannot set any credible testimony against the resurrection of Christ: if that is not a μετάβασις εἰς ἄλλο γένος, then I do

not know what Aristotle meant by this term.'[24] This is the outcome of his argument, with its foreshadowing of Kierkegaard's leap: 'That, that, is the ugly broad ditch which I cannot get across, however often and however earnestly I have tried to make the leap. If anyone can help me over it, let him do it, I beg him, I adjure him. He will deserve a divine reward from me.'[25]

I have quoted this argument and tried to analyse it in rather great detail, for it is a very important one, and one not properly understood, least of all by theologians. For they are wont to take the ditch to be one of our own digging, whereas my understanding of Lessing is that it is a logical one. And the implications of this need to be seen. If the ditch were of our own digging, then we could say at least that God could jump over it, and, perhaps, by His grace, we might even be enabled to jump over it also, i.e., take a leap of faith. But where the ditch is a logical gulf of the type that Lessing has described, then we cannot even say that God can jump over it without there being a lacuna somewhere. To bridge the gulf without there being this lacuna which demolishes the whole structure is a *logical impossibility*, and to claim that God can perform what are logical impossibilities leads not to the paradoxes of faith but to the absurdities of nonsense. To adapt an old illustration, someone who wanted to claim this for God would have to answer the question: Can God dig a ditch He cannot jump over?

This argument, then, amounts to the *reductio ad absurdum* of the view that ordinary historical assertions are at all relevant to necessary eternal truths, and insofar as theologians of a later time have accepted Lessing's way of putting the problem, there is only one way of pursuing their task. That way is to give up ordinary historical assertions as theologically instructive, and this was Kierkegaard's conclusion. And if this line is taken, and clearly Lessing himself took it, then the patient work of the biblical scholar is irrelevant for theology and faith, and, as subsequent scholarship has discovered, a great gulf yawns between biblical scholarship and dogmatics.[26] For this line, Lessing's classic thesis becomes an axiom: 'Accidental truths of history can never become the proof of necessary truths of reason.'[27]

There are three points, finally, to be noticed about this line in Lessing's thought. Firstly, he has noticed and drawn sharp attention to what is a genuine historical problem about New Testament exegesis, namely that there are assertions of events which bear no direct analogies to present experience, and thus an acute question is raised as to establishing the historicity of these alleged events. If the theologian wants to maintain that the historicity of these events, or certain of them, is essential to Christian theology, and there is a good case for his doing so if that theology is to count as Christian, then he cannot avoid these problems.

Secondly, Lessing's argument about the 'ugly, broad ditch' means that historical assertions and necessary truths have no essential relevance to each other. For his asserting that to pass from one class to another is a μετάβασις εἰς ἄλλο γένος means that on his terms one is not only forbidden to make such a transition in argument, but one cannot adapt, form or alter one's 'metaphysical and moral ideas' in relation to them. It is not just a matter of fallacious *argument;* it is a matter of irrelevance of content.

Thirdly, the cogency of Lessing's conclusion hinges upon his assumption, for it is an assumption, that theological statements come into the class of 'necessary truths of reason.' He has implicitly accepted the former as *a priori;* he demands that they should be capable of proof where by proof means the sort of deductive demonstration such as one finds in Euclid, for he quotes Euclid frequently. For all his rejection of historical apologetic, indeed that might be a sign of it, Lessing is a product of eighteenth-century rationalism. For him, reason in each of us furnishes us with the essentials of religion, which are simply to recognise God, forming only the noblest conceptions of Him, and bearing these in mind in all thought and action. Yet it is necessary, 'conventionally,' for people to single out certain things and ideas, although in truth they are unessential to this natural religion, and to come to some agreement about them. 'Out of the religion of nature, which was not capable of being universally practised by all men alike, a positive religion had to be constructed, just as out of the law of nature, for the same cause, a positive law has been constructed.'[28] 'This positive religion received its sanction through the distinction of its founder, who claimed that the conventional elements in it came from God, only mediated through him, just as certainly as the essential elements in it were immediately derived from God through each individual's reason.'[29] Here is a more explicit affirmation of the rationalist *a priori* character of theological statements which we saw assumed by the distinction between *historical proof* and what can be *demonstrated* essential to his analysis of the 'ugly, broad ditch.' My whole argument has been that if Lessing's identification of theological assertions with necessary truths of reason is conceded, then his gulf must be fixed in his way, and it is indeed unbridgeable, no matter how hard we leap.

But need Lessing's identification be accepted? There seem to be good grounds for rejecting it, and the Christian, at any rate, would seem to be bound to reject it. Otherwise God's *actions* would simply be assimilated to necessary implications of the Divine essence, and thus the fundamental notion of *grace* would be rendered meaningless. But if this is so, then we can only learn of the actions of God *a posteriori* (hence the emphasis upon Scripture, and history), and they can never be logically necessary. It was this dependent-upon-grace feature of

theological statements which Kierkegaard was struggling to elucidate in the 'experiment in thought.' Yet we must remember that he
did so in reaction to the Hegelian system in which religious language
was considered logically necessary, being the description under the
religious 'form' of the unfolding of necessary implications of the Divine essence. Now, when this dependent-upon-grace feature of theological statements is insisted upon, they are then categorised as
'eternal truths' quite wrongly. They likewise are *a posteriori*, and
thus, when theological assertions are seen in this different logical
category, then the sharpness of Lessing's ditch disappears. It is no
longer a question of basing an eternal consciousness upon an historical point of departure, not because the historical point of departure is
given up, but because the *a priori* rationalist notion of 'an eternal consciousness' based upon a notion of 'eternal truths' is rejected on theological grounds. This is not to say that there is not still a proper logical
distinction between theological and historical assertion, and that
their relations do not still require a great deal of careful investigation. But at least questions of relevance can again be asked. Not all
logically distinct types of assertion are irrelevant, as Lessing himself
saw when discussing historical and immediate knowledge.

The result of this discussion of the validity of the problem which
the 'experiment in thought' seeks to answer is in the negative. The
Kierkegaardian leap, which Lessing saw he could not make, is logically impossible, and further, is required only on an understanding of
the nature of theological statements which is incompatible with the
inevitable contingency introduced by the Divine freedom and grace.
Or to put it even more sharply, because he has followed Lessing's
way of putting the problem, Kierkegaard's very commendable attempt
to think through the consequences of accepting the Moment as decisive in our learning Truth is incompatible with his account of the
nature of the leap of faith.

It is through his acceptance of Lessing, for all the latter's use of
'a bit of cunning,' that Kierkegaard can applaud him for opposing
'what I would call an attempt to create a quantitative transition to a
qualitative decision.'[30] On this it needs to be pointed out that in fact
in quite ordinary language a quantitative change of sufficient degree
is enough for us to claim that there has been a qualitative change.[31]
Of course, to cite this everyday fact of language does nothing in itself
to settle the question which is really at issue here, viz. the nature of
the relevance of matters of historical trustworthiness to matters of
faith. But at least it suggests that the issue is not simply another example of an allegedly invalid transition from quantity to quality as
such. Each transition which arises for discussion, and here we are
concerned with that from historical evidence to commitment of faith,
must be taken on its merits. The possibility of such a transition must

not be ruled out *a priori*. Kierkegaard's objection, upon which he depends for his notion of a 'leap,' only stands if he follows Lessing to the extent of identifying theological assertions with 'eternal truths,' an identification which would cut across the great weight he wishes to give to the Divine grace manifest in the decisiveness of the Moment.

Nevertheless, and perhaps precisely because of his desire to give this weight to the Moment, Kierkegaard is aware that some sort of question at least must be admitted with respect to the Absolute Paradox, or else decision could never arise. The question he admits is this: 'How does the learner come to realise an understanding with this Paradox? We do not ask that he understand the Paradox, but only that this is the Paradox. . . . It comes to pass when the Reason and the Paradox encounter one another happily in the moment; when the Reason sets itself aside and the Paradox bestows itself.'[32] The third entity in which this happy union is realised—a union contrasted with the offence of the unhappy consciousness—he calls Faith, which is another name for the gift of the condition for understanding the Truth.

At this point we should take note of the fact that Kierkegaard uses 'faith' in two senses. On the one hand, 'faith' is part of the intellectual equipment of any historian. For he defines the historical as that which is subject to becoming. When an observer is looking at a star, he does not *believe* that the star is there; he sees it. But the moment he reflects upon its coming into being, the 'elusiveness which is implicit in all becoming' has to be reckoned with. At this point faith comes in to overcome the uncertainty of this elusiveness. 'The elusiveness pertaining to an event consists in its having happened, in which fact lies the transition from nothing, from non-being, and from the manifold possible "how."'[33] So then, the historical, as such, is not open to direct perception and immediate knowledge. Again, what is known immediately simply is; it is not immediately known *as an effect*. That it is an effect is a matter of belief, since it is subject to the uncertainty of becoming, in other words, to doubt. But when faith resolves to overcome this doubt, to do away with the doubt implicit in the manifold possible 'how,' it is not making an inference, as if this were a matter of cognition, but is exercising a free act of will. 'The conclusion of belief is not so much a conclusion as a resolution, and it is for this reason that belief excludes doubt.'[34] This act of resolution is the characterisation he gives of faith as the general instrument by which the historical is apprehended.

On the other hand, Kierkegaard uses 'faith' in a 'pre-eminent sense,' to mean the condition of understanding eternal Truth given in the decisive Moment. The issue which now arises concerns the naming of these two things by the one name. If faith as the condition for apprehending eternal Truth is *a preeminent sense* of faith as the resolution for overcoming the uncertainty of the historical, there must be some real analogy between this condition and this resolution. And to insist on this is to insist that for all his talk about sheer leaps, Kierkegaard is *really* embarked on a close analysis of the relation between theological and historical judgments. This is the logic of what he is saying here, though this line of thought is perhaps implicit rather than explicit, and his talk of sheer leaps would appear to be inconsistent with what I have suggested from his usage of the word 'faith.' And this being so, he is here pursuing a constructive line of investigation, compatible with my critique of Lessing's problem, which has not properly been taken up in modern times. For this constitutes his real answer to Lessing and, this being so, an appeal to Kierkegaard, in spite of his talk about sheer leaps, by those who tend to minimise the relevance of historical questions for theological issues[35] is at best to ignore this other line in his thought which does offer the possibility of constructive development.

The ground of the analogy between the two senses of 'faith' Kierkegaard finds in the notion of reducing possibility to actuality. We have seen how this problem of the historical, *i.e.*, of what has *become*, is resolved not by an inference but by an act of will. This resolution of the historical problem is different from both the aesthetic and intellectual principle, which seeks to resolve the *esse* of some reality into its *posse*, and the ethical principle, which is concerned with the *posse* in order to assimilate it to the *esse* of the individual's own life of decisive becoming. In dealing with the historical neither principle is involved by itself, yet there are similarities with both. 'The historical is ever only so much raw material, which only he who appropriates it to himself can reduce to its *posse* in order then to assimilate it in its *esse.*' The point about understanding the historical is that in faith the individual decides for certain possibilities and rejects others, and in so doing the historical question has been settled in connexion with his own reality, and thus it constitutes a summons to him to realise its possibilities. These are the reasons behind Kierkegaard's apparent disparagement of the factuality of the historical event. This is why he says 'It is intelligent to ask two questions: (1) Is it possible? (2) Can I do it? But it is unintelligent to ask these two questions (1) Is it real? (2) Has my neighbour Christopherson done it?'[36]

Likewise, the Absolute Paradox when proclaimed is a scandal, at which either I take offence, or which I decide to believe. But in this faith, faith in the pre-eminent sense, there is realised in me the condition of understanding the Eternal Truth so that I am involved in my reality with the Moment in which the Paradox confronts me. In this sense, the history of Christ represents the Paradox which summons me to realise the possibility of learning the Truth which the Teacher is wanting to confer upon me. Corresponding to the two analogous senses of faith, there are two senses of history: history in the general sense, 'historical in the first degree'[37] and history in the special sense of the Christian revelation, 'history in the second degree.'[38] Faith in the pre-eminent sense corresponds to this second sense of history; it is a sense 'in which the word can be used only once, *i.e.*, many times, but only in one relationship.'[39] This unique sense of faith cancels the difference which in respect of the first relation exists for those of diverse temporal situations. By this means, Kierkegaard considers the time gap to be insignificant. The real gap, over which faith must leap, is the gap represented by the Paradox, with its promise of eternal truth.

The general result of this sort of emphasis upon realising the possibilities of history in me is the depreciation of ordinary historical investigation. To Kierkegaard this belongs to the objective problem concerning the truth of Christianity, and, as we have seen, his thesis is that to treat Christianity objectively is to miss its essential point. But now, in particular, we must ask whether Kierkegaard carries through his emphasis upon the creative personal decision, which believes in the meaning and truth of the fact, to cover belief in the factuality of the event itself. As Diem says, 'This would mean in effect that the believer simply postulates the fact of revelation as an historical fact through his believing insight into the eternal truth.... How are we to avoid changing the Gospel proclamation which flows from the self-attestation of Jesus into the communication of a luminous, albeit paradoxical, truth of existential philosophy?'[40] Again, as Diem sees, this is one of the burning issues of modern biblical and theological discussion, especially as it rages around Bultmann. If we go on to say that the believer does *not* postulate the *factuality* of the event which it is claimed has a revelational character, then at this point at least, there is a genuine objective problem concerning the truth of Christianity which the theologian cannot ignore, yet which is in principle open to the non-believing historian to investigate.

But what about Kierkegaard? As Diem points out in his answer to his own question, Kierkegaard insists that 'the absolute fact is also an historical fact. Unless we are careful to insist on this point our entire hypothesis is nullified; for then we speak only of an eternal fact. The absolute fact is an historical fact, and as such it is the object of faith. The historical aspect must indeed be accentuated, but not in such a way that it becomes decisive for individuals ... though when so understood it involves a contradiction; for a simple historical fact is not absolute, and has no power to force any absolute decision. But neither may the historical aspect of our fact be eliminated, for then we have only an eternal fact.'[41] This makes it clear that Kierkegaard has no intention of giving up the historicity of the fact about which the disciple says 'I believe and have believed that (so-and-so has taken place), although it is a folly to the understanding and an offence to the human heart.'[42] Yet it does seem as if he does not keep to his own analysis. If the absolute fact, *i.e.*, the fact of revelation, is an historical fact, *as such* it is an object of faith, but faith here is faith *in the ordinary sense* which applies to the facts of the life of Caesar as well as to the facts of the life of Jesus.

This being so, Kierkegaard has not said as much as he thinks he has said when he points out, what has been clear from at least Hume onwards, that all knowledge which historico-critical methods can yield is merely an approximation. On his own analysis, any historian is faced with uncertainty and doubt which he can only resolve by an act of faith. Let us look at his comment: 'What a piece of good fortune it is that this wishful hypothesis, this beautiful dream of critical theology, is an impossibility, because even the most perfect realisation (of its aim) would still remain an approximation. And again how fortunate for the critics that the fault is by no means in them! If all the angels in heaven were to put their heads together, they still could only bring to pass an approximation, because an approximation is the only certainty attainable for historical knowledge—but also an inadequate basis for eternal happiness.'[43] We will let pass here his oft repeated point that eternal happiness, personal knowledge of eternal truth, faith in the pre-eminent sense cannot be built upon historical knowledge. I have already criticised this. What I want to contend here is that if the historicity of the fact which has absolute significance is to be preserved, then there is no escape from the detailed work of 'approximations' even though the issue has to be concluded by an act of 'faith.' This faith is simply the historian's inference, and it is not blind. The historian chooses this conclusion rather than that because of certain evidence. Now, of course, Kierkegaard is right in insisting that no accumulation of evidence can ever amount to an *unfalsifiable* demonstration of the fact of revelation, or of any other fact either. And if it is true that historico-critical theologians of his day thought it did, then Kierkegaard was within his rights in reminding them of the true nature of the situation. But to insist that the historian firms to his conclusion in a way that is not strictly deducible from the evidence, in a way which involves some inference-leap, is no ground for saying that the weight of evidence is irrelevant to the issue of the factuality of the events in question. That the historical is subject to a leap of faith in this sense does not mean that historico-critical methods are irrelevant to the question of the historicity of the revelatory events.

Despite all this, it is clear that Kierkegaard wants to make great profit from his discovery of the inference-leap of the historian. 'I assume now the opposite, that the opponents have succeeded in proving what they desire about the Scriptures. . . . Because these books are not written by these authors, are not authentic, are not in an integral condition, are not inspired (though this cannot be disproved, since it is an object of faith), it does not follow that Christ has not existed.'[44] Now as a matter of logic, Kierkegaard is right in this. Even if there be no evidence whatever that a certain Eliezer Gephoups lived in Windsor Castle from the year 1900 until 1932, I can still say that this does not rule out the possibility that he did. I can still say with great passion and conviction that he did, if I want to. But why would I want to? The only answer would be that *to me* saying this has some great significance. But then, the assertion about Eliezer Gephoups does not really say anything about a person who lived in Windsor Castle; it says something about me. And the 'creative personal decision' not only brings belief in the meaning and truth of the fact; it brings belief in the factuality of the fact itself.

What I am saying here about Kierkegaard applies equally well to much modern theology, for these doctrines of Kierkegaard have greatly influenced nearly all contemporary discussion. Using Kierkegaard as our basis, we can put a dilemma to this modern theology:

On the one hand, the factuality of the revelatory facts may be insisted upon. In this case ordinary historical questions can be raised about them, and faith in the pre-eminent sense is sundered from the rationalist ideal of eternal truths. It must now be seen as somewhat dependent upon faith in the ordinary sense, which in turn is guided by matters of weight of evidence. Thus faith cannot be sealed off from 'natural inquiry.'

On the other hand, Lessing's setting of the problem may be accepted. Then the factuality of the revelatory facts is quite incidental, the real issue being concerned with the reality of the believer. In this case the Moment has ceased to be decisive, we have returned to the Socratic situation, and the fact of revelation is simply part of the mythology postulated by the believer as the mere occasion for the learning of certain eternal truths which really are known implicitly all along.

This dilemma consists of *either* one side of Kierkegaard's thought, with the two senses of faith intimately related, *or else* Lessing's yearning after eternal truth, with its turning of revelation into the education of the human race, and without Kierkegaard's attempt to leap what Lessing rightly saw could not be leaped. If we learn the lesson posed by this dilemma, though it is not the lesson usually learnt from Kierkegaard, and though it is not at all the lesson he thought he was teaching (indeed, as I said, his lesson is that we should stop trying to learn lessons about the nature of Christianity), we will have done quite well.

FOOTNOTES

1. Cf. Hermann Diem: *Dogmatics.* See also the role this problem plays in J. M. Robinson: *A New Quest of the Historical Jesus* for one example.

2. *Ph. Fr.*, p. 5.

3. *Ph. Fr.*, p. 6.

4. *Ph. Fr.*, pp. 6-8.

5. *Kierkegaard's Dialectic of Existence*, pp. 58-59.

6. In line with this he disclaims any intention to be putting forward an opinion which he hopes others will adopt. Cf. Preface, p. 3.

7. *Ph. Fr.*, p. 9.

8. *Ph. Fr.*, p. 12.

9. *Ph. Fr.*, p. 25.

10. Cf. *Ph. Fr.*, p. 25. It is interesting to note that this is defended by an argument which only holds if there be a direct analogy between human love and the divine.

11. *Ph. Fr.*, p. 37.

12. Cf. *Ph. Fr.*, p. 92.

13. Diem, *Kierkegaard's Dialectic of Existence*, p. 81. Cf. his *Dogmatics*, p. 20.

14. *Ph. Fr.*, p. 47.

15. *Ph. Fr.*, p. 87.

16. For a full and brilliant analysis of his position, cf. Barth: *From Rousseau to Ritschl*, ch. 3. This article, however, should be read in the light of the criticisms I make of Lessing's position, criticisms more radical than those Barth himself makes. Indeed it can be suggested that Barth's willingness to follow Lessing's setting of the issues as much as he does is an instance of how Lessing's approach to the problem has dominated modern theology.

17. *Theological Writings*, IV, 169 quoted in Barth, *op. cit.*, p. 129.

18. Cf. Barth's citations from Lessing's *Theological Writings*, p. 134 and 'On the Proof of the Spirit and of Power' in *Lessing's Theological Writings*, trans. H. Chadwick.

19. 'On the Proof of the Spirit and of Power,' trans. Chadwick, *op. cit.*

20. *Ibid.*

21. *Ibid.*

22. *Ibid.*

23. *Ibid.*

24. *Ibid.*

25. *Ibid.*

26. This indeed is Diem's concern. Cf. his *Dogmatics*.

27. *Op. cit.*

28. 'On the Origin of Revealed Religion,' sect. 5, in *Lessing's Theological Writings*, trans. H. Chadwick.

29. *Ibid.*, Sec. 6.

30. *Concluding Unscientific Postscript*, p. 88.

31. That the distinction between quality and quantity is an absolute one is often taken for granted, despite this fact, and especially by theologians. The discussion by Hegel of this matter is much sounder. Cf. his discussion under 'Measure': *Lesser Logic* 98-99.

32. *Ph. Fr.*, p. 47.

33. *Ibid.*, p. 67.

34. *Ph. Fr.*, p. 69.

35. Cf. e.g. John Knox, *Faith and Criticism* and R. Niebuhr, *Faith and History*.

36. *Con. Unsc. Post.*, p. 286f.

37. *Ph. Fr.*, p. 72.

38. *Ph. Fr.*, p. 72.

39. *Ph. Fr.*, pp. 71-72.

40. *K.'s Dialectic of Existence*, p. 89.

41. *Ph. Fr.*, p. 84.

42. *Ibid.*, p. 86.

43. *Concl. Unsc. Post.*, p. 31.

44. *Concl. Unsc. Post.*, p. 31.

PART TWO

REASON AND FAITH

Introduction

The heart of SK's philosophical work resides in his *Philosophical Fragments* and *Concluding Unscientific Postscript.* The significance of his work—and indeed of these two titles—can only be appreciated when contrasted to the dominant philosophy of his day, Hegelianism. The thought of SK must be understood as a revolt against that of Hegel, and that on two separate counts.

First, Hegel's philosophy defined truth as the whole. This meant that no truth was obtainable apart from a completely coherent system, and this meant, in turn, that no individual could ever attain the truth. For Hegel the individual was almost entirely insignificant, because he was viewed as only a tiny particle in the vastness of a coherent, all-inclusive system. Second, Hegel's philosophy defined truth as objective. This meant that truth is by definition independent of the individual knower's relation to it. Thus, once again, the individual is viewed as superfluous with respect to truth and knowledge. In short, for Hegel, truth was defined in terms of a philosophical system and an objective, or scientific, study of reality.

As the titles of the two books mentioned above would indicate, SK's position was exactly the reverse of Hegel's. He argued that truth is always "fragmentary" (as opposed to being systematic) and therefore can never be essentially objective, but must be viewed as basically "unscientific." SK argued that Hegel's philosophy systematically eliminated the role of the individual knower in the knowing process by doing away with the need for commitment on the knower's part. Following Augustine, SK maintained that "Unless you believe, you shall not understand." Thus the heart of SK's philosophy is his position on the relation between reason and faith. The remainder of this introduction will be devoted to tracing out the main steps of the argument which he offers for his position.

The first move—the beginning point—of SK's religious epistemology is that truth is a function of subjectivity. By this he would appear to mean that the crucial question about any given truth is the quality of the knower's relationship to it. What good is purely objective truth if it is not appropriated into the life of the knower? To give mere mental assent to a propositional truth is hardly sufficient to qualify one as a knower of the truth. What is needed to obtain true knowledge in any field is the total commitment of the knower. In this sense, truth is subjectivity. It is to this claim that the author of the first essay of Part Two (Chapter Five) addresses himself. Just how is SK's claim that truth is a function of subjective commitment to be understood and justified?

The second move—or premise—in SK's overall argument is that subjectivity is a function of paradox. The idea here seems to be that the more a given claim demands of the subject by way of total commitment and concomitant risk, the more truth must be said to reside in the claim. Although it is not altogether clear whether SK means 'paradox' and 'contradiction' to be taken as synonymous, he does maintain that paradoxical claims demand the most risk and commitment from the individual subject who attempts to believe them. Thus, subjectivity is a function of paradox. The second essay of this part (Chapter Six) focuses the reader's attention upon this claim. The crucial question is: does the acceptance of paradox necessitate an irrationalist position? If not, how does one distinguish between paradoxes which contain truth because they demand high risk and those which demand high risk because they are nonsensical?

The third move—or final premise—in SK's position involves the claim that the acceptance of paradox is a function of faith. Here he seems to mean that from a human (or strictly rational) point of view it is impossible for an individual to believe a paradox apart from religious faith—which must be supplied by God. When this claim is coupled with SK's other contention that the Christian gospel expresses the most outlandish of all paradoxes ("God was in Christ"—a man), it becomes easier to see why he maintained that faith alone provides the basis for religious truth. The third essay of this part (Chapter Seven) discusses the nature and implications of such a view of faith, and argues against its cogency.

On the basis of the foregoing analysis of the individual moves in SK's argument, one may summarize the argument as follows:

(1) All cases of truth are cases of subjectivity

(2) All cases of high subjectivity are cases of the acceptance of paradox

(3) All cases of the acceptance of paradox are cases involving faith
Therefore:

(4) All cases of truth are cases involving faith
Moreover:

(5) Since the Christian gospel, in expressing an absolute paradox requires the most faith, it also can be said to involve highest truth.

In addition to the many profound questions that can be raised regarding each of the individual steps of this argument—most of which are examined in the essays comprising this volume—there is also a more fundamental issue which concerns the argument as a whole. Although this issue is implied in several of the essays, it is met head-on in the final essay (Chapter Eight) of Part Two. There seems to be a basic, and even fatal, tension between (1) SK's argument that because faith is beyond reason it cannot be and need not be rationally defended and (2) the fact that this two major philosophical works, especially *Concluding Unscientific Postscript*, do present a rational defense of faith. The argument of Chapter Eight is that the only way to save SK from this tension is to interpret his philosophical efforts as ironic—as attempts to show the utter futility of developing an existentialist system of thought. This interpretation gains some support when it is recalled that SK wrote his dissertation on the *Concept of Irony*, and that he made constant use of indirect literary techniques to express his ideas in a style consonant with their main thrust. Thus, here is yet another possibility for interpreting SK's thought on the relation between reason and faith.

CHAPTER FIVE

ON KIERKEGAARD'S CLAIM THAT "TRUTH IS SUBJECTIVITY"

by Arthur E. Murphy

I propose in this paper to examine the claim of Kierkegaard that "truth is subjectivity," as this thesis is expounded and defended in his *Concluding Unscientific Postscript,* in an attempt to discover (a) what it means and (b) what grounds, if any, there are for believing that what it says is true. Kierkegaard's discussion of this subject is characteristically devious and I cannot hope, within the limits of this paper, to cover all that he has to say about it. His thesis, however, is of some philosophical interest, since it purports to be not only a devastating refutation of Hegel but a way of showing the incapacity of philosophy to enlighten the ultimate issues of human existence. The considerations offered to support it have impressed many contemporary thinkers, including some philosophers, as both pertinent and profound. It seems proper, therefore, for those of us who are engaged in the common work of philosophical inquiry to make the best attempt we can to understand it. Those who regard it not as a proper subject for common understanding but as a work of esoteric edification will not find this a rewarding undertaking. They will be well advised at this point to turn their attention to matters more congenial to their taste and temperament.

The point of Kierkegaard's discussion of "truth," I take it, is to offer a justification of faith, in his special sense of "faith," by showing that the believer is "in the truth" subjectively in his groundless affirmation of what is rationally absurd, because this affirmation both brings him into the right relation to "the truth" on which his eternal happiness depends and "potentiates" his inwardness in existing to the highest degree. So to exist is to be "in the truth," whether what is affirmed is "objectively" true or not, and faith is thus justified by the truth subjectively "in" the believer, not by grounds (in this case, it is argued, there can be no grounds) for believeing that what is affirmed —the being of God—is actually the case. "When the question of truth

From Arthur E. Murphy, "On Kierkegaard's Claim that 'Truth is Subjectivity'" in REASON AND THE COMMON GOOD: Selected Essays of Arthur E. Murphy, edited by William H. Hay, Marcus G. Singer and Arthur E. Murphy, (C) 1963. Reprinted by permission of Prentice-Hall, Inc., Englewood Cliffs, N. J.

Read at the Fifth Inter-American Congress of Philosophy, Gallaudet College, Washington, D. C., July 1957. Previously published in *Reason and the Common Good.*

is raised in an objective manner, reflection is directed objectively to
the truth as an object to which the knower is related. Reflection is
not focussed upon the relationship, however, but upon the question of
whether it is the truth to which the knower is related. If only the object to which he is related is the truth, the subject is accounted to be
in the truth. When the question of truth is raised subjectively, reflection is directed subjectively to the nature of the individual's relationship; if only the mode of this relationship is in the truth, the
individual is in the truth even if he should happen to be thus related
to what is not true."[1] A footnote adds, "The reader will observe that
the question here is about eternal truth, or about the truth that is
essentially related to existence, and it is precisely for the sake of clar-
ifying it as inwardness or as subjectivity that this contrast is drawn."

"When the question of truth is raised in an objective manner..."
What question? The question whether it is the truth to which the
believer is related—whether there is any such "eternal truth" as faith
affirms? That would be the "objective" way of putting it, the way that
Kierkegaard reprehends. To *this* question he has no answer at all,
except to say that it should never have been asked. "When the question of truth is raised subjectively" the answer Kierkegaard has to
give shows at once that it is not the same question that is being raised.
For what he then tells us is that the believer is "in the truth" in believing even when what he believes is not the truth. To the question,
"Is what my belief affirms true?" the answer is, "You are truly existing in believing it to be so even if it is not." If the believer is concerned about the object of his belief, the reality of God, this is no
answer at all. It becomes an answer only if he can be persuaded that
"the truth" that matters here is the tension, inwardness and existential profundity of his own manner of being (as contrasted with the
aesthetic, ethical and that of "religiousness A"). The point of the
whole discussion of truth as "subjectivity" is to recommend this
change of reference.

This may be contested by those who like to regard Kierkegaard's
thesis as a justification of faith in the more familiar sense of ground
for believing that what the faith affirms is true, but there can really
be no doubt about it. Kierkegaard, on this point at least, has been at
pains to make his meaning clear. "Objectively we consider only the
matter at issue, subjectively we have regard to the subject and his
subjectivity; and behold, precisely this subjectivity is the matter at
issue. This must constantly be born in mind, namely that the subjective problem is not something about the objective issue, but is the
subjective itself" (p. 115). "Objectively the interest is focused on the
thought-content, subjectively on the inwardness. At its maximum
this inward 'how' is the passion of the infinite and the passion of the
infinite is the truth. But the passion of the infinite is precisely subjectivity, and thus subjectivity becomes the truth... Only in subjectivity"

is there decisiveness; to seek objectivity is to be in error. It is the passion of the infinite that is the decisive factor, and not its content, for its content is precisely itself. In this manner subjectivity and the subjective 'how' constitute the truth" (p. 181).

Thus to say that "truth is subjectivity" is not to bring any new support to the claim of religious faith to objective truth. It is rather to shift attention from this issue to another—that of the existential status of the individual in believing, and to call this manner of existing "the truth." The conceptual determination of truth (when subjectivity is the truth) is this: "An objective uncertainty held fast in an appropriation-process of the most passionate inwardness is the truth, the highest truth attainable for an existing individual...But the above definition of truth is an equivalent expression for faith." (p. 182). The man of faith is "in the truth" because his inwardness in believing *is* the truth (as subjectivity) and "behold, precisely this subjectivity is the matter at issue." The point of Kierkegaard's discussion lies in *making* it "the issue," for the existing individual the *only* issue in which he is existentially involved, the issue of his own existence. Given his definitions of "subjectivity," "truth," and "faith," it seems to follow, as he claims, that such a "faith" *is* the truth, though why this self-centered passion should be identified as religious faith rather than sheer egocentricity is so far hardly clear. And why it should be dignified as the highest truth attainable for an existing individual is a further question. To this question we now turn.

Why is faith, or being subjectively *in* the truth, the *highest* truth attainable for an existing individual? Becuase (a) it potentiates "inwardness" to the highest degree and such inwardness is the highest manner of existing for an existing individual. And (b) it is the highest manner of existing because it brings man into the right relationship to "the truth" on which his eternal happiness depends, a truth which infinitely transcends his present temporal condition as an existing individual. Let us consider these points in order.

The "leap of faith" intensifies inwardness because it is a tremendous risk, and objectively groundless affirmation of the rationally incredible. Such affirmation generates passion and, by its objective absurdity, throws upon the individual the whole responsibility for the decision for or against eternal truth. This decision is the supreme expression of his decisiveness as an individual. To be in this way an individual is truly to exist; it is the mode of being proper to man as a synthesis of the eternal and the temporal situated in existence. In this sense, only the man of faith *truly* exists, though of course there are others who "exist" also—in their fashion. Here "truth" is a kind of being and the ontological superiority of this mode of being for the existing individual is the justification of faith.

Surely there is something wrong with this picture. If "the truth" is subjectivity, then the believer runs no risk when he leaps; he has it, or rather *is* it, in the very act of leaping. For the truth here in question is "eternal truth," the truth essentially related to man's existence, and Kierkegaard claims to have shown that *it* is inwardness or subjectivity. But if this is the case then eternal truth is not a transcendent goal but a present possession; the passionate individual is now in the highest state of existence he could possibly attain. Verily he *has* his reward, and his condition is one not for soul-searching but for self-congratulation. This note of self-congratulation is not absent from Kierkegaard's account of faith.

But this is surely very dialectical indeed. For if the believer has the truth he seeks where is the tension? If no tension, where is the inwardness? And if no inwardness, no authentic faith. So it looks as though, if truth is inwardness, the man of faith is not in the truth precisely in virtue of being in the truth. But then he is of all men most miserable and so after all is in the truth because he is not in the truth. Perhaps it would be better to say that he is in the truth only because he does not understand that to exist in passionate inwardness is to be in the truth and therefore, through a misunderstanding of Kierkegaard's theory, goes on leaping for a truth he still supposes he does not possess. This would prove once more, and on a higher level, the importance of a lack of understanding to faith as inwardness. I offer it to the dialectical theologians for such use as they may care to make of it.

On a more mundane level it is pertinent, I think, to point out that, here as elsewhere, the alleged dialectic arises through a failure to make some elementary distinctions. In his discussion, Kierkegaard uses "the truth" to mean *both* the eternal truth at which the believer aims, which is emphatically *not* subjectivity since it infinitely transcends the believer's present state of being ("God does not exist, He is eternal") (p. 296) *and* the subjective condition of the believer is his agonizing separation from this truth (his "situation in existence") when he groundlessly affirms it. To be "in the truth" is not to possess this truth, but endlessly, and in this life vainly, to be trying to attain it. It is precisely because the believer is infinitely concerned with a truth that is not subjectivity and with its infinite transcendence that he is in the truth in his passionate and tortured affirmation of it. Kierkegaard recognizes this at times and even makes a point of it. "To ask with infinite interest about a reality that is not one's own, is faith, and this constitutes a paradoxical relation to the paradoxical ... The believer differs from the ethicist in being infinitely interested in the reality of another (in the fact, for example, that God existed in time)" (p. 288).

Now the fact that God existed in time is not a fact of the believer's state of being; and his being "in the truth" (passionately decisive) in affirming it sheds no light on what he is here passionately concerned about, that this *is* a fact and one on which he can properly stake his chance of an eternal happiness. Thus being "in the truth" is no confirmation whatever of "the truth" that he is infinitely concerned about —the reality of another. In a way, this must be good news for Kierkegaardians. For this, once recognized, should drive the individual still further back into himself and potentiate inwardness to an even higher degree. But this is new evidence that he is in the truth in believing, and if subjectivity is the truth, then once more he has it and now in overflowing measure. In seeing that Kierkegaard's answer is no answer one becomes still more subjective and this, perhaps, is the Kierkegaardian answer. As he puts it in a revealing passage: "It is impossible to express with more intensive inwardness the principle that subjectivity is truth, than when subjectivity is in the first instance untruth, and yet subjectivity is the truth" (p. 191). We must add, however, that it is not merely "in the first instance" but eternally that subjectivity is not "the truth" that for example Christianity proclaimed. For it is not a truth about God but a state or existential condition of the believer and only a believer more concerned about his own inwardness than about God could find in it an adequate goal in his quest for religious truth.

There is good reason to conclude, I think, from the whole tenor of his life and writing that Kierkegaard was that kind of a believer. The point of his discussion is not that he has offered grounds for belief in the truth of *what* the Christian faith affirms but that, by shifting the reference of religious truth from God to man, he has shown that the groundlessness of faith fits his own unhappy inwardness and is, *in this way*, the truth. "Subjectivity culminates in passion. Christianity is the paradox, paradox and passion are a mutual fit, and the paradox is altogether suited to one whose situation is, to be in the extremity of existence" (p. 206). Nietzsche unkindly described Kant's practical reason as "a special kind of reason for cases in which one need not bother about reason." I think we might with more justice say that Kierkegaard has given us a kind of truth for cases in which we are told not to bother about truth. The paradox of this position is that it is only because we are profoundly bothered about the objective truth of faith that we are in the condition (passionate inwardness) which is here offered as the highest existential substitute for the eternal truth we seek. Whether such a paradoxical condition is existentially profound or merely self-defeating is a further question.

That what Kierkegaard has to tell us about faith fits the facts of his own subjectivity is clear enough. Rarely has a man been more persuasive in projecting his private ailments as "existential" profundities. His relations to his father and to Regina Olsen take on ontological significance, as the commentators love to tell us, and his fears and frustrations are dignified as an embodiment of the highest truth attainable to man—the truth of subjectivity. But *is* this condition of recessive inwardness the highest truth that is humanly attainable?

If human existence is the incongruous juxtaposition of temporal and eternal that Kierkegaard says it is, if the Being on whom man's eternal happiness depends is an offense to his reason and (compare *Fear and Trembling*) to his morality as well, and if to embrace this offense without being offended is his only hope for salvation, *then* the unhappy passion of this desperate affirmation is indeed the response appropriate to his condition. But are any of these the case? The subjectivity of faith does not warrant their affirmation, for it is only if they are accepted as objective truth that faith is even subjectively justified as suited to man's existential situation. If what they assert is not the case then Kierkegaard's suffering is like the agony of a man self-submerged in two feet of water who refuses to stand up and breathe good air because his prostrate posture is the one appropriate to the situation in existence of a drowning man. "But this," as Kierkegaard likes to say, "is comic." Suppose that this were objectively true. And why are we not to suppose it? Because in so doing we should be existing only objectively, which is not truly to exist at all. What then is the criterion of "true" existence? Subjective inwardness. Why so? Because such inwardness is proper to man in the extremity of existence. Is he in such an extremity? In the state of passionate inwardness he feels himself to be and in faith affirms it. Is this affirmation true? It is true in the sense that in making it he is *in* the truth, that is, in the subjective condition proper to a man in the extremity of existence. This could go on almost endlessly, and in the *Postscript* it does.

The point I wish to make is that while it ostensibly turns away from the issue of objective truth, Kierkegaard's procedure presupposes such truth at every step in its retreat into recessive inwardness. His subjectivity is parasitic for its "existential" significance on the assumed objective truth of a doctrine about man and God whose right to claim such truth it strives at every point to discredit. Not only does it bite the hand that feeds it but it calls this questionable procedure faith. For whatever feeds recessive inwardness feeds faith. "Religiousness is indeed inwardness in existing and everything which serves to deepen this determinant heightens the religiousness, and the paradox-religiousness is the ultimate" (p. 506). This is the best that Kierkegaard has to offer. There is no better reason for believing that this is the highest existential condition attainable by man than for believing in the objective reality of God (as Kierkegaard describes Him), and for this, he has been at pains to tell us there is no reason whatever. What have we left? Just subjectivity itself, as devoid of ontological as of divine support. "Subjectivity is truth; subjectivity is reality" (p. 306). Whose subjectivity? Kierkegaard's. And there the matter ends. Whether it is a dead end or an ultimate disclosure of reality, is for the reader to decide. But he will do well to remember that it can be at best a disclosure of the reality, not of God, but of Kierkegaard.

Of course faith is not knowledge and a man cannot fairly be asked to demonstrate the truth of that which, in the circumstances of his creaturely existence, he must accept on faith or not at all. But faith is at least an affirmation of the objective truth of what is believed, and objectivity, as a human attitude, is the concern that what is thus affirmed shall in fact be true and credible as such by such standards as are humanly available. It is unreasonable to limit such standards to the procedures of mathematics and the empirical sciences, since these would be inappropriate to the relation between God and man if such a relation did in fact exist. But to reject not merely a too narrow objectivity but a concern for the objective truth itself, and to make an existential virtue of the inflexible determination to retain a preconceived opinion at all costs is a danger not so much to reason as to faith itself. For when faith loses its concern for objective truth, it loses its transcendent reference and that means that it also loses its transcendent object. Only subjectivity is left. It is the peculiar merit of Kierkegaard's account that it has made this truth so explicit that hereafter it can hardly be missed. The remaining question is whether the substitute object now offered—subjectivity—is one that a man of faith, in the more usual sense of that term, can accept as the proper goal of his religious quest.

Kierkegaard frequently speaks of faith, as he understands it, as a God-relationship. The propriety of this description is questionable at least. It seems rather to be a self-relationship in which the believer, through the repulsion of the paradox, is driven back into himself. The ostensible object (God) serves as a kind of opaque surface which turns back the light and presents to the believer only a reflection of himself as inwardly existing. Here faith indeed has *found* an object, "whose content is precisely itself." But this is not the faith that is the substance of things hoped for, and the evidence of things not seen.

And finally, *of course* reason is not faith, nor a proper substitute for faith in the lives of men who, if they are to live at their human best, must reach for truth not seen as yet. But reason may nonetheless be an essential aid to any faith that aims at any truth beyond its own "existential" occurrence. It can, for example, resolve some of the dialectical paradoxes that are Kierkegaard's stock in trade in his attempted proof that religious truth must, for man as a rational creature, be absurd. It can remind us, in the judicious words of Whitehead, that the discovery of a contradiction in an argument proves nothing except that a mistake has been made somewhere, and that the borrowed dialectic on which Kierkegaard depends to discredit human reason is itself a misuse, not a proper use, of reason. As a way of *finding out* about the world in which our subjectivity is involved, reason can bring light into dark places, a light that only those who love their own opinions more than truth need be afraid to face. And at its objective best it guarantees an openness to truth in all aspects and dimensions of experience that can give us a larger world to live in, not with a fragment of our minds and hearts but with the whole of them. This wholeness, above all else, is what we miss in Kierkegaard. The *Philosophical Fragments* is well named, and the *Postscript* is a postscript to the *Fragments*. Kierkegaard has not shown that a rational faith is unattainable. But he has shown conclusively, I believe, that it requires a different method and a different object than those that such fragments of philosophy can articulate or understand.

REFERENCES

1. S. Kierkegaard, *Concluding Unscientific Postscript*, translated by David F. Swenson, completed after his death and provided with an introduction and notes by Walter Lowrie (Princeton: Princeton University Press, 1941), p. 178. All further page references are to this book.

CHAPTER SIX

KIERKEGAARD: "PARADOX" AND IRRATIONALISM

by Alastair McKinnon

I

There can be few opinions in philosophy so widespread and apparently well-founded as the view that Kierkegaard was an irrationalist. My purpose in this paper is to show that, appearances notwithstanding, this interpretation is quite groundless and mistaken. I propose to do this by means of an examination of the various senses in which he actually employed the term "paradox." I proceed in this way because this interpretation appears to be based mainly upon his repeated use of this and certain similar terms[1] and because thus far at least, there has been almost no attempt to discover precisely what he means by it.[2]

It may be well to begin with a word of explanation. Kierkegaard employs the term "paradox" primarily in connection with his defense of religious and, more specifically, Christian belief. He constantly urges his reader to accept Christianity as a paradox if not, as some have supposed, because it is actually a paradox. This is not to say that the points he wishes to make cannot be generalized, but it does mean that the various senses in which he uses this term are most readily seen in this context.

"Irrationalism" is a vague term and needs further specification. Of course, we do not equate it with the acceptance of Christian belief as such; that would be a strange if perhaps not altogether unknown use. But neither do we intend it simply as the opposite of classical rationalism. The reasons for this are found in Kierkegaard's thought and they are both simple and instructive.

The great rationalists of the past believed that logic was grounded in the nature of reality, or, put another way, that reality is itself fundamentally rational. They believed that logic and reality were essentially connected. The denial of this claim we shall call *ontological* irrationalism. This is the doctrine that existence or reality is somehow chaotic, indeterminate, and nonsystematic. Now Kierkegaard would no doubt have agreed that existence often strikes us in this way[3] but, unlike those still standing within the classical tradition, he would not have concluded that it was therefore irrational.

Reprinted with permission from Alastair McKinnon and JOURNAL OF EXISTENTIALISM, Spring 1967.

There are perhaps a number of reasons for this but the fundamental one is his sharp distinction between the realms of possibility and actuality, and, again, between those of thought and reality. Thought may or at least should be logical; reality is neither logical nor illogical, neither rational nor irrational. These are categories which simply do not apply. This is fundamental to Kierkegaard's thought and he makes the point many times[4] without, however, suggesting that reality is therefore somehow illogical, irrational, or absurd. Indeed, the two realms being entirely distinct, it could not possibly be so. This is illustrated in some references to Christianity. *Being* a Christian involves one in paradox (in one peculiar but interesting sense of that term) but it is only Christianity as a *doctrine* or *teaching* which could be itself paradoxical. In short, rationality could be a property only of some thought or system of thought. But existence or reality is not a thought, and for Kierkegaard it makes no sense to ask whether or not it is rational. Of course, one might reject his underlying assumption but once this is granted, it becomes pointless to ask whether he was an ontological irrationalist. In any event, we do not intend to pursue this particular question.

The very different kind of irrationalism of which Kierkegaard might more plausibly be accused has already been suggested. As we have noted, he constantly strives to lead his reader to an acceptance of Christianity regarded as a paradox. The question, therefore, is whether in doing so Kierkegaard is urging his reader to accept something which he does and must find logically self-contradictory. It is whether he holds that we can accept or believe a claim which is and must remain logically incompatible with our underlying conceptions. The view that this is possible I shall call *epistemological* irrationalism. Whether Kierkegaard actually held this view is the different but still substantial question with which we are here concerned.

There are certain other preliminary considerations which must at least be noted even in this brief comment. For example, though Kierkegaard uses "paradox" to make a number of points about specifically Christian belief, there is no doubt that at least most of these are equally relevant to the broader question of the sources and limitations of human knowledge as such. Nor is there any doubt that Kierkegaard was much concerned with this question. Considerations of space preclude explorations along these lines, but we can at least remark that he was generally opposed to a number of traditional rationalist claims. Of course, it goes without saying that this is no evidence whatsoever that he was an irrationalist in the present or, indeed, any significant sense of that term.

It is also important to recognize that Kierkegaard's conception of paradox is in large measure a response to Hegel's account of Christianity, at least as he understood it. In his view, Hegel had completely falsified its nature. He had transformed it from an existence communication into a doctrine asking only to be understood. He had identified it with certain values belonging properly to natural man and only falsely ascribed to reason. He had presented it as a mere illustration of the eternal truth expressed in his own philosophy, and hence ultimately as a product of Hegelian Reason. Kierkegaard saw this as intolerable condescension, and, ever the master of wit and parody, declared Christianity to be instead a Paradox.[5] It was, in fact, his way of denying many of the things which he understood Hegel as asserting. This goes far to explain why Kierkegaard's "paradox" is such a rich and variegated concept; it was a kind of focus or center for a number of related but nevertheless quite separate points or protests.

Equally relevant are some of the distinctive features of Kierkegaard's "authorship." Its primary concern was not the articulation of some doctrine or teaching. It was rather to lead the reader from one existence stage to the next; a transition which he typically described as "from the aesthetic, through the ethical, to the religious." This is why the majority of his works employ indirect communication and are ascribed to one or other of his many pseudonyms. But also, and more immediately relevant, it is why his works deal not with the state of belief but rather with the *transition* to belief. Their focus is the *process* of coming to believe. This is crucial to our argument and we shall return to it later.

Of course the irrationalist interpretation of Kierkegaard has sources other than his use of the word "paradox." There is, for example, the generally accepted interpretation of *Fear and Trembling* as endorsing action which is not in accord with universalizable maxims. More precisely, there is the unblinking and surely doubtful ascription of this view to Kierkegaard.[6] There is also his central if perhaps "background" doctrine of the stages, and, especially, his representation of the Religious, particularly Religiousness B, as standing in the sharpest contrast with the Ethical defined as action in accord with rational or universalizable maxims. Then, too, there are those notorious phrases such as "Subjectivity is truth," "the crucifixion of the understanding" and "the martyrdom of faith." At another level, there is the continuing influence of Christoph Schrempf and, in our own time, the impact of Barth, particularly in his early *Epistle to the Romans*.[7] Nevertheless it seems clear that Kierkegaard's use of "paradox" had been the chief source of the irrationalist charge and that this is where one must begin if he seeks to answer it. In any event, there is reason to hope that insight gained in this way may lead to a reassessment of its other sources.

II

Kierkegaard used the term "paradox" in a great and indeed bewildering variety of senses; a variety of which he was not himself, I suspect, ever fully aware. I do not claim to have discovered all these senses nor do I presume that my account of any one of them is exhaustive. I believe, however, that I have succeeded in identifying those most relevant to the charge before us, and that the various accounts are at least adequate for our present purpose.

Kierkegaard's uses of "paradox" fall into two quite distinct types which we can provisionally classify as the existential and the logical respectively, a division which, incidentally, accords with and reflects his own distinction between reality and logic. When these uses have been described we can then ask whether they tell for or against the irrationalist interpretation of our author.

What we have called the existential sense of "paradox" represents Kierkegaard's perhaps most distinctive and characteristic use of this term. Though not directly relevant to our immediate concern it expresses an important aspect of his general position and should promote the understanding and correct appraisal of the various logical senses.

Unlike these others, the existential sense stems entirely from the fact that the knower is, in Kierkegaard's language, "an existing individual." This can be brought out most clearly by reference to Socrates who, at least in Kierkegaard's view, provides the proper introduction to Christianity precisely because of his emphasis upon the fact that the knower is all the time an existing being. This and nothing else explains why the truth is a paradox in this particular sense. "Socratically the eternal essential truth is by no means in its own nature paradoxical, but only in its relation to an existing individual."[8] ". . . the fact that the truth becomes a paradox is rooted precisely in its having a relationship to an existing subject."[9] Again, in an important *Journal* entry he speaks of paradox as "an ontological definition which expresses the relation between an existing cognitive spirit and eternal truth."[10] The sense in which "paradox" is here used seems quite clear; at least it is if we recall Kierkegaard's assumption that the realms of existence and logic, and therefore truth, are totally separate and distinct. "Paradox" is in fact used to stand for the relation resulting from the bringing together of these two realms; in this case, their bringing together in the experience of an existing individual. It is, in fact, the relation resulting from this particular juxtaposition of existence and truth.

It is worth noting that, according to Kierkegaard, Christianity is paradoxical in precisely this same sense, or, rather, it is even more obviously and clearly so. The reason is that Christianity accentuates existence yet more strongly than the Socratic point of view. It does so because, unlike that point of view, it is also paradoxical in the various logical senses of that term. The fact of this connection is most instructive: reality and logic may be totally disparate, but at least the corresponding senses of "paradox" are not entirely unrelated.

When we turn to the logical senses of "paradox" the situation becomes rather more complicated. Here there are no less than five distinct senses. These can be marked as follows: the dialectical, the systematically incomprehensible, the *Self*-contradictory, the historically dependent, and the apparently contradictory. These are rough indicators: it remains now to describe these senses more precisely. For the sake of brevity I shall quote only where documentation seems necessary or his own words provide the most convenient summary.

The first or dialectical sense appears in the following *Journal* entry.

> The paradox is really the *pathos* of intellectual life, and just as only great souls are exposed to passions it is only the great thinker who is exposed to what I call paradoxes, which are nothing else than grandiose thoughts in embryo.[11]

In fact, this early entry, and particularly its closing words, fails to do justice to the complexity of Kierkegaard's use of "paradox." Nevertheless the sense intended is quite clear. "Paradox" here stands for a thought containing a contradiction which nevertheless can and should be unwound. The entry as a whole is therefore a declaration that purely logical contradictions can and should be untied; indeed, that it is the precise business of great thinkers to untie them. Kierkegaard continued in this confidence throughout his life but it is worth noting that this particular use of "paradox" belongs primarily to his youth and reflects the Hegelianism of that period. He never lost sight of the point expressed by this use but the fact is that in the "authorship" it is much less common than any of the other senses.

The second sense, the systematically incomprehensible, appears in another *Journal* entry together, be it confessed, with our earlier existential sense. The following is part of that entry.

> ... the inexplicable, the paradox, is a category of its own ... it is the duty of the human understanding to understand that there are things which it cannot understand, and what those things are. Human understanding has vulgarly occupied itself with nothing but understanding, but if it would only take the trouble to understand itself at the same time it would simply have to posit the paradox. . . .[12]

It is clear that Kierkegaard's central concern here is to make a point about the nature and operation of the human understanding as such. He is insisting that any coherent understanding rests and must rest upon something which cannot itself be expressed in terms of that understanding. He is saying that any system of understanding rests ultimately upon something which cannot be understood in terms of that system; upon something which, as we have put it, is systematically incomprehensible.

This same point has been made in our own day with particular reference to deductive systems. It is now generally recognized that such systems rest upon certain primitive postulates which, because they are primitive, cannot be defined in terms of the system. This does not mean that they are unintelligible *per se*. It means only that, as the foundation of the system, they cannot be meaningfully explained in terms of it. Kierkegaard is making this same point but within the broader context of the operation of the human understanding. As he remarks, an understanding which took the trouble to understand itself "would simply have to posit the paradox." This is perhaps a novel use of this term, but, at least with this explanation, it is surely neither improper nor misleading.

The third or *Self*-contradictory sense is more closely associated with Christianity and, particularly, Kierkegaard's conception of it. It reflects his assumption that there is an implacable opposition between the goals of Christianity and those of natural man, and further that, as in the Hegelian philosophy, the latter are identified and bound up with human reason. Whether these are in any sense rational is really beside the point. For Kierkegaard, Christianity is a contradiction of the natural self and hence can only be experienced and accepted as paradoxical in the sense of *Self*-contradictory.

The historically dependent sense is closely linked with the preceding, but it is concerned less with the content than the form of Christianity. More particularly, it is connected with the fact that it is an historical religion and that the believer must in some sense base his faith upon certain merely historical facts. Kierkegaard has Hegel particularly in mind, but the point he wishes to make can perhaps now best be illustrated by comparison with Hume. Against the Hegelian claim that the historical facts of Christianity are merely helpful illustrations of timeless and eternal truths, Kierkegaard insists that these facts are absolutely vital since apart from them we could never have imagined or conceived these truths. Like Hume, he wants to make the point that certain of our beliefs are really dependent upon the facts of experience. But there is one important difference. We may be annoyed that our knowledge of the properties of bread rests only upon experience, but we are bound to be offended by the insistence that even in much more crucial matters we are similarly dependent. That, indeed, is one of the reasons why, particularly in the *Fragments*,[13] the concept of paradox is so closely linked to that of offense. Our rationalist hopes or, perhaps, illusions are denied; we are offended because Christianity proposes to base our salvation upon some merely historical fact.

What I have called the apparently contradictory sense is much more familiar, straightforward, and, of course, closer to common use. It is also the one which figures most largely in Kierkegaard's authorship. When he declares Christianity to be a paradox in this sense his point is really quite simple: it is that Christianity, or any other new view for that matter, *appears* to the would-be believer as a contradiction. Kierkegaard is not saying that Christianity actually is logically contradictory in and of itself. His point is simply that, as a new view, it necessarily conflicts with the would-be believer's earlier conceptions, and that one can *become* a believer only by first accepting a claim which, because of this conflict, is or at least appears to be logically self-contradictory. Many of Kierkegaard's reiterations that Christianity must be accepted as a paradox are to be understood at least primarily in this way.[14]

It may be worth noting that this particular use of "paradox" is very close to Kierkegaard's concept of the absurd. That the eternal has come into being in time, that God has existed in human form, that the eternal is the historical—all these are referred to as both paradoxical and absurd.[15] Here, too, Kierkegaard's way of presenting the absurd suggests that it is somehow essentially self-contradictory. He speaks of "the contradiction that something which can become historical only in direct opposition to all human reason, has become historical." And, he continues, "It is this contradiction which constitutes the absurd, and which can only be believed."[16] This might prompt one to suppose that such claims are really unthinkable and genuinely self-contradictory. But this impression stems from the peculiar focus and concern of the authorship. Indeed, as I hope to show, Kierkegaard's position is that even those claims which appear to unbelief as absurd or contradictory are not essentially, permanently, and incorrigibly so. But this is a view for which the evidence has yet to be provided.

I do not wish to claim that Kierkegaard had clearly distinguished all these senses in his own mind, nor do I wish to suggest that he always used the term "paradox" in a clear and unambiguous way. I would merely suggest that these senses mark the principal points he was concerned about making in his repeated references to Christianity as a paradox. It now remains to ask whether in advocating Christian belief thus conceived, he was in fact guilty of irrationalism as here specified.

III

It should be clear that there is no suggestion of such irrationalism in what we have called the existential sense. "Paradox" in this sense is simply Kierkegaard's way of describing the relationship of the truth, which belongs to one realm or sphere, to the existing individual, which belongs to another. The truth becomes a paradox in such cases simply because, as already stated, the two realms are essentially distinct. "Paradox" may be a peculiar name for the result, but neither the use of this term nor the point it is intended to convey constitutes evidence of irrationalism of the kind with which we are concerned.

The charge is equally implausible in connection with the first of our five logical senses. Real intellectual life does have a pathos in Kierkegaard's sense, and those who are intellectually alive are constantly attempting to iron out the contradictions in their thought. These are the facts of life and their admission can hardly be an offense, intellectual or otherwise. The important thing is the confidence that, with reflection, these contradictions can be removed. This sense assumes that they can, and to that extent, it reflects Kierkegaard's view that our beliefs can be made internally consistent. Hence this sense of "paradox" is really evidence against rather than for the irrationalist charge.

At first glance it might seem that the systematically incomprehensible sense is tinged with a kind of irrationalism, but this reflects what is at best surely a pious rationalist hope. We now know that any deductive system is based upon postulates which cannot be defined in terms of that particular system. Kierkegaard is making or rather recognizing the same point in connection with belief. He sees that any coherent belief system rests upon certain fundamental commitments and that it cannot therefore ever be fully justified or explained. This concession may be disappointing to some but it is a properly logical point and scarcely open to doubt or dispute.

The same general conclusion appears to hold with respect to the *Self*-contradictory sense. In the course of human history the reason may have become identified with the values of natural man, but in fact this association is merely accidental. Kierkegaard does not for a moment suppose that there might be a clash respecting values between Christianity and the reason as such. Indeed, as Swenson[17] long ago pointed out, his conception of reason renders such a conflict quite inconceivable. In fact, reason does not have any values and can enter this particular fray only by aligning herself with values not in any sense her own.

The significance of the historically dependent sense seems equally clear. The point of this sense is simply that even in matters of religious belief we are dependent upon the facts of history. But this is simply to grant one of Hume's points and certainly does not constitute any endorsement of self-contradiction.

The case of the apparently contradictory sense is admittedly less clear. Indeed, it might seem an obvious instance of the very irrationalism we have been attempting to deny. That it is actually not so follows from one peculiar but important feature of the "authorship."

As already mentioned, and as Kierkegaard repeatedly insisted, his work was specifically concerned with the process of coming to believe and this as something distinct from the state of belief. This is especially true of the works of Johannes Climacus with which this last sense is particularly linked. But Kierkegaard, or rather Climacus, does not use it to claim that Christianity is in itself logically contradictory. His point is rather that, in the process of coming to believe, the unbeliever must necessarily experience it as contradicting his former conceptions. But, again, this is simply a function of the process of coming to believe. It is something necessarily involved in moving from one life-view to another. Kierkegaard made his point with special reference to Christianity, but it seems clear that he saw it as an instance of the general point that the adoption of a new outlook necessarily involves something which, at the moment and in the process of transition, seems paradoxical or absurd.

This crucial point is borne out by a relatively late *Journal* entry in the midst of which we are given a rare glimpse of the real Kierkegaard, the hidden figure who stood behind the authorship and its sometimes deliberate contortions. The entry is a long one and it begins in a familiar way. It insists that for the unbeliever the content of faith is absurd and that in order "to become a believer everyone must be alone with the absurd."[18] But suddenly, and in the very midst of these claims, we find this single sentence: "While naturally it is a matter of course that for him who believes it is not the absurd."[19] Now, obviously, the fact of belief cannot alter or dissolve the second, third, or fourth of the logical senses of "paradox;" these are permanent and inescapable features of Christian belief as such. But the fact of belief can change the situation regarding this last sense. This is because it is possible to revise our conceptions in the light of our claims; because real belief is, by its very nature, internally consistent and logically coherent. Kierkegaard recognizes this and the present aside is simply an obvious consequence; that, indeed, is why he says "naturally it is a matter of course." This is because the claim follows from the very nature of belief. The claims of Christianity do seem absurd in light of our natural conceptions but it is possible to take these claims seriously and revise our conceptions in their light. It is possible to render belief internally consistent. In short, at least so far as this is a purely intellectual matter, we can move beyond paradox in this particular sense.

That Kierkegaard did in fact hold this view is further attested by an unpublished fragment directed against a theological adversary.

> When the believer believes the absurd is not the absurd—faith transforms it.... The passion of faith is the only thing capable of mastering the absurd.... In the category of the absurd rightly understood, there is therefore absolutely nothing terrifying.[20]

The words "rightly understood" offer the clue. "Rightly understood," the absurd or the paradox is not at all intellectually terrifying; it is not a plea for absurdity or irrationalism. It can be mastered; it can be transformed so that it is no longer absurd. The believer is not committed to a life of permanent and incorrigible self-contradiction. In some sense at least it is possible to achieve the state of belief and in that state all properly logical or conceptual conflicts can be resolved. Though he says almost nothing about it, Kierkegaard assumes the possibility of such a state; that, indeed, is why he was prepared to lavish such exquisite care and skill upon an "authorship" devoted primarily to leading his reader through what he took to be its necessary preliminaries.

It is now clear that none of these senses of "paradox" provide support for the irrationalist interpretation of our author. The existential and the dialectical sense can be set aside; the former because, as already noted, it has nothing to do with the acceptance of logical contradiction, and the latter because it eventually falls under the final one. The second, third, and fourth logical senses all conflict with certain traditional rationalist assumptions but they are not irrationalist in any significant or proper sense. The fifth or last is conceivably so but, as we have seen, it is a function of the transition to belief rather than a feature of belief as such. It is then clear that Kierkegaard's conception of paradox offers no real evidence for the irrationalist charge. Indeed, rightly understood, it provides strong evidence against it.

I conclude with a general comment which may help to put the irrationalist interpretation in proper perspective. Kierkegaard was equally and perfectly clear on two points particularly relevant to our present concern. He saw that any substantial change of belief must involve the would-be believer in the acceptance of a claim which was apparently contradictory. But he also saw that real belief involved the revision of our conceptions in the light of our claims and hence the disappearance or overcoming of paradox in this particular sense. His assessment of the needs of his own time prompted him to emphasize the former insight and neglect the latter; indeed, his tacit admission that there actually is a state of belief comes, as we have seen, almost in passing. But this is a result of his assessment of the times and the demands of the "authorship." In fact, a careful reading of his works reveals that the Kierkegaard behind that "authorship" attached no less importance to one insight than to the other.

REFERENCES

1. The other term is, of course, "absurd" (in Danish, *Det Absurde*). I have chosen to concentrate upon the broader and more comprehensive term "paradox" *(Paradox)*. Generally speaking, as will appear, "absurd" is linked with the last of our six senses of this term.

2. The actual state of affairs is well described in the following: "It is indicative of the sorry state of Kierkegaard studies—at least in the English speaking world—that no one has as yet raised these questions or has attempted to make clear how Kierkegaard uses the technical term 'paradox.' An exception is "Kierkegaard's Doctrine of the Paradox" by N. H. Soe in *A Kierkegaard Critique*, ed. by Howard A. Johnson and Niels

Thulstrup (New York 1962, pp. 207-77). But here, as in other discussions of Kierke-gaard's doctrine of paradox, the properly philosophical question about the precise mean-ing of the concept is not raised." Richard Schmitt, "The Paradox in Kierkegaard's Re-ligiousness A," *Inquiry*, Spring, 1965, p. 133. In fact, the situation seems little better in Denmark. For example, the most recent complete edition of Kierkegaard's works (Gyl-dendal, 1962-64) includes a *Terminologisk Ordbog* in which five different types of par-adox are noted. These are, respectively, the ethical, the intellectual, the absolute, the psychological, and the transitory. However, this classification is neither very satisfac-tory nor helpful.

3. In fact, Kierkegaard dwells upon our experience of the world as chaotic and uncertain; see, for example, *The Concept of Dread* and various entries in his *Journals*. Elsewhere I have argued that his concern with this experience, together with his ability to come to terms with it, is the source of much of his interest and relevance for modern thought. Cf., Alastair McKinnon, "Søren Kierkegaard," in *Architects of Modern Thought*, C. B. C., 1962.

4. Cf., e.g., *The Concept of Dread*, pp. 12ff., *Journals*, 584, 1054. Cf. also *Journals* 636 where he records his indebtedness to Trendelenburg and 959 (3) where he expresses his agreement with Kant.

5. To my knowledge the first person to have made this point was the late D. F. Swenson.

6. I say "doubtful" because Kierkegaard expressly denied responsibility for the views expressed in the pseudonymous works. In "A First and Last Declaraion," which he attached to the *Postscript*, he deals with the entire (to that date) pseudonymous production. But the status of *Fear and Trembling* is particularly suspect. Consider, for example, his "Had I had faith I should have remained with Regine," (*Journals*, 444) and, equally, his subsequent repudiation of the disjunction between the ethical and the religious which this work presupposes.

7. Elsewhere I have attempted to show that Barth's interpretation of Kierkegaard does less than justice to its subject. Cf. Alastair McKinnon, "Barth's Relation to Kierke-gaard: Some Further Light." *Canadian Journal of Theology*, October, 1966.

8. *Postscript*, p. 184.

9. *Ibid.*, p. 176.

10. *Journals*, 633 Cf. also, "The paradox emerges when the eternal truth and exis-tence are placed in juxtaposition with one another; each time the stamp of existence is brought to bear, the paradox becomes more clearly evident." *Postscript*, p. 186.

11. *Journals*, 206.

12. *Ibid.*, 633.

13. Cf. especially, "Appendix: The Paradox and the Offended Consciousness," *Frag-ments*, pp. 39-43.

14. This is a claim which I argue at the end of the paper; I do not assume that it has as yet been established.

15. *Fragments*, p. 50, *Postscript*, pp. 188-194.

16. *Postscript*, pp. 189f.

17. Cf. especially, D. F. Swenson, *Something About Kierkegaard*, pp. 220f.

18. *Journals*, 1084.

19. *Ibid.*

20. Papirer X[6] B 79, quoted by Cornelio Fabro, "Faith and Reason in Kierkegaard's Dialectic" in *A Kierkegaard Critique*, ed. Johnson and Thulstrup, pp. 182f.

CHAPTER SEVEN

KIERKEGAARD ON FAITH

by Brand Blanshard

At the center of Kierkegaard's thought is the idea of human life as lived on various plateaus, each with its special characteristics. The idea probably came from Hegel. Just as Hegel recognized three main stages on the way to the Absolute—being, essence, and the notion —so Kierkegaard distinguished three "stages on life's way," the aesthetic, the ethical, and the religious. The first two were preparatory stages, rungs on the ladder that led to the third, where the clearest and surest insights of which men are capable were to be reached. This highest stage was again divided into two, A and B, each with its special features. Of these it is 3B, the last stage of all, that is of most interest to the philosopher, since it carries us to the highest summit that man's knowledge can attain.

But Kierkegaard insists that this summit is not attained through any process of reflective thought. The final step is a passionate, non-rational "leap of faith," a commitment of feeling and will. What is the commitment *to?* Not to a way of life merely, as some readers have supposed, but also to Christian belief. And the central Christian belief, he holds, is the belief in the incarnation. "The object of faith is thus God's reality in existence as a particular individual, the fact that God has existed as an individual human being."[1] This is the distinctive fact of Christianity, which marks it out from all other religions. And according to Kierkegaard it is a fact incapable of establishment by any process of objective thought. You can never *prove* the existence of any past fact. It might seem, then, that the proper attitude is one of doubt and suspended judgment, just as it would be if we were asked to accept the existence of King Arthur. The two facts, however, are not comparable. For the unique Christian fact, if a fact at all, is one of overwhelming moment, upon whose acceptance our eternal happiness depends, and if there is any chance of its reality, an attitude of reserve and detachment would be flippancy. So, "while objective knowledge rambles comfortably on by way of the long road of approximation without being impelled by the urge of passion, subjective knowledge counts every delay a deadly peril, and the decision so infinitely important and so instantly pressing that it is as if the opportunity had already passed."[2] The decision is what James called a

Reprinted with permission from Brand Blanshard and THE PERSONALIST, Winter 1968.

"forced option"; we cannot evade it, since with so high a prize at stake, to evade decision is in effect to reject the offer as illusory.

Faith as Non-Rational. The man who attempts to make this decision on the ground of evidence is in an even worse position than we have suggested. For the incarnation is not a fact of more or less probability; to our reason it is an impossibility. Kierkegaard admits it to be a "contradiction that God has existed in human form."[3] It is not knowable or even thinkable. "To speculate upon it is a misunderstanding, and the farther one goes in this direction the greater is the misunderstanding. When one finally reaches the stage of not only speculating about it, but of understanding it speculatively, one has reached the highest pitch of misunderstanding."[4] The attempt to know religious truth by the intellect is thus fundamentally misguided because destined to defeat by the nature of its object. "For the absurd is the object of faith, and the only object that can be believed."[5]

Fortunately this defeat of intelligence does not leave us without recourse. Faith remains. But there must be no looking back, no longing for the unprofitable old fleshpots of rational understanding and certainty. One must recognize the sophisticated intellect for the dangerous thing it is, and be content to become a child again. "When faith requires of a man to give up his reason, it becomes equally difficult for the cleverest and the most stupid person to believe, or it becomes in a sense more difficult for the clever."[6] The difficulty must be overcome, not by thinking more critically, which is futile, but by a resolute act of will. The leap of faith is a daring, passionate non-rational commitment to the paradoxical and the unintelligible. "Faith begins where thought leaves off."[7] "Without risk there is no faith." "The truth is precisely the venture which chooses an objective uncertainty with the passion of the infinite ... the above definition of truth is an equivalent expression for faith.... Faith is precisely the contradiction between the infinite passion of the individual's inwardness and the objective uncertainty."[8] "Faith is what the Greeks termed divine madness."[9]

We shall say more in a moment about such faith as a means of insight in theology. But Kierkegaard's best known illustration of the meaning of faith is drawn not from theology, but from morals. The ultimate source of right and wrong is the will of God, and "the knight of faith," like the knights of the Round Table, will at every moment of life be in the service of his royal master. Not that he needs to renew the appeal to this will at every moment consciously; for the lower-level guidance of his own ethical faculties will normally suffice. The ethical level, says Kierkegaard, is the level of "the universal." By this cryptic pronouncement he seems to mean one or other of two things; either that the moral man will, in Kantian fashion, ask what conduct could in principle be consistently adopted by everybody, or, in Hegelian fashion, ask what the community would generally approve. Most modern moralists would regard either of these appeals as hopelessly inadequate, but Kierkegaard had little grasp of ethical theory. His chief contribution to it is to say that at times it breaks down, and that when it does, our resort must to be to a "teleological suspension of the ethical" at Divine behest. The nature of this behest can be ascertained only by faith.

The Crucial Case of Abraham and Isaac. How is he to show that our natural faculties do break down in morals? The most effective way would be to show that our clearest moral judgment may stand in radical conflict with the divine will. Can any case of such conflict be cited? Yes; we find it in scripture itself. The most revolting act of which a human being is capable is to destroy his own flesh and blood. In the book of Genesis we find Abraham commanded by God to do just this, to take his only son, the son of his old age on whom the joy and hope of his life were concentrated, to the summit of Mount Moriah, to bind him, cut his throat, and use his body as a burnt offering. Anthropologists who have studied this legend have considered that it is probably a relic of the custom of human sacrifice which once held in many parts of the world, and apparently even in the prehistoric past of the Hebrew people. However that may be, Kierkegaard takes it in all historic and symbolic seriousness. Is it not the point of this story, which is clearly inspired, that is was Abraham's duty, and may at any moment be ours, to trample down the affections of the natural man and all his nicely calculated goods and evils? Kierkegaard's answer is an emphatic Yes.

In his essay *Fear and Trembling* he goes into the matter with gusto and in detail. After a "Preliminary Expectoration," as he calls it, in which he spews philosophy, ethics and even reflective theology out of his mouth as incompetent to deal with the case, he goes on to consider what is implied in the command to Abraham. There have been cases in history and literature in which a father's killing of a child may in some degree be reconciled with out moral sense. Brutus ordered the execution of his sons, but they were, after all, guilty of treason, and does not a general's duty to the state take precedence of his own affections? Jephthah made a grateful vow to Heaven to offer as a sacrifice the first person he met on his return from victory, and if this happened to be his daughter, he would nonetheless be breaking a sacred oath by sparing her. If Agamemnon kills Iphigenia, it is to appease the wrath of Artemis, who holds the power of destruction over his fleet and army. These are not, therefore, pure cases of "the teleological suspension of the ethical"; in all of them the killing of the child is dreadful, but it is not entirely pointless. The great thing about the act demanded of Abraham was that it was pointless absolutely. Isaac was wholly innocent; Abraham loved him beyond anyone else in the world; no conceivable good to anyone could be anticipated from killing him. It was an act in which every human consideration was lined up on one side and on the other nothing at all but the command from on high to kill. Abraham bowed to it and drew his knife. The fact that at the last moment he was relieved of the need to strike is irrelevant in appraising him. Whether he actually killed or not, he showed that he possessed the one thing needful, namely the readiness to kill.

For Kierkegaard this makes him the perfect knight of faith. "Venerable father Abraham! Second father of the human race! Thou who first didst know that highest passion, the holy, pure, and humble expression of the divine madness..."[10] Abraham is "great by reason of his wisdom whose secret is foolishness, great by reason of his hope whose form is madness, great by reason of love which is hatred of oneself."[11] He surrendered himself to the "paradox which is capable of transforming a murder into a holy act well pleasing to God."[12] "Abraham believed and did not doubt, he believed the preposterous."[13] "He believed by virtue of the absurd; for all human reckoning had long since ceased to function."[14] He was called upon to renounce the moral for the religious, the finite for the infinite. "This is...clear to the knight of faith, so the only thing that can save him is the absurd, and this he grasps by faith."[15] Here is the meaning of that most deceptive phrase, "the teleological suspension of the ethical." "Teleological" means "for an end," but what Kierkegaard is praising here is the abandonment of all thought of ends and the doing of something that in every human point of view is productive of nothing but evil. "As soon as the will begins to look right and left for results, the individual begins to become immoral."[16]

Kierkegaard as a Moral Nihilist. What are we to say of a rhapsody (in forty thousand words) in praise of pure and holy murder, of a defense of the humanly immoral on the ground that it is religious duty? Kierkegaard, in choosing such ground, believes that he has cut off the possibility of rational criticism. And clearly if an appeal is taken to the unintelligible and the irrational, it is begging the question to protest against it on any grounds of sense or reason. Sense and reason have been deliberately left behind. But we can at least point out that the irrationalist defense is double-edged. If it undercuts its opponents, it also undercuts itself, in the sense that it has forgone all right to the rational criticism of others. If opponents claim a divine warrant for the opposite of what Kierkegaard proclaims, all he can do is denounce them as impostors.

Of course there have countless claims of this sort. There were Jewish leaders who claimed a divine imperative to destroy the Amalekites, man, woman, and child. There were Christians—St. Louis described himself as one—who thought the proper Christian reply to an argumentative Jew was to bury one's sword in him to the hilt. John Woolman felt a divine interdict against his preparing papers as a magistrate for the sale of a slave. John Newton, the hymn-writer, reported that some of his sweetest hours of communion with the divine were spent while he was the captain of a slave-ship, separated by a few planks from a weltering mass of human misery. Joseph Smith claimed to know that the divine will approved of plural wives; Mohammed made a like claim, but limited the divine approval to four; the Christian fathers limited it still further to one; and St. Paul construed it as favoring those who did not marry at all. St. Basil, St. Gregory of Nyssa and St. Ambrose thought it a divine imperative that one should not accept interest on loans. St. Abraham the hermit appears to have thought it the divine will that, beginning with the day of his conversion and continuing for fifty years, he should wash neither his face nor his feet. There are few practices too trivial or too eccentric to have been included among actions enjoined or prohibited by divine will. If claims to such guidance are to be above rational criticism, what we have is a chaos of voices, each announcing itself as authoritative, each denouncing its opponents as deceivers, and none of them able to defend themselves against the others.

Abraham was enabled by faith to see what ordinary men were unable to see. What exactly was this? It was that an act which, so far as the human mind could judge, was productive only of evil was nevertheless right—a duty because the will of God. For the person who possesses the insight, the principles and consequences involved in the act are held to be irrelevant; its character as seen by faith is its true character, which takes precedence of any judgment of our merely human faculties. Faith thus revealed to Abraham in the most dramatic and decisive way that it may be duty to reduce rather than to increase, to destroy rather than to create, the values recognized by reason and conscience.

Now when "the knight of faith" claims that he has had this kind of insight, can we credit what he says? It is hard to take the claim seriously. A person may *say* that it is really better that the powers of youth should be frustrated than fulfilled, that excruciating pain is better than pleasure, that sorrow and anguish are better than happiness, but can we believe that he has in fact seen these things to be true? The question is not, of course, whether pain, misery, and the destruction of life may be *means* leading to later goods; this is true enough, but is irrelevant here; for we are expressly forbidden to try to justify the divine command by any such considerations. What was presented as Abraham's duty, what he was honored for accepting, was the production of these evils without any thought of compensating goods. When the question is thus clearly put, one must take leave to doubt not only whether such insight occurs in fact, but whether it could possibly occur. For what the insight amounts to is that there is no such thing as good or evil, right or wrong, better or worse. If the killing of innocent youth without regard to consequences may be right, then anything may be right, since our moral sense has proved delusive at the very point of its greatest confidence. If pleasure is intrinsically evil and pain intrinsically good, if misery is in truth more desirable than happiness, then the clearest and surest judgments about values are worthless, and it is no longer possible to hold that anything is really better than anything else. The entire realm of values, including moral values, becomes a mirage. Now one may talk as if it were, but one cannot live or think accordingly. Daily and hourly we make choices implying judgments that it is better to be happy or enlightened or at peace than it is to be the opposite; indeed the person who chooses to affirm that nothing is better than anything else presumably assumes that it is better so to affirm than not to do so. The Kierkegaardian "knight of faith," in electing the "absurd," is divesting himself of the shackles of all insights. But to do that is to be not a saint, but a moral nihilist.

Rational Morals Repudiated. Those who accept Kierkegaard's knight of faith as the true saint may well pause over this conclusion. The popularity of his religious ethics in our schools of theology is a genuine anomaly. The Christian saint, we must admit, has at times been a strange character whose asceticism and other-worldliness have set him apart from the run of men and caused him to be regarded with uncomprehending wonder. Still, in the main he has accepted and exemplified the values most prized by his fellows and has been honored by them accordingly; he has believed in the superiority of love to hate, in the relief of human misery, in refusing to count his own good as more important than that of others. These are virtues that we can see to be virtues with our unaided human faculties. But for Kierkegaard as for Luther, these faculties are corrupt; all the principles laid down by them are open to a "teleological suspension of the ethical" imposed from above; they are subject at any moment to cancellation by "the absurd"; and if, in the face of such a suspension we retain our old adherence to love or loyalty or even conscience in its natural sense, the charge of immorality is compounded with a charge of impiety. Furthermore, the saint or knight of faith, according to Kierkegaard, is a man whose leading concern is not the welfare of others, but his own "eternal happiness," a description, incidentally that applied to himself. "If ever a person was self-centered it was Kierkegaard; he hardly ever thinks of anyone but himself."[17] What we have in this strange version of Christianity is thus an insistence on the selfish character of the religious motive, combined with an insistence that the values of the Christian life, so far as these can be understood, are provisional only, and may at any time be overridden. Kierkegaard revelled in paradox; "if anyone has ever used the slogan *credo quia absurdum*," says Emil Brunner, "it was Kierkegaard."[18] Those who love daylight, even in religion, will greet the absurd with less acclaim. To them it will still seem odd that one should have to become immoral in order to be religious. They may recall Halevy's remark that "virtue is more dangerous than vice, because its excesses are not subject to the restraints of conscience."

Rational Theology Repudiated. We have been dealing with the absurdity apprehended by faith in the field of morals. But it will be remembered that the central dogmas of the creed are also apprehended by faith, and are regarded as equally absurd. Sometimes the absurd is presented as the merely improbable. "Faith has in fact two tasks: to take care in every moment to discover the improbable, the paradox; and then to hold it fast with the passion of inwardness."[19] Sometimes, as we have seen, the paradox that must be held fast is more than improbable; it is impossible. The central fact of Christianity, Kierkegaard holds, is the incarnation. "The object of faith is...the fact that God has existed as an individual human being."[20] But he admits that by rational standards, this fact is inconceivable and inconsistent with itself. A being who is eternal or out of time cannot have measured out his life in human years. A being who is omnipresent could not be confined in his movements to a small area in the eastern Mediterranean. A being who is omniscient cannot grow in knowledge, or a being who is perfect grow in grace. A son who is a separate person from his father cannot also be one with the father; still less can three persons be one. So speaks logic. But faith requires us to put logic aside and accept what Kierkegaard admits to be a "contradiction."[21] "In my God-relationship I have to learn precisely to give up my finite understanding, and therewith the custom of discrimination which is natural to me..."[22] A man must somehow learn "to relinquish his understanding and his thinking, and to keep his soul fixed upon the absurd..."[23] He must achieve "a crucifixion of the understanding,"[24] and by a leap of faith embrace the improbable and even impossible as nevertheless certain.

The difficulty with this claim is to attach definite meaning to it. If we were told that though a certain belief were improbable, we should try to make ourselves believe it, that would be intelligible, whether ethical or not. If we were told that a belief, though beyond our present understanding was vouched for by others who did understand it, and that through provisionally accepting this assurance we might come to understand it ourselves, that too would make sense. But if we are told that although a belief is both unintelligible and self-contradictory, we shall see that it is absolutely true and certain if we commit ourselves to it passionately enough, we can only question whether the proposer knows what he is asking of us. The law of contradiction is not a principle that is valid in some cases and not in others; if it is invalid in any case, it is invalid *as such* and therefore in every case. But if it is thus universally invalid, then in no case does the assertion of something as true exclude the truth of its denial, and *nothing* is

true rather than untrue. And that makes assertion meaningless, for
what could one be asserting? Just as Kierkegaard's ethics implies the
denial of a realm of value, so his trans-logical truth undermines truth
as we know it. Not that he saw this implication or held to it. If he had,
he would not have argued at all. He was in fact proud of his prowess
as a dialectician, and took pleasure in pitting himself against Hegel.
But his philosophy terminates in a rejection of those very principles
of logic on which he proceeded as a philosopher. He can hardly have
it both ways. If the logic he assumes in his philosophy is valid, then
the faith which stands at the summit of "the stages on life's way" is
meaningless. If that irrational faith is accepted, the principles on
which reflection conducts itself are everywhere impugned. In that
case, Kierkegaard should merely smile like Buddha and remain silent.

What would he reply to all this? Probably that he was not concerned with the truth of doctrines at all; "Christianity is not a doctrine but an existential communication expressing an existential
contradiction."[25] He would fall back on his notion of subjectivity;
". . . the passion of the infinite is the truth. But the passion of the infinite is precisely subjectivity, and thus subjectivity becomes the
truth."[26] (This is of course an illicit minor, if logic still has any importance.) He would renew his attack on the attempt to understand,
insisting that "the objective acceptance of Christianity is paganism or
thoughtlessness."[27] He would remind us that religion is a commitment
of the will, that "Christianity wishes to intensify passion to its highest pitch,"[28] not to induce in us belief or comprehension. But we have
seen that this will not do. Christianity does include beliefs, and it
insists rightly or wrongly that these beliefs are true in the common
and ancient sense. To adopt Kierkegaard's new sense, peculiar to himself and inconsistently held, which reduces truth to a passionate commitment of feeling and will, would not save Christianity; on the
contrary, it would largely destroy it. For it implies that there are no
common truths for Christians to accept, no common principles by
which their lives may be guided, indeed no common Deity for them to
contemplate and worship. The Kierkegaardian subjectivity would
dissolve these things away into a set of processes in individual minds
where there would be as many Christianities as there were persons to
exercise their "inwardness" and their passion.

The Thinker and His Thought. In this review of Kierkegaard on
faith and reason, we have been examining the thought, not the man.
Ad hominem reasoning, besides being distasteful, is never conclusive
and is often self-defeating. But I do not wish to conceal my own belief
that psychological causes as distinct from logical reasons had much to
do with his conclusions. I cannot think that a psychopathologist would
have much trouble in connecting the irrationalism of his thought with
the irrationality of his temper. He said himself that his thought must

be understood through his personality, and his personality was profoundly abnormal—so abnormal as to have cut him off from his fellows, his friends, and his own family. His alternations of exaltation and depression, his temptations to suicide, the feverish activity of an over-pressed brain in darkened rooms, the hysterical-sounding claims to being "a genius in a market town" and his comparison of himself to Christ, the frantic excoriations of church and clergy in his later years, his own report that he had stood on the verge of insanity—it would be a mistake to pass over these things as if they were wholly irrelevant. They suggest, though with a force difficult to assess, that Kierkegaard's singularities of thought were less the product of judicial reflection than the by-product of a sick spirit.

I will take two examples that may serve to make clear what I mean. First, his overwhelming, persistent, and surely morbid sense of guilt. This was partly an infection from his father, who lived in terror of having committed the unpardonable sin, partly the reaction to youthful irregularities on the part of an excessively introspective mind brought up in a theological hothouse. Georg Brandes reminds us that "he lived his life through in an atmosphere saturated with theology and theological discussion; at least three fourths of his near acquaintances appear to have been theologians, chaplains, ministers, bishops, clerics of every rank." This atmosphere kept alive and flourishing in Kierkegaard's anxious mind a conviction which, if exposed to the air and light of free secular discussion, would probably have been dissipated, the inherited Lutheran conviction that we were born in sin, utterly corrupted by it, and doomed by it to condemnation unless faith could somehow be won. Kierkegaard, like his father, lived in fear. "The whole of existence frightens me; from the smallest fly to the mystery of the incarnation everything is unintelligible to me, most of all myself; the whole of existence is poisoned in my sight, particularly myself."[29] The cure for this fear was faith, and Kierkegaard was terrified that, by losing his faith, he might also lose his "eternal happiness"; he must therefore keep it at all costs.

He saw clearly the tendency of "objective thinking" to undermine and disintegrate this faith. Is there any wonder that an imaginative mind, living in a "sickness unto death" of fear, despair, and dread, should come to conceive of philosophy as the enemy? If one wished to preserve one's faith, it was safer not to play the philosophical game at all. "The ungodly calmness with which the irresolute man would begin in the case of God (for he would begin with doubt), precisely this is insubordination; for thereby God is deposed from the throne, from being the Lord. And when one has done this, one really has chosen another master, wilfulness..."[30] To argue the case with the philosopher is to risk defeat on an issue too important by far to be dealt with by a match of wits. It is better to ignore him, to insist that faith is one thing and reason another, and to settle the issue decisively by a leap of faith. That is the only escape from despair.

For the other example of how Kierkegaard's thought is rooted in his life, we may refer to his too celebrated love affair. Much in his philosophy seems to have been a rationalization, in the Freudian sense, of his conduct in this affair. He had long contemplated with growing passion a neighbor's daughter, a girl in her teens named Regina Olsen. He at last declared himself, led her on to a whole-hearted reciprocating passion, then threw her abruptly over and went off to Berlin where he wrote up his experience in *The Diary of a Seducer* and other edifying discourses. By merely secular standards, his behavior was that of a cad, and he seems to have realized this, for running through much of his work from this time on, there is a veiled attempt to justify himself. To his credit, he has occasional doubts. "If I had had faith, I would have remained with Regina," he once confided to his diary.[31]

But the line he more commonly took was that he threw her over because he did have faith, or at least because renouncing her would give exaltation to his spiritual life. He prefers to write about it in parables, but the reference is unmistakable. "Love for that princess became for him the expression for an eternal love, assumed a religious character, was transfigured into a love for the Eternal Being, which did to be sure deny him the fulfilment of his love, yet reconciled him again by the eternal consciousness of its validity in the form of eternity, which no reality can take from him."[32] In this treatment of her, the simple Regina was unable to share "the eternal consciousness of its validity in the form of eternity," and was broken-hearted. Kierkegaard probably realized that, as mentally and sexually abnormal, he was no fit person to marry at all, and if he had rested his desertion on such ground, one could understand it, though wondering why the discovery came so late. But such an explanation was not satisfactory to a mind in which a messianic egotism was mixed in unwholesome fashion with eroticism and piety. He had done wrong; he knew it; and if he was to retain his picture of himself as genius and saint, he must explain his action by lofty motives. He chose the loftiest. As Buber suggested, God was Regina's successful rival. The desertion was in obedience to a secret imperative from on high, which, like the hero of *Fear and Trembling*, he was ready to obey, whatever the cost in renunciation. Regarding this book, Professor Paton has passed judgment in terms with which, severe as they are, it is hard to disagree.

... What makes it nauseating as a professedly religious work is that, as he himself said, it is a "mystification" which reproduces his own life. In other words, it is an account of his unhappy love affair with Regina Olsen, an account in which his own deplorable behaviour is supposed to be similar to that of Abraham. We may pity his unhappy and diseased temperament, but neurosis is a poor qualification for setting up as a religious guide . . . Self-centeredness is the very antithesis of religion; and if the paradox of faith is—as he says—a willingness "to do the terrible and to do it for its own sake" (as well as as for God's sake), then the less of this kind of faith we have the better.[33]

Concluding Disillusioned Postscript. This is a grim note on which to end a study of Kierkegaard. He is a figure who of late years has received almost lyrical praise for the profundity of his thought and the penetration of his psychological insight. We have been assured that he "belongs to all time and to all humanity, just as surely as do Plato and Aristotle, Spinoza and Hume and Kant and Hegel."[34] We have been assured over and over of how profound he is. "Kierkegaard's explanation of the dialectical relation of freedom and fate in sin is one of the profoundest in Christian thought," and again, "Kierkegaard's analysis of the relation of anxiety to sin is the profoundest in Christian thought."[35] "Harnack's once celebrated essay on *The Essence of Christianity* seems incredibly trivial when one has read S. K."[36] I recall that, stimulated by such fair words, I approached his books with high expectation. My experience was like that of John Laird, who wrote, after a determined attempt on *Either/Or:* "By the time I had finished the first enormous volume I was sadly disconsolate. Even in a wide literary interpretation of 'philosophy'—and no other could be appropriate—I found very little that seemed to be worth stating in a formal way."[37] One reads a few puzzling pages with the feeling that the writer must be catching his breath and getting slowly under way; some definite point will soon emerge. It does not. One reads on with gathering disillusionment, coming in the end to realize that Kierkegaard, if a philosopher at all, is a distinct species of philosopher, and that it is useless to look for clearly stated theses, still less for ordered arguments in support of them. He combined an undisciplined intellect with a remorseless, facile, unchecked, limitless, compulsive loquacity; he was, as Disraeli said of Gladstone, "inebriated with the exuberance of his own verbosity." He is alleged to have written twenty-two books by the time he was thirty-five; and since they have no firm construction, no obvious beginning or end, or any internal reason why they should ever end, one can read them only by allowing one's critical sense to be lulled into drowsiness and one's mind to be floated along on the tide of words.

Unfortunately, no sooner has one made one's peace with the indiscipline of thought and style than one must begin the battle over again with the man himself. The self-absorption, the strange blend of piety and contempt (his two dominant emotions, Georg Brandes said), the dogmatism, the proclamations of unappreciated genius, the imprecations on church and clergy, the gospel of universal guilt and despair, the homilies on love from a mind that was simmering with hatreds, the scorn for those who, in religion, try to understand—these things have an effect that the reader must manage to suppress if he is to go on. He must remind himself that though this is a sick and twisted mind, such minds have, on occasion, shown a sharp eye for truth.

What was the truth that Kierkegaard saw? The great insight claimed for him is that in religion objective thinking breaks down and that the insight it seeks is obtainable by faith. As for the inadequacy of thought, a case can certainly be made for it, and such a case was actually presented with a force of statement and argument far beyond Kierkegaard's range by an English contemporary, Dean Mansel. Kierkegaard's own case is unimpressive. His contention that thought cannot deal with existence is put so obscurely that there is difficulty in extracting from it a meaning clear enough to refute. Furthermore, he seems never to have worked out what was involved for the normal exercise of reason by its breakdown at crucial points—for ethics by the suspension of its clearest rules, and for logic by the admission of contradictions to the status of higher truths. As a philosopher he employed with scornful confidence the reason which, as a theologian, he dismissed with equal scorn. He was too impatient to get on with his writing to declare a moratorium on it while he achieved coherence in this theory of knowledge.

What of the second half of the great insight attributed to him— that where reason fails faith succeeds? Unfortunately this is more obscure than the first. Perhaps it is inevitably so. When one has bid good-bye to reason and made the prodigious non-rational leap into the rarefied air of paradox, one should presumably say nothing, since anything one did say would have to be said in the distorting accents of the reason one has left behind. The silence, nevertheless, is a pity. Men struggle onward and upward along the stages on life's way; a hardy few reach the summit; and when they descend, the many waiting below ask a report on the splendid vision from the top. Kierkegaard, so voluble elsewhere, here finds his tongue at last tied. The stage that was supposed to cast illumination downward on all the others turns out to be strangely dark and empty. Practically, indeed, it is rather worse than empty. Kierkegaard insists that the love felt by the knight of faith is not mere human love, and if one can make any inference from his own practice, he was right, since the love displayed in that practice permitted a selfishness and harshness toward others —toward Hans Andersen and Regina and his mother and his brother and Bishop Mynster and the unfortunate "Christians" about him— which the lower love would not have allowed. Nor is the insight of faith into truth comparable with a merely human knowledge. Just as it gave Luther the power to see through and around Aristotle, so it gave Kierkegaard the power to see how superficial were all the systems of philosophy, and to see of science, without the need to study it, that if it differed from faith at any point, it was wrong.

In the end Kierkegaard stands, in his thought as in his life, a defeated figure. He was like a business man who builds up a commercial empire by condemning and buying up the businesses of all his competitors on the strength of promissory notes which he cannot redeem. He indicts reason; he indicts rational ethics; he indicts love and justice of the merely human variety; he indicts with eloquent contempt the Christianity practiced around him. He invites them all to accept subordination to one directing head in return for grandiose, even infinite, promises. But when they present their claims, they find the bank empty. The large promises of a new directorate are never fulfilled. Just how reason is to be rectified or ethics reformed, just what the new golden affections are that are to replace the old leaden ones, just what we are to believe or do or feel—these all-important directions never transpire. Faith has leaped so high that it has shot up beyond the earth's atmosphere to where thought and conscience can no longer breathe. These may be poor things, but we know them, and know that they have served us not badly. We shall do well to keep them, even when notes are flourished before us that are stamped in infinite denominations, unless we can be sure that the issuing bank is solvent. That assurance Kierkegaard never supplies.

REFERENCES

1. *Concluding Unscientific Postscript,* 290; hereafter referred to as CUP.
2. CUP, 179.
3. CUP, 38.
4. CUP, 339, note.
5. CUP, 189.
6. CUP, 337.
7. *Fear and Trembling,* trans. by W. Lowrie, 74.
8. *Ibid.,* 182.
9. Papirer, IVa, 109, as quoted by Thomte, *Kierkegaard's Philosophy of Religion,* 144.
10. *Fear and Trembling,* 37.
11. *Ibid.,* 31.
12. *Ibid.,* 64.
13. *Ibid.,* 35.
14. *Ibid.,* 47.
15. *Ibid.,* 57.
16. CUP, 121.
17. H. J. Paton, *The Modern Predicament,* 120.
18. *Revelation and Reason,* 310.
19. CUP, 209.
20. CUP, 290.
21. CUP, 38.
22. CUP, 159.
23. CUP, 495.
24. CUP, 496.
25. CUP, 339.
26. CUP, 181.
27. CUP, 116.

CHAPTER EIGHT

CHRISTIANITY AND NONSENSE

by Henry E. Allison

*My propositions serve as elucidations in the following way:
anyone who understands me eventually recognizes them as
nonsensical, when he has used them—as steps—to climb up
beyond them. (He must, so to speak, throw away the ladder
after he has climbed up it.)*

Ludwig Wittgenstein.

The *Concluding Unscientific Postscript* is generally regarded as the
most philosophically significant of Kierkegaard's works. In terms of a
subjectivistic orientation it seems to present both an elaborate critique of the pretensions of the Hegelian philosophy and an existential
analysis which points to the Christian faith as the only solution to the
"human predicament." Furthermore, on the basis of such a straightforward reading of the text, Kierkegaard has been both vilified as an
irrationalist and praised as a profound existential thinker who has
uncovered the only legitimate starting point for a philosophical analysis of the religious life and a Christian apologetic.

The aim of this paper is to suggest that any such reading involves
a radical misunderstanding of Kierkegaard's intent. Given the sup-
position that the *Postscript* is to be regarded as a contribution to religious or existential philosophy, the charge of irrationalism is
irrefutable. Viewed as an anti-idealistic philosophical thesis, the
"doctrine" that "truth is subjectivity" not only leads to a consistent
misologism, but also implies the ultimate identification of Christianity and nonsense. However, when this result is understood in light of
Johannes Climacus' (the pseudonymous author) self-proclaimed role
as a humorist, and of the discussion of indirect communication and
"double reflection" which is prefaced to the "argument," the doctrinal
content of the work must be regarded as an ironical jest, which essentially takes the form of a carefully constructed parody of the *Phenomenology of Mind*. Moreover, the real purpose of this jest is not to
convince the reader of a philosophical or religious truth, but to prevent him from theorizing, even in an "existential" sense about Christianity, and instead to help him to come to grips, in the isolation of his

Reprinted with permission from Henry Allison and THE REVIEW OF METAPHYSICS,
March 1967.

own subjectivity, with the question of what it means to become a Christian. Thus, far from being a contribution, good, bad or indifferent, to a philosophy of existence, the *Postscript* emerges as Kierkegaard's attempt at a *reductio ad absurdum* of any such enterprise.

I

The *Postscript* is essentially concerned with the problem of becoming a Christian. This is called the "subjective problem," and is sharply distinguished from the objective problem of the truth of the Christian religion. The latter question, which is the central concern of historical criticism and speculative philosophy, is rather cursorily dismissed with the reflection that an objective investigation of the historical claims of Christianity can never yield more than approximation (a certain degree of probability), and that any mere approximation is incommensurable with the "infinite personal interest in an eternal happiness" which characterizes a believing Christian. Furthermore, any such objective approach to Christianity is not only futile but perverse, for the disinterestedness demanded of an objective observer is diametrically opposed to the decisiveness and total commitment which constitutes the very essence of Christian faith.

This analysis of the two approaches to Christianity gives rise to the distinction between subjective and objective reflection, and it is within the framework of this distinction that the "argument" of the work unfolds. The tendency towards objective thought finds its culmination in Hegel. In the Hegelian philosophy we are shown the necessity of transcending our finite particularity and viewing things from the standpoint of the Idea. There one will come to see the unity of thought and being and the identity of subject and object. The goal of the *Phenomenology of Mind* is precisely to lead the individual along the "highway of despair," to see the inadequacy of all finite forms of consciousness, and eventually to the promised land of Absolute Spirit, where all finite oppositions are reconciled. From this standpoint it is incumbent upon the individual to "forget himself,"[1] in the sense of his finite particularity, to become disinterested in his personal existence and absorbed in the Idea.

It is precisely this viewpoint which is the main target of Climacus' attack. His basic objection, and here it must be remembered that his objection is directed as much against the Danish Hegelians, *e.g.*, Heiberg and Martenson, as Hegel himself, is that this ultimate conformity of thought and being can never be realized by an existing human being, for it is precisely existence which keeps the moments of thought and being, of ideality and reality apart. Thus, the attempt to realize their union and to achieve the standpoint of pure thought necessarily involves the comical attempt to forget that one happens to be an existing human being. Climacus epitomizes this contention with the reflection that: "If the Hegelian philosophy has emancipated itself from every presupposition, it has won this freedom by means of one lunatic postulate: the initial transition to pure thought" (p. 279).

However, while the objective thinker tends to lose himself in his speculations, the subjectively oriented thinker "is essentially interested in his own thinking, existing as he does in his thought" (p. 67). This means that the subjective thinker is not concerned with the results yielded by disinterested reflection, but with the realization of the truth in his own existence. Objective reflection is concerned with "the matter at issue," *i.e.*, whether a particular theory is true or false, but for the subjective thinker, his very subjectivity becomes "the matter at issue." Hence Climacus proclaims:

> This must constantly be borne in mind, namely that the subjective problem is not something about an objective issue, but is the subjectivity itself. For since the problem in question poses a decision, and since all decisiveness, as shown above, inheres in subjectivity, it is essential that every trace of an objective issue should be eliminated. If any such trace remains, it is at once a sign that the subject seeks to shirk something of the pain and crisis of the decision: that is, he seeks to make the problem to some degree objective. (p. 115)

With this the wedge is firmly placed between the two modes of reflection. They are not only heterogeneous, but incommensurable. Instead of the Hegelian both/and whereby the individual finds himself in the infinite after forgetting himself in the finite, Climacus offers the existential either/or wherein the forgetfulness of self, characteristic of speculative thought, is viewed as a fantastic flight from one's existential situation, and the authentic task of the subjective thinker is to "immerse himself in existence," *i.e.*, to become increasingly conscious of his existential situation.

Climacus offers several illustrations of what he means by subjective reflection or becoming subjective, and perhaps the most illuminating of them is his analysis of the question: "What does it mean to die," wherein he clearly anticipates the well known discussion of Heidegger. Objectively, Climacus suggests, we know all sorts of things about death. We know, for instance, that we shall die if we swallow a dose of sulphuric acid or if we drown ourselves. We also know from history books that Napoleon always went about with poison ready at hand, and that in certain circumstances the Stoics regarded suicide as a courageous act. Furthermore, we are all aware of the fact that we will eventually die, and even that it might happen at any moment. Yet to possess all these items of information, to objectively recognize the inevitability and the uncertainty of death, is not to have understood it. Such understanding is radically different from understanding any item of information. It requires the ability to so exist that one regards death as an ever present possibility. This does not mean, however, that one simply acknowledges in passing that one must think about it at every moment, but that one really does so think about it. This intensity of subjective reflection is necessary according to Climacus, for

> ... if I am a mortal creature, then it is impossible to understand this uncertainty in terms of a mere generality unless indeed I, too, happen to be merely a human being in general.... And if initially my human nature is merely an abstract something, it is at any rate the task which life sets me to become subjective; and in the same degree that I become subjective, the uncertainty of death comes more and more to interpenetrate my subjectivity dialectically. It thus becomes more and more important for me to think it in connection with every factor and phase of my life; for since this uncertainty is there in every moment, it can only be overcome by overcoming it in every moment. (p. 149)

II

This analysis of the two kinds of reflection leads Climacus to a consideration of the kind of truth appropriate to each. From the point of view of objective reflection, truth is viewed in the traditional manner as the conformity of thought and being. The precise meaning of this formula, however, is dependent upon an understanding of "being." Here Climacus recognizes two possibilities: either "being" is understood as real or empirical being or as ideal being. Because of the uncertainty of all empirical generalizations (an uncertainty which is grounded for Climacus, as for Plato, in the changing character of the world of sense), if "being" is understood in the former sense (as empirical being), truth becomes a *desideratum*, something to be approximated but never finally achieved by any existing individual. (Hence "an existential system is impossible.") If, however, it is understood in the latter sense (as ideal being) its conformity with thought becomes an empty tautology, "an abstract self-identity." In either case, however, the Hegelian attempt to mediate between thought and being must be rejected. Such mediation may be valid *sub specie aeterni*, but this is irrelevant to the poor existing individual, who is "confined to the straightjacket of existence" and cannot attain that exalted standpoint.

What is needed, therefore, is an explanation of how the eternal, *i.e.*, ethico-religious, truth is to be understood by an existing individual, and this is provided by the contention that truth lies in subjectivity. Since objective reflection necessarily leads away from the subject and culminates in a disinterested contemplation, a truth which is true for the subject, *i.e.*, existentially relevant, can only be acquired through inwardness or subjective reflection:

> The subjective reflection turns its attention inwardly to the subject, and desires in this intensification of inwardness to realize the truth. And it proceeds in such fashion that, just as in the preceding objective reflection,

when the objectivity had come into being, the subjectivity had vanished, so here the subjectivity of the subject becomes the final stage and objectivity a vanishing factor. (pp. 175-176)

Now inwardness culminates in passion, and it is only in the moment of passion that an individual is able to existentially realize the union of the finite and the infinite which is the goal of the Hegelian dialectic. "In passion," Climacus contends, "the existing individual is rendered infinite in the eternity of the imaginative representation, and yet is at the same time most definitely himself" (p. 176). This unique quality of passion is grounded in its dual nature as both the culmination of inwardness and the means to self-transcendence. Because of this dual nature Climacus can regard the individual during the moment of passion as at the same time fully at one with himself and in a genuine relationship with God. This conception follows from Climacus' definition of inwardness as "the relationship of an individual to himself before God" (p. 391) and points to Kierkegaard's oft expressed conviction that man, as a "synthesis of the finite and the infinite" is only really at one with himself when he exists in full consciousness of his God-relationship. Finally, since he often describes an individual's "God-relationship" as a "possibility relationship" and God as "infinite possibility," and since he regards imagination as the organ of possibility in man, it follows that for Climacus the union of God and man, the finite and the infinite, can only take place in the imagination.[2]

From this it can be readily seen that subjective reflection provides the only possible approach to ethico-religious knowledge, which is the only knowledge that has "an essential relationship to the existence of the knower." However, whereas from the objective point of view reflection is directed towards the result of one's investigation, conceived of as a body of truth maintaining its validity apart from the individual's relationship to it, subjective reflection is directed towards the relationship itself, with the paradoxical result that "if only the mode of the relationship is in the truth, the individual is in the truth, even if he should happen to be related to what is not true" (p. 178). In other words, one can say that while objective reflection is directed towards the "what" or content of a doctrine, subjective reflection is concerned with the "how," the way in which it is existentially appropriated by the individual. Thus, it is the "passion of the infinite," or the genuineness of the commitment which is decisive, and not the specific nature of that to which one is committed. As an illustration of this Climacus utters the well-known, yet highly misleading dictum:

> If one who lives in the midst of Christendom goes up to the house of God, the house of the true God, with the true conception of God in his knowledge, and prays, but prays in a false spirit; and one who lives in an idolatrous community prays with the entire passion of the infinite, although his

eyes rest upon the image of an idol: where is there more truth? The one
prays in truth to God though he worships an idol; the other prays falsely
to the true God, and hence worships in fact an idol. (pp. 179-180)

This statement is misleading because it appears to endorse the
unqualified rejection of the "what" of belief in favor of the "how"
with the obvious implication that it is better to be a "true," passionately committed Nazi than to be a lukewarm Christian. This, however,
is not Climacus' intent, and he goes to great lengths to obviate any
such misunderstanding. First, he endeavors to distinguish between
true inwardness and madness. Climacus points to Don Quixote as the
prototype of "subjective madness," and argues that the basic characteristic of such madness is the concentration of one's passion upon a
particular finite object, an *idée fixe*. Thus, madness becomes characterized as an "aberrant inwardness," wherein one becomes infinitely
concerned over something which is of no decisive significance. In contrast with this, true inwardness is always directed towards the infinite, *i.e.*, towards one's God-relationship, and, Climacus concludes:
"At its maximum this inward 'how' is the passion of the infinite, and
the passion of the infinite is the truth. But the passion of the infinite
is precisely subjectivity, and thus subjectivity becomes the truth"
(p. 181).

Second, and most important, this passionate "how" is so qualified
that Christianity, as the ultimate "what," becomes its only satisfac-
tory correlate, and thus, what began as an attack upon objective reflection, ends up as a rather peculiar "demonstration" of the subjective
truth of Christianity. This is not accomplished, however, by an immediate reconciliation of the "how" and the "what," the commitment
and its object, but by further accentuating their opposition, thereby
suggesting an eventual *coincidentia oppositorum*. The basic premise
of this "argument" is Climacus' contention: "An objective uncertainty
held fast in an appropriation process of the most passionate inwardness is the truth, the highest truth attainable for an existing individual" (p. 182).

This definition of truth which, Climacus tells us, is an equivalent
expression for faith determines the opposition between subjective and
objective reflection, "the fork in the road where the way swings off."
Just as the scientific quest for objective truth requires the rejection of
all subjective or private interests, so "when subjectivity is the truth,
*the conceptual determination of the truth must include an expression
for the antithesis to objectivity*" (p. 182). Thus, there is a direct correlation between objective uncertainty and subjective truth, the objective uncertainty serving to increase "the tension of that infinite
passion which is inwardness." When systematically applied such a
conception leads to a radical misologism, and as we shall see, this is
precisely the direction in which the discussion proceeds.

Climacus had begun his analysis of subjectivity by arguing quite cogently that the decisiveness of religious or ethical commitment is incompatible with the disinterested reflection of objective thought. Thus, one can neither speculate one's way into Christianity, nor treat the content of Christian faith in a speculative manner, à la Hegel, without completely perverting its very essence. However, where St. Thomas Aquinas was content to point out that one cannot know and believe the same thing at the same time, and where Kant sought to deny knowledge in order to make room for faith, Climacus argues for a direct relationship between theoretical implausibility and religious faith. Thus Climacus can assert: "Faith is precisely the contradiction between the infinite passion of the individual's inwardness and the objective uncertainty." Moreover, since such objective uncertainty is the inevitable lot of all existing beings, the attempt to deny it can only be regarded as absentmindedness, and thus the true believer "must constantly be intent upon holding fast the objective uncertainty, so as to remain out upon the deep, over seventy thousand fathoms of water . . . still preserving his faith" (pp. 182-83).

Armed with this conception of truth, Climacus returns to the problem of his earlier work, the *Philosophical Fragments:* the question of the relationship between the Socratic and the specifically Christian religiosity. Both here and in the *Fragments* Socrates is viewed by Climacus as the very prototype of the subjective or existential thinker outside of Christianity. His great merit over against both Plato and the modern speculative thinkers is that he never forgets that he is an existing individual, but rather "concentrates essentially upon existence."

The heart of Socratic thought is to be found in the notion that the truth lies within. As Climacus tells us in the *Fragments:* "In the Socratic view each individual is his own center, and the entire world centers in his views, his self-knowledge is a knowledge of God" (p. 14). Thus, the task confronting a Socratic thinker is to become subjective, in the sense of continually realizing in existence his God-relationship. This, according to Climacus, is the profound significance of Socrates' doctrine that knowledge is recollection, and which clearly differentiates it from the speculative use made of that doctrine by Plato. Existentially understood it means that the knower is potentially in possession of the eternal truth, *i.e.,* his God-relationship, and is confronted with no difficulty other than the fact that he exists. This minor difficulty, however, turns out to be decisive, and provides the clue to understanding Socrates' frequent professions of ignorance. This ignorance is viewed by Climacus as a consequence of the previously established contention that for one engaged in the business of existing, the eternal truth remains objectively uncertain. Moreover, since a total commitment is demanded to what is objectively uncertain, Climacus contends that from the point of view of the existing individual the truth becomes a paradox. This paradox was thoroughly grasped by Socrates, who totally committed himself to the truth despite his recognition of its objective uncertainty (the manner in which he faced death in the *Phaedo* being Climacus' favorite illustration), and for this reason: "Socrates was in the truth by virtue of his ignorance, in the highest sense in which this was possible within paganism" (p. 183).

But paganism is not Christianity, and although Climacus points to the analogies between Socratic inwardness and Christian faith, his main goal seems to be to show the superiority of the latter. The basic limitation of the Socratic position lies in the theory of recollection. This theory has a two-fold existential significance. First, as was shown in the *Fragments*, it clearly implies that neither an historical event nor another person can have any decisive significance for an existing individual. Since the truth lies within, one person can do no more than provide the occasion whereby another comes to recollect it (the slave boy incident in the *Meno* being the paradigm case), and thus the maieutic relationship is the highest possible between men. Second, because the truth lies within, temporal existence lacks any ultimate seriousness, for the possibility of "taking oneself back into eternity through recollection is always there" (p. 184). To be sure, Socrates with his passionate inwardness did not make use of this possibility, but according to Climacus its very presence serves to mitigate the seriousness of his inwardness.

This limitation raises the question of the possibility of a higher level of inwardness. Since the limitation of the Socratic position stems from the contention that the individual is initially in possession of truth, any deeper expression of inwardness or subjectivity must involve a denial of this possession. However, the denial that the individual is in possession of the truth is *eo ipso* a denial of the contention that truth is subjectivity, and thus we are led by the inexorable "logic" of Climacus to the paradoxical conclusion that the deepest possible expression of the notion that subjectivity is truth, is precisely the proposition that subjectivity is untruth. This, however, is not to be understood as implying a regression to the speculative standpoint, wherein subjectivity is also untruth, for the decisive characteristic of this level of ultimate inwardness is that here "subjectivity is beginning upon the task of becoming the truth through a subjectifying process, is in the difficulty that it is already untruth" (pp. 185-186). The result is not the abandonment, but the further accentuation of existence, and hence of inwardness. The subject cannot be regarded as eternally being in untruth, as this would apparently imply that he was created thusly by God, nor does it make sense to regard the loss of the "eternal essential truth" as the result of an unfortunate accident. Thus, the only explanation for the loss is that the individual brought himself into the condition in time, by a free act. If, however, the individual has in fact cut himself off from the eternal by a free act then the pathos of his existential condition is accentuated to the utmost possible degree.

Now it just so happens that this is precisely how Christianity, with its doctrine of original sin, views the human condition. From the Christian standpoint a man is born in sin and as a sinner. Thus, in contradistinction to the Socratic man who has access to the eternal by way of recollection, the Christian is profoundly aware of his alienation from the eternal, a situation poignantly depicted in Hegel's analysis of the "Unhappy Conscience." Furthermore, Climacus reflects: "If it was paradoxical to posit the eternal truth in relationship to an existing individual, it is now absolutely paradoxical to posit it in relationship to such an individual as we have here defined" (p. 186).

However, this is exactly what Christianity proclaims to have taken place through the entrance of God into history as the Christ. Thus, if for Socrates the paradox is to be found in the relationship between the eternal truth and the existing individual, for the Christian the eternal truth itself is inherently paradoxical. This is because for the Christian the eternal (decisive truth) is precisely that the eternal truth (God) has come into being in time. Hence, what for Socrates remained an objective uncertainty is for the Christian an objective absurdity: "The absurd is that the eternal truth has come into being in time, that God has come into being, has been born, has grown up, and so forth, precisely like any other individual human being, quite indistinguishable from other individuals" (p. 188).

This absurdity is the content of the Christian faith, the "what" corresponding to the "how" of Christian inwardness. It is the absolute paradox, or the paradox *sensu eminentiori* to which the Socratic paradox and its corresponding inwardness bear only a remote analogy. Since the starting point of the whole discussion was the affirmation of the direct correlation between objective uncertainty and inwardness, "the less objective security the more profound the possible inwardness," it would appear that it is only when the "what" becomes objectively absurd, and the more absurd the better, that the maximum degree of inwardness is attainable. Now since the requisite absurdity is found in the content of Christian faith, we are led to the conclusion that Christianity is the source of the maximum possible inwardness, and thus can be regarded as the "true" religion (subjectively understood), not in spite of, but precisely because of its objective absurdity! For, in Climacus' own words: "The absurd is precisely by its objective repulsion the measure of the intensity of faith in inwardness" (p. 189).

Despite the protest of several recent commentators this position must be regarded as radically irrationalistic.[3] The "argument" as it stands, with its explicit correlation between objective absurdity and subjective "truth" is clearly an expression of a consistent misologism or an "intellectualistic anti-intellectualism"[4] which finds its closest historical antecedent in the *"credo quia absurdum"* attributed to Tertullian. However, just as Hegel's panologism differs from the pre-Kantian rationalism of a Leibnitz or Spinoza by virtue of its dialectical structure, so Climacus' misologism can be viewed as an irrationalistic revision of the Hegelian schema. Thus, while Hegel rejects the absolute starting point of his predecessors and begins instead with the immediate, viewing absolute knowledge as the goal to be obtained through the demonstration of the inadequacy of all finite forms ("Of the Absolute it must be said that it is essentially a result."), Climacus, in his endeavor "to make the necessity of the paradox evident" (p. 191), begins with an analysis of the inadequacy of all lower stages of inwardness. This analysis, which traces the spiritual life of the individual, rather than the life of Absolute Spirit, from the lowest level, aesthetic immediacy, to the highest non-Christian expression, infinite resignation, and the consciousness of guilt before God, occupies the bulk of the *Postscript;* but its main purpose (suggested by the name Climacus) is to lead the individual up the dialectical ladder of inwardness to the point at which he can appreciate the uniqueness and absoluteness, as well as the absurdity of the Christian faith. Hence, one can say that for Hegel's conception of the necessary advance of the Spirit to absolute knowledge, Climacus substitutes the equally necessary (albeit in a different sense) advance of subjectivity to absolute paradox.

The necessity of this advance for the spiritual development of the individual is demonstrated by means of a further comparison of the Socratic and Christian forms of religiousness, here entitled A and B, or the "religiousness of immanence" and "paradoxical religiousness" respectively. The former is characterized by a "dying away from immediacy," the repudiation, or at least relativization of all one's finite concerns, and the devotion of all one's energies to the realization of one's "absolute telos," a phrase applied to both the individual's God-relationship and his eternal happiness, which seem to be identical for Climacus. Since the presupposition of this level of inwardness is the belief that the truth lies within, the individual is viewed as already potentially in possession of his God-relationship or eternal happiness, and his task is simply to transform his mode of existence so as to become in truth what he already is potentially. Hence, Climacus calls this level the "dialectic of inward transformation" (p. 494). The task of self-transformation, however, is soon shown to be far more difficult than it first appeared. Since this "dying away from immediacy" or "infinite resignation," cannot be accomplished once and for all, but must be undertaken at every instant, such a mode of existence essentially involves suffering. Moreover, since that which must be continually begun anew can never be completed, the decisive expression for this form of religiousness is the consciousness of guilt.

This consciousness of guilt, the awareness of being in the wrong over and against God, is the highest development of the religiousness of inwardness, and we are thus led to the paradoxical conclusion that the deepest expression of the individual's God-relationship is to be found in the consciousness of the dis-relationship.

It is at this point that the parallelism with Hegel once again becomes manifest. Just as the *Phenomenology of Mind* showed that one must traverse the "highway of despair" and experience the shipwreck of all finite forms of understanding before he is able to grasp the standpoint of the Absolute, so for Climacus, it is only the individual who has existentially striven to realize his God-relationship and has been shipwrecked upon the consciousness of guilt for whom the absolute paradox becomes meaningful. "Religiousness A," Climacus contends, "must be present in the individual before there can be any question of becoming aware of the dialectic of B" (p. 494). Only when existential pathos has reached its decisive expression in the consciousness of guilt can the venture into the absurd become an existential possibility. Just as it is the consciousness of the path which distinguishes the Hegelian conception of absolute knowledge from the dogmatic pretensions of his predecessors, for Climacus it is precisely the presence of this prior consciousness which distinguishes the venture into the absurd from superstition.

This implies that any speculative interpretation of the paradox involves a misunderstanding. The difficulty involved in becoming a Christian is not the intellectual difficulty of understanding how the eternal can be reconciled with the temporal, but the existential difficulty of committing oneself to the belief that one's eternal happiness is based upon something historical, and moreover, something historical which by its very nature cannot become historical. Such a commitment involves the complete sacrifice of one's reason, both theoretical and practical, for in addition to being inherently contradictory, the absolute paradox also violates the ethical integrity of the individual in that it places the locus of his eternal destiny in something external to him. The problem of the relationship between the ethical and the paradoxically religious modes of existence is one of the most interesting, yet generally ignored aspects of Climacus' analysis. Nevertheless he takes great pains to depict the proper relationship between them. The analogy, he argues, between faith and the ethical mode of existence is to be found in the "infinite interest" or "inwardness which distinguishes both from an aesthetic mode of existence." But the believer differs from the ethicist in being infinitely interested in the reality of another, *i.e.*, in the fact that God has existed in time" (p. 288).

This, Climacus asserts, can only be believed against the understanding, so that the believer's task is not to understand the paradox, but to understand that it cannot be understood. However, in view of the elaborate dialectical analysis which prepares the way for the apprehension of the paradox, it would seem that this itself requires a good deal of understanding, and is well beyond the ken of the "simple believer" whom Climacus is always praising at the expense of the pretentious speculative philosopher. This is no doubt the justification for those who regard the position of the *Postscript* as an "intellectual anti-intellectualism," and Climacus himself seems to admit as much when he proclaims that it is after all necessary for the Christian to make use of his understanding, "precisely in order to believe against his understanding" (p. 504).

Thus, the dialectical ascent to faith culminates in the "crucifixion of the understanding" (p. 500). Here, at the highest level of the spiritual life we encounter a total break with immanence. The individual has gone through the process of "infinite resignation," and has come to the realization of the shipwreck of his own resources, both intellectual and moral. His consciousness of sin makes him fully aware of his alienation from God and the hopelessness of his situation. Yet he nevertheless clings passionately to the absurd, and, so Christianity tells us, finds therein his salvation.

Climacus' analysis of subjectivity has thus brought us to the point where we can indeed recognize "the necessity of the paradox" in that we can see that its acceptance through an act of faith is the only solution to the human predicament. Moreover, with this insight we are also able to apprehend the return of objectivity. The analysis of the "how" has led us inevitably to the "what" of Christianity as its only true correlate, as the only content capable of satisfying the "passion of the infinite." Objectivity and subjectivity are reconciled in the inwardness of faith in a manner strangely reminiscent of the speculative reconciliation of consciousness and its object at the end of the *Phenomenology of Mind*, and Climacus is rapidly emerging as a rather queer sort of Hegelian. The essence of Climacus' position is to be found in a passage near the end of the work where the relationship between the how and the what is explicitly formulated.

> The thing of being a Christian is not determined by the what of Christianity but by the *how* of the Christian. This *how* can only correspond with one thing, the absolute paradox. There is therefore no vague talk to the effect that being a Christian is to accept, and to accept, and to accept quite differently, to appropriate, to believe, to appropriate by faith quite differently (all of them purely rhetorical and fictitious definitions); but to *believe* is specifically different from all other appropriation and inwardness. Faith is the objective uncertainty due to the repulsion of the absurd held fast by the passion of inwardness, which in this instance is intensified to the utmost degree. This formula fits only the believer, no one else, not a lover, not an enthusiast, not a thinker, but simply and solely the believer who is related to the absolute paradox. (p. 540).

With this Climacus' conviction of the uniqueness and incommensurability of the Christian faith with all other levels of inwardness receives its decisive expression. It thus is not true that it does not matter what one believes as long as one believes it with sufficient inwardness, for the only thing that can really be believed, *i.e.*, truly appropriated with the "passion of the infinite" is the absolute paradox. This aspect of Climacus' position is clearly expressed by Kierkegaard himself, who in a Journal entry for the year 1849, writes:

> In all that is usually said about Johannes Climacus being purely subjective and so on, people have forgotten, in addition to everything else concrete about him, that in one of the last sections he shows that the curious thing is: that there is a "how" which has this quality, that if *it* is truly given, that the "what" is also given; and that it is the "how" of "faith." Here, quite certainly, we have inwardness at its maximum proving to be objectivity once again. And this is an aspect of the principle of subjectivity which, so far as I know, has never before been presented or worked out.[5]

III

Viewed in the usual manner as an argument for the uniqueness, absoluteness and "subjective truth" of the Christian faith, Climacus' "apologetic" must be regarded as an utter failure. In terms of his misologistic orientation the "subjective truth" of Christianity is a function of the absurdity of its objective content. It is only because of the "repulsion of the absurd" that Christianity is able to intensify inwardness to the "utmost degree," and it is thus its very absurdity which allegedly qualifies it as the only "what" corresponding to the ultimate "how." But at this point the question inevitably suggests itself to us in our misguided role as objective thinkers: why this particular absurdity? Granted, for the sake of argument, that the belief that our eternal happiness is based upon an objective absurdity is necessary to raise the passion of the religious individual to its highest level, but does that really serve to prove that Christianity is the only absurdity which can really be *believed* (in the strong Climacian sense)? At the most this would seem to show that the passionate acceptance of Jesus of Nazareth as the Christ requires the highest level of inwardness, but so, it seems, would the acceptance of the claim of any of an untold number of deluded fanatics who have believed that they were God. Moreover, if Christianity is really as absurd as Climacus contends, if becoming a Christian really does require a "crucifixion of the understanding," then it is hard to see what criteria we could find to distinguish between this saving absurdity, and plain "garden variety" nonsense. Once the understanding is crucified in the radical manner which Climacus suggests, it is clearly no easy task to resurrect it.

Yet perhaps we are jumping to conclusions. Climacus does in fact attempt to distinguish between the absurdity of the absolute paradox and mere nonsense. The problem is discussed in passing in the *Fragments*. There he distinguishes between the paradox, and the, to him, nonsensical belief that Christ's initial disciples stood in a special relationship to him, that they received the "condition," *i.e.*, the inner witness of the Holy Spirit which makes faith possible, directly from him, and that they in turn were able to give this "condition" to the next generation of disciples. This view, which bears a curious analogy to the Roman Catholic and Grundtvigian conceptions of the Church as an objective authority and means of grace is distinguished from the paradox in that it is not only absurd, but self-contradictory, for it holds that "God is the God for the contemporary, but that the contemporary is God for the third party" (p. 27). Now, this would seem to suggest that the paradox differs from other absurdities in not containing a contradiction, but as we shall see, this hardly jibes with the analysis in the *Postscript*.

Again, in the *Postscript*, Climacus endeavors to distinguish between Christian faith and superstition or aestheticism, which may be regarded as a kind of nonsense. This is accomplished by means of an analysis of the dialectical structure of faith in its relationship to religiousness A:

> In case religiousness A does not come into the picture as *terminus a quo* for the paradoxical religiousness, religiousness A is higher than B, for then the paradox, the absurd etc., are not to be taken *sensu eminenti* (in the sense that they absolutely cannot be understood either by clever or by stupid people), but are used aesthetically of the marvelous among other marvelous things, which are indeed marvelous, but which after all can be comprehended. (p. 496)

Thus, to base my hopes for eternity upon my red hair, believing that this color is particularly pleasing to the gods, is the lowest form of paganism, totally lacking in inwardness. It is a rather superficial application of the aesthetic category of fortune, something at which the subjective thinker who has striven with all his passion to realize his relationship to the eternal could only laugh (or perhaps cry?). Now this is quite true, but it is also the case, as Climacus points out, that Christianity itself bears "a certain resemblance" to aesthetics:

> Religiousness B is discriminative, selective and polemical: only upon a definite condition do I become blessed, and as I absolutely bind myself to this condition, so do I exclude every other man who does not thus bind himself. This is the incentive to particularism in universal pathos. Every Christian possesses the pathos of religiousness A, and then this pathos of discrimination. This discrimination imports to the Christian a certain resemblance to one who is fortunate through favor, and when it is so conceived selfishly by a Christian we have the desparate presumption of predestination. (p. 516)

This resemblance is, however, according to Climacus, misleading. The fact that his happiness is based upon something historical, he contends, "makes the Christian's happiness or good fortune recognizable by suffering," and as a consequence, "the religious determinant of being God's elect is as paradoxically contrary as possible to being a Pamphilius of fortune..." (p. 516). But is it really? The essential difference between the Christian and the superstitious pagan is that the former believes "against his understanding" in full consciousness of its absurdity, and hence with suffering, while the latter (our red-headed Pamphilius of fortune) simply affirms his good fortune with a naive self-confidence. Now this certainly serves to distinguish between the "way" of believing or the levels of inwardness of the Christian and the pagan, but it hardly enables us to make any judgments concerning the *contents* of their respective beliefs. According to Climacus' analysis it would seem that they both believe absurdities, with the rather dubious advantage of the Christian being simply his awareness of the absurdity of his belief.

Finally, we must consider the passage in the *Postscript* where Climacus specifically endeavors to distinguish between the absurdity of Christianity and nonsense. As we have seen, Climacus argues that the proper use of understanding for a Christian is to make sure that he believes against his understanding. From this he concludes:

> Nonsense therefore he cannot believe against the understanding, for precisely the understanding will discern that it is nonsense and will prevent him from believing it; but he makes so much use of the understanding that he becomes aware of the incomprehensible, and then he holds to this, believing against the understanding. (p. 504)

This passage has been cited as evidence against the charge that Kierkegaard is an irrationalist, and it is suggested that Christianity is here distinguished from nonsense as being (in terms of the traditional distinction) above rather than contrary to reason.[6] It is clear, however, that such a contention hardly fits the argument of the *Postscript*. In addition to the fact that Climacus constantly emphasizes the need to believe against the understanding, rather than merely something which transcends it, the whole analysis of the *Postscript* is geared to showing the contradictory nature of the paradox. Traditionally, the realm of the *supra rationem* was held to be incomprehensible for the finite understanding, but not inherently contradictory. It was, for instance, precisely in terms of this distinction that Leibnitz endeavored to reconcile faith and reason in the *Theodicée*. Climacus, however, maintains that the paradox contains not one, but two "dialectical contradictions": first the basing of one's eternal happiness upon the reality of something historical, the contradiction here being between the approximate nature of all historical knowledge, and the total commitment demanded by faith; and second, the "fact that this historical datum is compounded in a way contradictory to all thinking..." (p. 513).

It is true that these contradictions are called "dialectical" and the first instance at least this seems to suggest a juxtaposition of incongruous concepts, a kind of "category mistake," rather than a simple logical inconsistency. In the second instance, however, where the reference to the fact that the historical datum is one which by its very nature cannot become historical, is clearly a case of logical contradiction, and thus we are led once again to the recognition of the irrationality of the paradox.

With this we are back to our original question: If the pardox here viewed simply as "the incomprehensible" is indeed irrational and even contradictory, how is this peculiar kind of irrationality to be distinguished from mere nonsense? According to the cited passage this distinction is recognized by the understanding of the believer, but this raises two fundamental difficulties. The first is again the oft mentioned problem of criteria. Climacus has so strongly emphasized the absurdity of the paradox that it would seem that any effort to distinguish its objective content from mere nonsense is bound to fail. One could, of course, retort that these objective considerations are irrelevant, and that it is its subjective or existential significance for the believer which distinguishes the paradox from nonsense. This, however, gets us nowhere, for it amounts to the admission that *objectively* there are no criteria, and hence that the only difference between Christianity and nonsense is that the former happens to be taken seriously by some individuals while the latter is not. Moreover, we must remember that according to Climacus the distinction is recognized by the understanding. But if this is indeed the case, has not objectivity once again reared its ugly head in a decisive, albeit a perverse manner? From the standpoint of subjective reflection, with its direct correlation between subjective truth and objective uncertainty, would not the recognition, assuming it could be made, that "the incomprehensible" is not nonsense, actually serve as a check, rather than an inducement to inwardness? The only way to avoid this conclusion, and to distinguish between the paradox and mere nonsense, would be to suggest that the former is in some sense even more irrational than the latter. This would mean, however, that for the Hegelian demand to go beyond faith, Climacus is substituting the rather dubious demand to go beyond nonsense!

Secondly, and even more fundamental, Climacus' contention that the understanding will discern nonsense and *prevent* one from believing it, while a reasonable enough statement, stands in blatant contradiction to the distinction between will and intellect, subjectivity and objectivity, which is central to his whole "doctrine." In discussing the problem of historical knowledge in the *Fragments*,

Climacus draws attention to the uncertainty involved in all statements about the past. Arguing against the Hegelian conception of history as the necessary process of Spirit in the world, he contends that since the past has come into existence it "has the elusiveness which is implicit in all coming into existence" and thus cannot be regarded as necessary. Now if this be the case, Climacus continues, "the organ for the historical must have an analogous structure. It must comprise a corresponding somewhat by which it may repeatedly negate in its certainty the uncertainty that corresponds to the uncertainty of coming into existence." This condition is met by faith or belief *(Tro)* because as an act of the will "there is always present a negated uncertainty, in every way corresponding to the uncertainty of coming into existence" (pp. 100-101). Furthermore, precisely the same reflection is applicable to doubt, the negative correlate of belief. According to Climacus the radical doubt of the Greek sceptics was not the result of cognition, but a free act of the will, and on this basis he argues against both Descartes and Hegel that doubt cannot be overcome by reflection but only "by a free act of the will" (p. 102). However, if belief and doubt are viewed as acts of will, and as such sharply distinguished from forms of knowledge, it seems rather difficult to see just how our understanding of anything, even nonsense, could "prevent" our belief.

Moreover, lest one suppose that our pseydonymous author has changed his position in the later work, we can readily see that the whole critique of the objective approach to Christianity in the *Postscript* is dependent upon the distinction between the decisiveness of will characteristic of Christian faith, and the disinterestedness of speculative understanding. It is on this basis that Climacus is able to argue that religious commitment (subjectivity) does not follow as a matter of course from objective considerations, but requires a "leap." But if an act of will, a religious commitment, necessarily involves a break with the understanding, how can one maintain that intellectual considerations, *i.e.*, the recognition that something is nonsensical, can "prevent us from believing it"? If belief really is an act of will, which by its very nature involves a "leap" beyond the understanding, then far from inhibiting belief, the recognition of the nonsensical character of a doctrine would seem to provide an inducement to inwardness, and hence be a potential source of "subjective truth." Thus, we are led to the conclusion that not only does Climacus' misologism fail to provide criteria in terms of which the understanding can distinguish between the Christian absurd and nonsense, but that even if such criteria were available they would be irrelevant to the "subjective thinker."

IV

We have attempted to find within the *Postscript* a relatively straightforward albeit bizarre argument for the "subjective truth" and uniqueness of the Christian faith, and we have come to the conclusion that viewed as such it is a colossal failure. Yet this conclusion raises more problems than it solves. The argument appears to be so bad that we can question whether it could have been seriously meant. Thus, we find ourselves confronted with a decision, which Kierkegaard would no doubt have found amusing: either we must dismiss him as an extremely muddleheaded thinker, who in opting for a subjectivist position, tried and failed to posit criteria in terms of which we can distinguish between Christianity and nonsense, or we shall have to make a new and more strenuous effort to come to grips with that enigma called Kierkegaard.

Now even apart from a consideration of Kierkegaard's frequent but not overly consistent treatment of the question of the precise status of the Christian absurd in his other writings, it is apparent from the structure of the work, its pseudonymous character, and the *First and Last Declaration* which Kierkegaard appended to it in his own name, that such a straightforward, undialectical reading of the *Postscript* involves a serious misunderstanding. As is well known, Kierkegaard proclaims in this "Declaration" that none of the teachings of the pseydonymous are to be regarded as his.

> So in the pseudonymous works there is not a single word which is mine, I have no opinion about these works except as a third person, no knowledge of their meaning except as a reader, not the remotest private relation to them, since such a thing is impossible in the case of a doubly reflected communication.

This is no doubt somewhat of an overstatement, and is to some extent contradicted by his analysis of his authorship in *The Point of View*, but it does provide us with an important clue for understanding the *Postscript*. Let us begin then with a consideration of the character of the pseydonymous author. The name, Johannes Climacus, is that of a sixth century monk of the monastery at Sinai, and the surname was derived from the title of his work: *Scala Paradisi*. Thus, Kierkegaard's use of the pseudonym clearly suggests the notion of climax, or ascent from purely human to specifically Christian categories. It has been suggested that the pseudonym represents Kierkegaard's own attitude during his student days at the University.[7] But within the context of the *Postscript* he repeatedly describes himself as a non-Christian humorist who is concerned with the subjective problem of how to become a Christian. This raises the question: to what extent are Climacus' external, *i.e.*, non-Christian perspective and humoristic orientation reflected in the structure of the work?

Climacus defines humor as a boundary stage between the ethical and religious modes of existence, corresponding on a higher level to irony, which is the boundary between the aesthetic and the ethical. The essential quality of the humorist is his ability to recognize contradiction, and specifically the contradiction between the inwardness of the religious life and all its outward manifestations. The humorist, Climacus contends,

> ... sets the God-idea into conjunction with other things and evokes the contradiction—but he does not maintain a relationship to God in terms of religious passion *stricte sic dictus*, he transforms himself instead into a jesting and yet profound exchange-center for all these transactions, but he does not himself stand related to God. (p. 451)

Thus, the humorist knows something about the existential difficulties of the God-relationship. He is able to recognize objectivistic or superstitious perversions of this relationship, but he comprehends in an intellectual, *i.e.*, objective, sort of way, what the believer appropriates existentially. Since the God-relationship lies in subjectivity, his very awareness of the difficulties of such a relationship requires a certain degree of inwardness, but since he does not himself make the "leap," but rather withdraws into the realm of jest, he is obviously lacking the decisiveness of the truly committed person. Now given Climacus' own description of the stance of the humorist *vis-a-vis* Christianity, one would expect to find this reflected in his own analysis of faith, *i.e.*, one would expect this analysis to be in its very essence humorous, and therefore to some extent objective.

The humorous aspect of the argument is suggested by the curious parallelism to Hegel, and this suggestion is further strengthened by a Journal entry wherein Kierkegaard writes: "Hegel is a Johannes Climacus, who did not, like the giants, storm the heavens by setting mountain upon mountain, but entered by means of his syllogisms."[8] Thus, both Hegel and Climacus are stormers of the heavens, searchers for the Absolute, and the main difference between them lies in their respective routes to this exalted goal. The one proceeds by way of speculative philosophy, the other by means of "the principle of subjectivity." Yet both attempts are equally futile, for despite the difference of their approaches, they both end up at the same place, viz., the identification of Christianity and nonsense. This follows for Hegel because the attempt to mediate between philosophy and Christianity destroys the decisiveness which is the very essence of the Christian faith, and it follows for Climacus because the attempt to locate the paradox on a scale of subjectivity, undercuts any possible means of determining the uniqueness of the Christian absurd.

In light of these considerations is it outlandish to view the whole "argument" of Climacus as a kind of perverse parody of Hegel? The dialectical structure of the analysis, and the "objective" concern for the ultimate reconciliation of the "how" and the "what" in Christian faith, which parallels the culmination of the *Phenomenology of Mind* in Spirit's consciousness of itself as Spirit, the reconciliation of subject and object in Absolute knowledge, certainly suggest such an interpretation. Moreover, this reading enables us to view the "argument" of the humorous Climacus as a jest, and thus, to overlook the philosophical absurdity of his position. But it naturally gives rise to the question: what is the point of the jest? Why should Kierkegaard's critique of Hegel take the form of a parody? Is he simply playing with us, or is he perhaps asking us to reconsider the possibility raised by the failure of Jacobi and Lavater to understand Lessing's earnestness: "unless it should happen to be the case that one cannot understand earnest without understanding jest" (p. 66)?

The answer, if it is to be found, may very well lie in Kierkegaard's conception of the problem of existential communication, and the recognition of the need for such communication to employ indirection and "double reflection." This possibility becomes very appealing when we recall that in his "Declaration" Kierkegaard characterized his pseudonymous works as examples of "doubly reflected communication," and that within the *Postscript* itself, Climacus begins his account of the "subjective problem" with an analysis of that very concept.

For Climacus, the problem of communication is grounded in the recognition of the different goals of objective and subjective reflection. Objective reflection, as we have seen, is concerned only with results, *i.e.*, with the attainment of a body of authenticated truths. As results they can be directly communicated in a series of propositions. The subjective thinker, on the other hand, is not concerned with the acquisition of a given body of truths, with "finding something out," but with "existing in 'the truth,'" appropriating it existentially. This different goal demands a different type of reflection, "the reflection of inwardness or possession, by virtue of which it belongs to the thinking subject and no one else" (pp. 167-168). This uniquely personal quality of subjective reflection brings with it two consequences which determine the problem of existential communication. First, since the subjective thinker is concerned with the task of living in the truth he is constantly in the process of becoming. "Subjective truth," *e.g.*, religion, faith, is not the sort of thing which one can simply acquire once and for all, but rather it requires a continual effort at re-appropriation. Thus, "subjective truth" can never be a permanent acquisition in the form of a result: "Subjective thought puts everything in process and omits the results." Second, the reflection of inwardness demands a "double reflection," both an intellectual reflection which leads to recognition, and an existential reflection which leads to appropriation. "In thinking," Climacus writes of the subjective thinker, "he thinks the universal; but as existing in his thought and as assimilating it in his inwardness, he becomes more and more subjectively isolated" (p. 68).

Thus, it is the very essence of subjective thought or existential reflection that it cannot be directly communicated, for to do so is to translate it into a result, and thus to contradict its "existential" character. Climacus offers several examples to illustrate this point, the most interesting of which is the analysis of the attempt to express the by now familiar conviction: "Truth is inwardness, there is no objective truth, but the truth consists in personal appropriation" (p. 71). How then is this "doctrine" to be proclaimed? An enthusiast, Climacus suggest, may expend great zeal in the propagation of this truth. He may make a special point of proclaiming it on every possible occasion. He may publish it in a learned treatise, and as a result gain many new adherents to his "doctrine," who in turn would strive to win others to the cause. However, as a consequence of such an endeavor, the champion of subjectivity succeeds only in rendering himself comical. In propagating the doctrine in this manner he has turned it into a result —an objective truth, a theory *about* the significance of subjectivity, and thus contradicted himself.

But how is this situation to be avoided? How is it possible for the subjective thinker, for one who really believes that the existential appropriation of the truth is the essential factor, to communicate this conviction without contradicting himself, without turning his conviction into a theory about subjectivity? According to Climacus the first requirement of such a communication is that it be expressed in such a way so as not to induce an immediate intellectual assent. Its goal is not the coercion of the recipient to a point of view, but his emancipation so that he may come to understand it inwardly, and as Climacus tells us: "The inwardness of understanding consists in each individual coming to understand it for himself" (p. 71). Such a goal, however, precisely because it is formulated in recognition of the freedom of the other cannot be achieved directly. Here Climacus is in thorough agreement with the Socratic contention that the only authentic relationship between individuals is the maieutic one, and it is because of this that he holds that any communication of a "personal" truth must be indirect, and that this indirection requires both artistry and self-control.[9]

The artistry is expressed in the form of the communication, and it consists in the elusiveness which forces the individual to reflect back upon himself. This elusiveness is the negative element in the process of communication, and it is decisive, for operating as a repellent factor, it prevents one from regarding such communication as a straightforward objective presentation of a doctrine. It is in terms of these considerations that we must understand "the subtle principle" of subjective thought: ". . . that the personalities must be held devoutly apart from one another, and not permitted to fuse or coagulate into objectivity. It is at this point that objectivity and subjectivity part from one another" (p. 73).

If this conception of the nature of existential communication is applied to the content of the *Postscript*, some interesting results follow. The book, as we have seen, points to the difficulties of becoming a Christian. It contends that in the ethical and religious spheres "truth is subjectivity," that subjectivity or passion stands in a direct correlation with objective uncertainty, and finally, that as an objective absurdity, Christianity is the objective correlate of the maximum degree of inwardness, and thus, can be regarded as the "true" or ultimate form of religiousness. We further saw that despite Climacus' protestations to the contrary, this view led to a consistent misologism, which ends with the identification of Christianity and nonsense. In proceeding in this way, however, it would seem that like the vast body of Kierkegaard's commentators, and "existential philosophers" in general, we have become "town criers of inwardness." We have attempted to treat as a philosophical proposition ("truth is subjectivity") what by its very nature cannot be regarded as such without contradiction. Is it any wonder then that qua philosophical proposition it reduces itself to an absurdity? The absurd consequences of this consistently misologistic position can now be seen to provide the repellent factor, the elusiveness necessary to indirection, which the author has artistically devised in order to avoid achieving a "result," and to throw his readers back upon themselves.

In light of these considerations let us return to Climacus' argument. The starting point of his trouble, the decisive passage which gives rise to the misologistic consequences is the assertion: "When subjectivity is the truth, the *conceptual determination* of the truth must include an expression of the antithesis to objectivity." The key words here are "conceptual determination" for they make clear that Climacus' misologism is a direct consequence of the conceptualization of the "principle of subjectivity"! But to conceptualize is to objectify, and, as we have seen, to speak objectively about inwardness (and Christianity, it will be remembered, is the highest form of inwardness) is stupidity. Thus, unless we are to view Kierkegaard as guilty of the very stupidity which he went to such great lengths to condemn, we must view the whole "argument" as a jest, as an expression of the author's artistry, the intent of which is not to "prove" the superiority of Christianity or even to show us in a theoretical way that the absolute paradox makes a kind of sense as *supra rationem* which is lacking in garden variety nonsense, but rather to help us realize existentially what it means to become a Christian, and to see that the only valid concept which we can form about Christianity is that it defies conceptualization. Moreover, it is only in light of these considerations that we can appreciate the significance of Kierkegaard's reflection: "Dialectically it is easy to see that Johannes Climacus' defense of Christianity is the most extreme that can be made and only a hair's breadth from an attack."[10] It is the most extreme that can be made because it consists essentially in pointing to its utter incommensurability with all human categories, and the "hair's breadth" which distinguishes this from an attack is nothing more than the double reflection of the subjective thinker. If this be omitted, and the *Postscript* viewed as an essay in existential apologetics, then it is indeed an attack for it leads to the ultimate identification of Christianity and nonsense.

Thus, as a genuine subjective thinker, for whom "everything is dialectical," and whose main work contains "not only a conclusion but a revocation" (p. 547), Kierkegaard remains perpetually elusive. Like Socrates, of whom he was a life long admirer, he believed that his task was not to expound but to sting, and hence any attempt to pin him down, to look for results in the form of an existential philosophy or Christian apologetic in his writings is, to use Climacus' analogy, "like trying to paint Mars in the armor that made him invisible," the supreme irony being, as Climacus points out and the whole history of Kierkegaard scholarship verifies, that such efforts seem to have "a partial success" (p. 73).

REFERENCES

1. Hegel, *The Phenomenology of Mind*, trans. by J. B. Baillie (London and New York, 1931), p. 130.

2. My interpretation of this passage, and especially the phrase "in the eternity of imaginative representation" *(i Phantasiens Evighed)* is indebted to Professor Louis Mackey.

3. Cf. the essays of James Collins, Cornelio Falio and N. H. Søe in *A Kierkegaard Critique*, ed. by Howard A. Johnson and Niels Thulstrup (New York, 1962) and Heywood Thomas, *Subjectivity and Paradox* (New York, 1957). The interpretation of these commentators is also attacked along similar lines by H. M. Garelick in his *The Anti-Christianity of Kierkegaard* (The Hague, 1965).

4. This frequently reiterated charge seems to have been most explicitly formulated in relation to the *Postscript* by Thorsten Bohlen in *Kierkegaard's tro och Kierkegaard-Studies* (Copenhagen, 1944). For a discussion of Bohlen's position see Søe's "Kierkegaard's Doctrine of the Paradox" in *A Kierkegaard Critique*, pp. 208-210. A similar position is very forcibly argued by Richard Kroner in "Kierkegaard's Hegelverstandnis," *Kant-Studien*, Bd. 46, Heft 1, 1954-55, pp. 19-27.

5. *The Journals of Søren Kierkegaard*, ed. by Alexander Dru (London, 1931). No. 528.

6. Søe in *A Kierkegaard Critique*, p. 290.

7. T. H. Croxall, *Assessment*, prefaced to his translation of *Johannes Climacus*, or *De Omnibus Dubitandum Est* (Stanford, California, 1958), pp. 18-19.

8. Papirer II A 335, Thulstrup's Commentary, *Philosophical Fragments*, 2nd ed. (Princeton, 1962), p. 148.

9. In this connection it is interesting to note that in the very year of the publication of the *Postscript* we find Kierkegaard commenting in his Journal: "The reason why several of Plato's dialogues end without results is more profound than I used to think. It is an expression of Socrates' maieutic art, which makes the reader or the hearer himself active, and so does not end in a result, but in a sting." *The Journals*, no. 528.

10. *The Journals*, no. 994.

PART THREE

THE ETHICO-RELIGIOUS
Introduction

It can be argued that SK's most widespread and lasting influence ultimately will be traceable to that part of his work which lies outside his strictly philosophical efforts. In addition to displaying an extremely creative literary ability, SK offers deep insights into psychology, ethics and religion. The essays of Part Three focus on these three fields of study. Since each of the issues to be discussed in the following essays takes its significance from SK's analysis of the "three spheres of existence," it is appropriate to summarize briefly this analysis.

For SK there are four ways of "being in the world" and four appropriate modes of expressing each of these ways. First, there is that mode of existence which is "psychically determined." This mode is characterized by stability, order, and objectivity; it is termed "psychical" because it is, in the broadest possible sense, a way of "life," but it does not involve the awareness of the possibility of being a self. The mode of expression which appropriately portrays this "form of life" in the artistic realm is spatial representation, as in painting and sculpture. (*Either/Or*, Vol. 1). Intellectually, logical and sensory representation could be said to express this way of being. It was dominant in classical Greco-Roman and in Medieval culture and, with a little distortion, could be said to be displayed in contemporary positivism.

SK conceives of the second mode of existence as "spiritually determined." This characteristic is shared by the stages which stand beyond this second mode and it involves a special relation to the possibility of selfhood (spirit), consciousness, and expression. This mode —called *the Aesthetic*—is one of movement, disorder, and "immediacy." Here one refuses to become a self *(Sickness Unto Death)* by living a life of immediacy and being constantly on "the go." The appropriate artistic expression of this mode is music, which is a constant, on-going tumult and allows no opportunity to stop and reflect—it has no tenses. This way of life became viable after the breakdown of the ancient and medieval worlds. The sensuality of *Don Juan* is taken as the epitome of the Aesthetic mode *(Either/Or*, Vol. 1).

Third, SK designates *The Ethical* mode of existence, distinguished from the Aesthetic by the fact that it involves a reflective decision to become a self *(Sickness Unto Death)*. Such a decision implies an awareness of both the Aesthetic and Ethical alternatives, and a responsible acceptance of the latter. This Ethical mode is characterized by reason, self-determination, and "equilibrium" (*Either/Or*, Vol. 2). The appropriate mode of expression is the responsible use of language, for it is only language (through tenses and pronouns) which gives rise to self-consciousness. Like the Aesthetic, the Ethical mode only became an important option following the dissolution of the ancient and medieval worlds. The Ethical mode could be said to be reflected in rationalistic humanism from Kant on. Marriage is the symbol of this mode (*Either/Or*, Vol. 2). The shortcoming of this sphere of existence is that the person living it is under the delusion that he can be a self *by himself!*

Finally, SK delineates the fourth (third of those that are spiritually determined) and highest mode of existence—*the Religious*. This form of life may be viewed as a synthesis (a la Hegel) of the Aesthetic and Ethical stages, in that it negates each (Neither/Nor) while including each. SK labels the act of negation "infinite resignation" since it involves giving up the attempt to become a self. And yet, in the act of faith—a total commitment to the Absolute—which goes beyond infinite resignation, the individual becomes a self by means of his relation to the Absolute (*Sickness Unto Death*). In this act of faith the values of the other modes of existence find their place. There is no mode of expression which is especially appropriate to the religious mode of existence, for all expressions are finite. It is impossible to recognize "the knight of faith"—he is at home in all other modes—and yet is above them all. This form of life was made possible by the Judeo-Christian religion, and SK points to Abraham (*Fear and Trembling*) as one who lived it. Contemporary expressions of the religious mode remain a possibility.

The first essay in the third part (Chapter Nine) is concerned to trace out the various relationships to selfhood implied by the foregoing spheres of existence. There are important and difficult psychological and philosophical matters which need sorting out about the concept of the self. SK's approach to this concept is powerfully, if truncatedly, summarized in the opening paragraph of *The Sickness Unto Death:*

> Man is spirit. But what is spirit? Spirit is the self. But what is the self? The self is a relation which relates itself to its own self, or it is that in the relation [which accounts for it] that the relation relates itself to its own self; the self is not the relation but [consists in the fact] that the relation relates itself to its own self. Man is a synthesis of the infinite and the finite, of the temporal and the eternal, of freedom and necessity, in short it is a synthesis. A synthesis is a relation between two factors. So regarded, man is not yet a self.

Also, in *The Sickness Unto Death*, SK analyzes the human condition apart from religious faith. He sets out the relationship between sin, ignorance, and despair quite thoroughly. It is precisely this relationship that provides the basis of discussion in the second essay of Part Three (Chapter Ten). The essay examines SK's related work, *The Concept of Dread*, in order to underline the logical connection between despair, anxiety, and guilt. It argues that much of what has been propagated about "existential angst" in SK's name is essentially non-Kierkegaardian.

The application of SK's major emphases to theology in general and to Biblical interpretation in particular has been a particularly fruitful and influential enterprise. This application has come most forcefully by way of the existentialist philosophy of Martin Heidegger into the theological perspective of Rudolph Bultmann. Heidegger set forth in systematic fashion a Kierkegaardian analysis of the elements (the "existentials") of human existence, and of the factors which distinguish authentic from inauthentic existence. Bultmann brought this analysis and the message of the New Testament together in an effort to cast light upon how the latter must be interpreted so as to be meaningful to modern man. He argued that the New Testament needs to be "demythologized," or more accurately "remythologized," in terms of the categories offered by existentialist philosophy. The third essay (Chapter Eleven) asks how Bultmann's adaptation of existential motifs for New Testament interpretation jibes with the main emphases of SK's analysis.

Finally, how do SK's views on the relationship between faith and understanding in general, and between the "modes of existence" in particular, relate to the ongoing connection between religious faith and theological endeavor? If faith is not essentially based in rational activity, and if the religious sphere of existence is a function of commitment and existential authenticity, rather than of systematic analysis, then of what value are theological questions and doctrines? The final essay in this collection, rather than being an essay about how SK would answer such matters, is an effort to deal with them from within a Kierkegaardian perspective. The essay is an excellent example of a Kierkegaardian approach to an issue which has both lasting and particularly contemporary relevance. In addition, it displays some of the implications of SK's analysis of the ethico-religious dimension of existence.

CHAPTER NINE

KIERKEGAARD AND THE SEARCH FOR A SELF

by Frederick Sontag

1. The problem of knowing the self.

We owe to the existentialists the valuable service of reminding us that our severest difficulty is not that we have a self and do not remain loyal to it, but that most often we cannot even locate within us a genuine self worthy of such consideration. It is bad enough to fail to live up to what we know to be right for our own nature, but it is an even more serious state of affairs when we cannot find out what that self is which we are seeking to become. Existentialism has succeeded in making the problem of the self more crucial than we had thought it was.

According to either the romantic or the idealist views of man, which dominated our thinking for more than a century, a man's self and his future were almost automatically unfolded under the pressure of history, culture and necessity. If one had talent, it was for a specific public accomplishment, and genius would unfold itself to be discovered by all in due process. History's purpose would reveal itself through you and give you your nature, if only you did not thwart your own development. All sense of the contingent, the empty, the indeterminant is lost in such a romantic view, but recently the existentialists have created a new literature based upon the discovery of a perilous contingency as being the distinguishing feature of reality, a contingency so widespread that the self tends to become lost in it.

Both romanticism and idealism stressed man's role in the world as a spirit, but what good is that if the majority of men live without being conscious that they are or can become spiritual beings? Moreover, not only do we sometimes fail to recognize ourselves as potentially spiritual, but we often talk confidently about spirit as if what we are most sure of were our own nature. Man is a spirit, we say. But what does it mean to be a spirit? Spirit is the self, we answer. But what is the self? The value of existentialism is that it brings us back to basic questions, makes us realize just how far we really are from knowing individually what it is that we really are or ought to become.

Reprinted with permission from Frederick Sontag and JOURNAL OF EXISTENTIAL-ISM, Spring 1967.

2. The problem of the loss of the self.

Nowhere does the basic insecurity involved in the attempt to discover a self become more clear than in the existentialists' constant stress upon the fact that the self may be lost. According to the optimism of most of the nineteenth century, the self was carried along securely in its knowledge of the steady development and progress of which it was a necessary part. Then Kierkegaard revealed the sequence of life to be one which is constantly threatened with interruption, and gaps appear in the temporal process through which the self may slip away at any moment. Before, life was threatened only by the cataclysmic climaxes of world history; now we turn to the individual in his solitude and realize that "a single little mistake is capable of throwing life's prodigious balance sheet into confusion."[1] Before, history and the self-development of the individual had been thought to be in the grip of an inevitable necessity; now suddenly an infinite expanse of possibilities is spread, out of which we are at a loss to choose. Although possibility and contingency are just what can allow breathing space for the soul, so are they also precisely that indefinite area in which the self can become lost. "Instead of summoning back possibility into necessity, the man pursues the possibility—and at last he cannot find his way back to himself."[2]

The route to find the self lies through the heart of danger. The self has no opportunity to know its limits until it does become fully aware of the range of possibility open to it. No self is realized until a synthesis is made between possibility and necessity, infinity and limitedness, freedom and determination. When the immensity of this task is realized, the crucial moment of decision has come in which the self is either forged or split apart.

> Dread is the dizziness of freedom which occurs when the spirit would posit the synthesis, and freedom gazes down into its own possibility, grasping at finiteness to sustain itself. In this dizziness freedom succumbs.[3]

> The self thus leads a fantastic existence in abstract endeavor after infinity, or in abstract isolation, constantly lacking itself from which it merely gets further and further away.[4]

> If possibility outruns necessity, the self runs away from itself, so that it has no necessity whereto it is bound to return—then this is the despair of possibility.[5]

> He lost himself, owing to the fact that this self was seen fantastically reflected in the possible.[6]

Here is the irony: the self needs to try alternative ways of life in order to explore its own possibilities. Yet this can only be accomplished by letting go of both the discipline and the necessities derived from an ingrained moral life. The trick is to venture into possibility, then to return to know necessity, and to synthesize the two without losing the self in the transition. What is unfortunate is that the venture into new possibilities creates excitement and novel results so that it becomes extremely difficult to be sure the self is not lost in the process, especially since a loss of this kind is not something of which the external world is likely to be aware. Since the self is not visible, its absence can be obscured by the presence of exciting new possibilities.

> But in spite of the fact that a man has become fantastic in this fashion, he may nevertheless ... be perfectly well able to live on, to be a man, as it seems, to occupy himself with temporal things, get married, beget children, win honor and esteem—and perhaps no one notices that in a deeper sense he lacks a self. About such a thing as that not much fuss is made in the world; for a self is the thing the world is least apt to inquire about, and the thing of all things the most dangerous for a man to let people notice that he has it. The greatest danger, that of losing one's self, may pass off as quietly as if it were nothing; every other loss, that of an arm, a leg, five dollars, a wife, etc., is sure to be noticed.[7]

> In spite of the fact that a man is in despair he can perfectly well live on in the temporal, in fact all the better for it; he may be praised by men, be honored and esteemed, and pursue all the aims of temporal life. What is called worldliness is made up of just such men, who (if one may use the expression) pawn themselves to the world. They use their talents, accumulate money, carry on worldly affairs, calculate shrewdly, etc., etc., are perhaps mentioned in history, but they have no self, no self for whose sake they could venture everything, no self before God—however selfish they may be for all that.[8]

If the self becomes lost through an inability to pull itself out of the possibilities spread open before it, although this is often not directly evidenced, it can sometimes be detected through the person's inability to be decisive. This lack of the power of decision can be expressed by saying that he can talk but not converse. Such persons are able to say a great deal, but they lack the factor of personal appropriation. "Appropriation is precisely the secret of conversation,"[9] so that while such people can talk a great deal they lack any factor of personal attachment and conviction.

What complicates this discovery is that it has become so popular to talk in certain fashionable ways about some fundamental experiences. It is not enough to enjoy worship privately, to appreciate good art or to enjoy music or a novel; not just the critic, but everyone must be able to discuss these affairs in acceptable terms. Since such experiences are vital to man, it is possible to learn to talk in such a manner that the deception involved in your own lack of personal conviction goes unnoticed, provided that the style used is in fashion.

> In fact, spiritlessness can utter the same words the richest spirit has uttered, only it does not utter them by virtue of spirit. Man when he is characterized as spiritless has become a talking machine, and there is nothing to prevent him from learning a philosophical rigmarole.[10]

Many a person hides behind the barrier of a learned pattern of words, fending off with a barrage of jargon all who try to see his nakedness. The real art of conversation is the attempt to induce a person to remove the barrier of words and to reveal his thoughts, but this is a painful process if one has neither discovered himself nor found any thoughts which he can genuinely call his own. The difficulty here is that we tend to fight such self-revelation for fear that some contradiction will be discovered in our nature. Yet the presence of paradox is precisely that which generates the thinker's passion, that which alone allows him to be decisive and to overcome the internal contradiction. "The thinker without a paradox is like a lover without feeling;"[11] but, being afraid to admit that such difficulty is present within our nature, we lose the very source of energy which alone might hold us together.

"So much is said about wasted lives—but only that man's life is wasted who lived on, so deceived by the joys of life or by its sorrows that he never became eternally and decisively conscious of himself a spirit, as self."[12] The reflection by the self of nothing but its great and good external crusades is precisely an admission by the self that it is internally empty. Not to be able to be one's own self is despair, and yet we often stave this off by continuing to act out the routine provided by the external structure into which we were born. When one is forced to be a self which he does not will to be, his torment is that he cannot get rid of himself. If he could attain the self he wills to be, this would be delight; but cut off from that he despairs because he cannot get rid of himself, cannot become nothing. This is the problem of the loss of the self.

3. The danger of finding a self.

If the existentialists have broken the romantic spell and convinced us that contingency makes it possible to lose the self and turn it to exterior activity as a camouflage for its interior emptiness, it would seem natural that if finding a self is such a crucial matter we would bend every effort in that direction. Unfortunately, in the same moment that the urgency for establishing a self is made clear, we also see that a danger is involved in the process of finding a genuine interior self.

Nothing reveals the lack of a stable self so quickly as proximity to one who has the power and conviction in himself of his own synthesis of possibility and necessity. To have established the self in the face of contingency has the result of judging those who have not faced the problem and this makes others uncomfortable. Seeing this and feeling the natural desire to be at ease with others, we either intentionally fail to synthesize a self within or else conceal it, as Nietzsche says, behind a mask in order to render it mild and acceptable. Realizing that the establishment of a self itself involves difficulties in our relations with others, we often prefer never to attempt the arduous discovery.

> By seeing the multitude of men about it, by getting engaged in all sorts of worldly affairs, by becoming wise about how things go on in this world, such a man forgets himself, forgets what his name is (in the divine understanding of it), does not dare to believe in himself, finds it too venturesome a thing to be himself, far easier and safe to be like others, to become an imitation, a number, a cipher in a crowd. This form of despair is hardly ever noticed in the world. Such a man, precisely by losing himself in this way, has gained perfectability in adjusting himself to business, yea, in making a success in the world.[13]

> So it is too that in the eyes of the world it is dangerous to venture. And why? Because one may lose. But not to venture is shrewd. And yet, by not venturing, it is so dreadfully easy to lose that which it would be difficult to lose in even the most venturesome venture ... one's self. For if I have ventured amiss—very well, then life helps me by its punishment. But if I have not ventured at all—who then helps me? And, moreover, if by not venturing at all in the highest sense (and to venture in the highest sense is precisely to become conscious of oneself) I have gained all earthly advantages ... and lose my self! What of that?[14]

Furthermore, the same qualities which render a self unpleasant to others also tend to make it a difficulty for its possessor. Since the problem of the self is that it must explore contingency and possibility and synthesize this with stability and necessity, the self that results will have well-defined limits and a strong sense of necessity beneath its flexible range. Such an inclusion of necessity within the self would force us to abandon dreams and the far ranges of possibility. Necessity is demanding and thus sometimes unpleasant, so that it is much easier for the moment to drift through fancies of the possible selves you might be, rather than to face the more exacting task of fusing a limited area of possibility with the demands of necessity in the self. The infinite, the stuff of which dreams are made, must be limited and cut off; but this is a process involving some disenchantment and disillusionment about the possible selves we might have been. Innocence is ignorance and a perfection one ought not wish to recover, yet innocence is natural if we seem unwilling to make the painful effort to remove ignorance—even if it means that we must postpone the discovery of ourselves.

In addition to the unpleasant judgment which a true self makes upon each of us simply by existing, we resist the process of synthesis due to the painful transitional state involved. It is easy enough to say that all you have to do is take the range of possibility before each self, weld it to some necessity, and thus cause the possible to pass over into the actual self. "In reality it is not so easy, and an intermediate determinant is necessary. This intermediate determinant is dread."[15]

Dread comes in the painful moment of transition when, looking down into all of the possibilities before us, we realize that the self could all too easily merely slip into nothingness rather than emerge as a concrete synthesis. Thus, we avoid the transition because of the pain caused by dread, which alone is strong enough to be the necessary determinant. It is not pleasant to be medically treated, and so we avoid this feeling of emptiness which could bring forth the true self, cramming in objects and activities that prevent the realization of dread. Unfortunately, this self-defeating tendency is all too human. "In spiritlessness there is no dread. It is too happy and content for that, and too spiritless."[16]

Another factor which acts to restrain us from the formation of a self is that it also produces demands upon us which we can no longer escape. As long as we wander aimlessly among a loose collection of possible selves, there is no real self upon which anyone can place binding demands. A game of hide and seek takes place among the possibles open to the self, so that if one is agile it is impossible ever to catch him long enough to pin him down. If one could stop long enough to clear his head and think, he might actually long to find himself, but the dance goes on because he is unwilling to pay the price of being always in one place long enough to receive commands. "To have a self, to be a self, is the greatest concession made to man, but at the same time it is eternity's demand upon him."[17]

Much of this natural aversion to any necessity takes place under the guise of a search for freedom, but this represents an identification of freedom with possibility. Instead, freedom is actually a dialectical element between necessity and possibility. That is, freedom cannot be genuine without a self, and no self can be produced out of the merely possible until it is limited by being welded to some necessity.

It is of course true that if necessity takes over complete possession, freedom will be lost. This is just why freedom is such a difficult concept. In sheer possibility freedom is present, but without a self to enjoy it and preserve it. The trick is to find a way to synthesize possibility with the necessity required to constitute a self, and this is why freedom is neither possibility nor necessity, but a dialectical relation between them as difficult to maintain as it is to establish.

> But upon close inspection it is really necessity the man lacks. Actuality is unity of possibility and necessity. Nor is it merely due to lack of strength when the soul goes astray in possibility. What really is lacking is the power to obey, to submit to the necessary in oneself, to what may be called one's limit.[18]

Yet all of this talk about the establishment of the self still rests upon a romantic assumption that the self will be worth having once it is found. When Kierkegaard says, "This is the sorry ludicrous condition of the majority of men, that in their own house they prefer to

live in the cellar,"[19] his assumption here is that there really is more
to every house than a cellar. Instead, perhaps some people prefer to
avoid the painful process of establishing a self, precisely because
they have looked inside and cannot foresee the emergence of a self
worth possessing. In addition to not wishing to offend their friends by
the definiteness of a true self and face the difficulty of accepting necessity as an element in the self, some avoid the transition stage of
dread because they do not find the self they see within to be worth all
that trouble.

Much good is produced by those who firmly establish themselves,
but some dangerous men have also found themselves and gained terrifying powers in the process. The synthesis of a self alone does not
guarantee that it will be a good self, so that sometimes it is better not
to have a self than to produce such a mixed blessing. The Christian
doctrine of the necessity for a second birth is precisely a recognition of
the problem that sometimes the natural self is not worth having, in
which case only a radical regeneration could render the self acceptable.

4. The problem of the self before God.

There is no question that Kierkegaard's solution, in so far as this
problem admits of one, is to place the self before God. Actually, "to
place" is not a very good term, since according to Kierkegaard one
can accomplish a relationship to God only through leap of faith. The
self can realize itself only before God, since this relation is the union
of finite and infinite; but one comes into relation with God not through
rational argument but in the positing of oneself as an act of the will
in faith.

There is a serious question here whether or not Kierkegaard
calls upon the self to do someting which it does not have the power to
do, since it seems that he has simply transferred the idealist's unbridled optimism about what reason can do into a demand upon the
will to accomplish the same thing through its limited energy. Leaving
this difficult question aside for the moment, one further unanswered
question for Kierkegaard is how one knows what God's nature is, so
that one can know in which direction to leap, granting that he has the
energy and the willingness to do so. The religious genius will turn
toward himself, "for by the fact that he turns toward himself he turns
eo ipso toward God."[20] But what if one does not even know in which
direction God lies, then how will he know in which direction to turn?

Kierkegaard says little about the nature of God, but he seems to
assume that we are aware of what God is like and that our only problem is the decision to turn toward Him. Actually, the problem is more
subtle and complicated than this. All of the traditional arguments
and proofs for God's existence are not so much designed to produce
belief in a God already recognized as to convince the listener that God

is really of such a nature as the argument claims. The question of belief in God's existence is a question of trying to find a conception of
God adequate to the intellect and acceptable to the person.

Even within the Christian tradition there is no unified description of God's nature, so that the listener has the double problem of
trying to arrive at an acceptable description of God before he can really take the problem of his own personal belief seriously. Most objec-
tions to any belief in God have at their basis an assertion that the
description of God offered is not adequate. In many cases the real
problem seems to be not that the proofs are not interesting but that
the God produced in the proofs is not yet acceptable. Granted the
diversity of the descriptions of God's nature, if the characterization
offered of God were plausible, belief would not be nearly so difficult a
problem.

Kierkegaard's solution in placing the self before God is an oversimplification, since many gods are offered to man and he is never told
which description is the true one. Kierkegaard is right in that it is
only by an act of faith in positing oneself before God that one can find
a test for the validity of his conception of God; but this does not really
solve the problem of multiplicity of the self, since conceptions of God
are only slightly less multiple than conceptions of the self.

All of this indicates a further difficulty in Kierkegaard's view
that the self defines itself in its relationship with God, because what
he has assumed is that man is essentially religious by nature and
that the religious self is man's only true self. Then, in addition to the
multiplicity of conceptions of God we must admit that man is not
singularly and unambiguously religious. Even granting the seriousness of the religious problem to man, it is far from being his only problem, because the religious self is far from being his only self. In this
case, even to discover an adequate conception of God might define
part, if surely not all, of the self. Our possible selves are indefinitely
numerous, but our true selves are still more than one.

5. The complication of the multiplicity of the selves.

Despite the tortuousness of his writing, Kierkegaard's position
seems too simplified. On every page he treats man as if he were totally
a religious being, and even the ethical side of man is introduced via
the religious. This view is too uncomplicated, since one of man's basic
problems is whether or not he shall become religious in the first place,
although certainly there is often a strong basic tendency in that direction. One small look at the world at large is enough to convince anyone that the majority are far from seeing the problem of the self in
religious terms, so that the first step is often to try to induce men to
see the self in such a light. And this is not as easy as it might be; there
are also the aesthetic self, the ethical self, the human self, the professional self, the intellectual self, and so on.

To find one self is not to find them all. Surely, it is all too common an experience that many successful people have found one self, often either a self of personal enjoyment or a professional self, and then concentrate on this particular self to the exclusion of all others. Met on one plane, such people seem genuine and valid, but when seen in a different setting they are disappointing, always trying to carry over one side of the self to another level of life where it does not belong. Nor is it always easy even to force anyone to see the problem of the multiplicity of selves. The answer to any claim that the problem of the self still remains unsolved on numerous levels is often countered with the reaffirmation of a self which has been made concrete, which of course avoids the issue.

Kierkegaard makes man an individual, and it is true that it is in the interior where the decisive battle takes place. On the other hand, man also lives his life through others, so that no interior struggle is ever decisive, however hopeful it may make the situation appear. We are vulnerable not only because we may fail to synthesize some necessity with the possibility in our own nature, but also because of our dependence upon others in many areas of the life of the self. Kierkegaard casts the problem almost entirely in terms of the interior religious self, whereas actually there are many interior selves, as well as some exterior dependencies, from among all of which we are forced to choose and to strike a balance. If the self were not so multiple by nature, the problem would be far less serious.

6. The clue to be found in the objects of love.

It has become common to distinguish between two types of love. One is desire, as Plato describes it in the *Symposium*, and the nature and status of men can be characterized by the fact that there are necessarily many things for which men must be continually striving. The other form of love is often identified as Christian love, although the Christian stress upon it does not give them exclusive rights to it. This is self-sacrificing, outgoing, generous love which seeks to benefit not itself but its objects. Plato recognized this form of love in his classic phrase "Goodness is diffusive of itself."

Love of this kind cannot help but go out from itself, whereas desire seeks constantly to draw objects to it for its exclusive possession. Now the introduction of these two forms of love, present in various proportions in everyone, suggests a possible solution of the dilemma of finding a self, a solution not out of sympathy with Kierkegaard's own analysis of love, even though he did not himself suggest it. He confined his analysis of love primarily to his devotional writings, although if transferred into systematic form it can relieve some of the tension in the problem of the self. This is as it should be, since the stress upon divine love is equal in the New Testament with the stress upon the divine judgment of human sin.

In the *City of God* one of Augustine's points is to tell us not to be superficial in the way we organize and classify men. Families, races, geography, business, clubs and schools—all these are the exterior and simplified groupings in which we place men when we wish to do so without deeper thought. Actually, it is none of these easily observable characteristics that designate the union and separation of men in common bonds. Instead, men are most profoundly grouped according to the objects and orientation of their love.

Here, then, is a tenuous but valuable clue to the discovery of a genuine self. First, one's inner nature is manifest in the objects of his wants. The next step is the crucial one, since desire reveals only a surface self. Does desire exhaust his capacity to love? If it does, then this indicates the shallowness of his personal self. On the other hand, if it begins to become clear that he can find some person, object, or cause to which his affection naturally goes out without an equal desire for possession, if he begins to discover within himself areas in which he finds it natural to be generous, then here is the formative area for the genuine self. This may take a religious form, as Kierkegaard seems to think it always does, or it may be cultural, educational, humanitarian, or political. In whatever area or areas a generous and self-less love begins to appear, here is the place to begin the cultivation and discovery of a genuine self, since it is according to the objects of their love that selves are really to be known and classified.

Some interesting results follow from such a view, one of which is that while we must think about the self, actually the self is never to be found wholly within thought. It is still important to remember that it is thought which finds the self, so that thinking cannot be abandoned; but it is in feeling (primarily in the form of love) that the self is finally to be located, if at all. Kierkegaard says that "the supreme paradox of all thought is the attempt to discover something which thought cannot think. This passion is at the bottom in all thinking,"[21] but this is too strong a statement. Passion is present and we must locate its source and direction if we are to know the self, but it does not follow that because love isn't made of thought alone it cannot be discovered rationally and thought about. It is no paradox, except to a Hegelian, to have reason able to know something different from itself. Reason becomes foolish only when it tries to transform everything into its own image, rather than recognizing passion for what it is, that is, as something other than thought.

Another consequence of using outgoing love in order to discover the self is that self-love is revealed as self-defeating and, in effect, literally impossible. The self is never really constituted until it goes out from itself in generous love. As long as it either stays within itself or knows love only as a desire to bring things to itself, it is in the paradoxical position of having no real self to love or to bring things to. It is a psychological fact that some people are incapable of generosity, but they are to that extent to be pitied since they will continually frustrate themselves by trying to love and dress up a self which really isn't there.

Of course, it is true that this doctrine of the necessity for outgoing love as the required basis for constituting the self is no more than a modern commentary on the Biblical phrase, "For whosoever will save his life shall lose it; but whosoever shall lose his life for my sake and the gospel's, the same shall save it." (Mark 8:35) Such a view requires an adventure and a gamble before response to outgoing love can bring any enjoyment to the self established by the venture, and, of course, there is no guarantee against ending up in bankruptcy. Religiously phrased, this doctrine means that, if the self learns to love God, it can define itself by going far enough out from itself to venture, and thereby discover, which God it actually believes in.

7. The necessity for solitude and denial.

It is easy enough to say that one can gain a clue to the nature of the self through discernment as to the kinds and directions of its love, but it is another thing to show how this can be actually accomplished. The paradox is that after the self is clearly evident and made known, it is easy to see its line of development after the fact. Yet, when one is trying to discover the self's nature, he is in a state of some personal confusion—precisely the condition which prevents clear insights. Repeated endeavor is the only general answer which can be given here, since only those are hopelessly lost who have abandoned the search for a self and relaxed into either boredom or constant anxiety.

However, one specific answer here is that the proper conditions must be provided, conditions that are conducive to discovery. Denial enters here, too, for when one grants passions their every desire, it is too easy to confuse the self with the objects that it buys in the world. Solitude and denial cut away the growth and confusion around the self and allow the directions of its love to be expressed and understood. Whether the self will be found to be desirable when it is uncovered is, of course, another question.

By stripping life of its trappings, either mentally or actually, one narrows the possibility that some external substitute can be offered for the self one is not able to find. Incapable of finding a solid self, there is a natural tendency to offer overt products and accomplishments in its place. Solitude and denial may make possible for one to discover that his salvation may not lie essentially in external order and arrangements, however desirable, advantageous, and enjoyable these might be in themselves. In solitude, if there is no self there is nothing, whereas in an ornamented life this emptiness can be more easily escaped. It is natural enough to want to become something else, if one's only alternative is to be nothing at home, although it is always necessary to return home sooner or later. And home is far enough away to go. The interior life is sufficiently rich in examples, "if only one understands how to see; one need not journey to Paris and London—that is of no avail when one cannot see."[22]

8. A more radical interpretation of a traditional doctrine.

One who is discerning will object that this whole discussion has been merely an elaborate commentary on the Biblical question: "What shall it profit a man if he gain the whole world and lose his own soul?" (Mark 8:36) Such an objection would be well taken if it were not for one minor but important exception. The analysis given here actually changes the passage so that it now should read: What shall it profit a man if he gain the whole world and never succeed in finding himself?, or, What shall it profit a man if he gain the whole world and never know the feeling of possessing a self which can be lost?

The original wording of the traditional phrase seems to imply that one knows and enjoys the possession of a self from the beginning and then trades it way in the marketplace. Although this may happen occasionally, the more serious and fundamental problem is that we are often unable ever to find a self in the first place, so that actually we seek to gain the world as a substitute for an internal impoverishment which we are unable to overcome. The activity in the world would be much less frantic if one really did know what the self was from birth, but the problem is precisely that life does not make this crucial bit of information at all clear to us. The self must be discovered before it can be traded away. Unfortunately, the clamor and attraction of the marketplace, to which we are driven to buy something we can call our own, is for many the least likely place in the world where a genuine self can be found. Where the real self is each man can only find alone—until his love turns away from himself. In loneliness the soul can be lost, but it is there it may also be found.

REFERENCES

1. S. Kierkegaard, *The Concept of Dread*, trans. W. Lowrie. Princeton: Princeton University Press, 1946, p. 68.

2. Kierkegaard, *The Sickness Unto Death*, trans. Lowrie. New York: Doubleday & Company, 1954, p. 170.

3. Kierkegaard, *The Concept of Dread*, p. 55.

4. Kierkegaard, *The Sickness Unto Death*, p. 165.

5. *Ibid.*, p. 169.

6. *Ibid.*, p. 170.

7. *Ibid.*, p. 165.

8. *Ibid.*, p. 168.

9. Kierkegaard, *The Concept of Dread*, p. 15.

10. *Ibid.*, p. 85.

11. Kierkegaard, *Philosophical Fragments*, trans. Swenson. Princeton: Princeton University Press, 1952, p. 29.

12. Kierkegaard, *The Sickness Unto Death*, p. 159.

13. *Ibid.*, pp. 166-67.

14. *Ibid.*, p. 167.

15. Kierkegaard, *The Concept of Dread*, p. 44.

16. *Ibid.*, p. 85.

17. Kierkegaard, *The Sickness Unto Death*, p. 154.

18. *Ibid.*, p. 169.

19. *Ibid.*, p. 176.

20. Kierkegaard, *The Concept of Dread*, p. 96.

21. Kierkegaard, *Philosophical Fragments*, p. 29.

22. Kierkegaard, *The Concept of Dread*, p. 67.

CHAPTER TEN

MAN: ANXIOUS OR GUILTY?
A SECOND LOOK
AT KIERKEGAARD'S

The Concept of Dread

by Kenneth Hamilton

Dread reveals Nothing.... In the trepidation of this suspense where there is nothing to hold on to, pure Da-sein *is all that remains.*

—Martin Heidegger[1]

Man as man in every civilization is anxiously aware of the threat of non-being and needs the courage to affirm himself in spite of it.

—Paul Tillich[2]

Anxiety is to be approved. It is a reason for hope.

—Karl Jaspers[3]

Christian doctrine traditionally has described man in his present condition as a sinner: he is *guilty* man. But, ever since Kierkegaard's writings began to influence twentieth-century thought, *The Concept of Dread* has provided a new interpretative key to man's nature. As the above quotations illustrate, man is now often taken to be *anxious* man.

A recent work, *The Fear of God* by Fred Berthold, Jr.,[4] has undertaken to show the relevance of this view for Christian faith and doctrine. Its author believes that the doctrine of Original Sin should no longer occupy the center of the theological picture. He writes:

Man's anxieties, particularly those which directly express a religious content, suggest that it is not correct simply to say man is separated from God by sin and death. Rather the situation appears to be more complex and dialectical. Man is threatened with separation. He is aware of and anxious about the threat, anxious *because* he also feels that that which he is in

Reprinted with permission from Kenneth Hamilton and THE CHRISTIAN SCHOLAR, Winter 1963.

danger of losing is good.... Apparently, then, the experiences of anxiety suggest that, even for natural or "sinful" man, the positive bond between man and God is not severed. There appears to be, at least implicitly, a desire for God.[5]

Here man's relationship with God is conceived to be one of real, though not continuous, communion. The older view that found the king-pin of Christian anthropology in Romans 7:18 ("For I know that in me, that is, in my flesh, dwelleth no good thing") is repudiated. It seems that we are not fallen creatures so much as creatures who fear the possibility of a fall. Instead of having been turned out of Paradise already, we still live there and are upset at the thought that we may be evicted. Thus Paul's use of the Psalms to make the statement of Romans 3:11 ("There is none that seeketh after God") is misapplied. We all seek after God, desiring to be with Him. The universal fact of religion proclaims as much, showing that none of us is without the intuition of the divine that reaches out in love toward the Source of all good.

Since these ideas are symptomatic of a whole trend of present-day thinking, they invite examination. And, since they are manifestly post-Kierkegaardian ideas, we might be well advised to assess them only after taking a second look at *The Concept of Dread*. It was Kierkegaard who introduced the notion of human life being permeated with *angst*, and expounded it in his most influential book. Yet there is no reason to assume that he found existential anxiety to be the hopeful and positive sign of spirituality which some "existentialist" writers today take it to be, or that he ever believed that the category of anxiety could replace the category of sin as a more exact determinant of man's nature.

In his exposition of anxiety as an implicit desire for God, Berthold mentions Kierkegaard rather briefly, explaining that "it is, in a sense, almost too easy to claim him as an ally."[6] But where in Kierkegaard does he find support for his opinion that "it is not correct simply to say man is separated from God by sin and death?" Instead of leaving behind traditional doctrines of sin for something "more complex and dialectical," Kierkegaard builds upon them. *The Concept of Dread* carries the subtitle *A simple psychological deliberation oriented in the direction of the dogmatic problem of original sin*, and its Introduction declares:

> The present work has taken as its theme the psychological treatment of "dread" in such a way that it has *in mente* and before its eyes the dogma of original sin. It has therefore to take account, although tacitly, of the concept of sin.[7]

If Kierkegaard departs at all from the program here outlined, it is in taking account of sin more than tacitly; for elsewhere he admits that the book is one which does not remain within the psychological frame of reference but deals openly with dogmatic material.[8] At any rate, anxiety[9] is always treated in *The Concept of Dread* in relation to sin. In this relation, anxiety appears in three phases: first, before sin comes into the world, where anxiety appears as the presupposition of sin; second, when sin has "posited itself" and holds universal sway, where anxiety appears as the consequence of sin; and third, after faith (which is the opposite of sin) is known, where anxiety turns into a "saving experience."

Berthold overlooks these successive roles played by anxiety, and so he totally misrepresents Kierkegaard's teaching. He tells us that

> anxiety which is the result of sin also expresses a dynamic dissatisfaction with the life of sin. For this reason Kierkegaard believes that the only cure for anxiety is anxiety. Anxiety is God's "school," weaning us away from sin.[10]

The facts are quite otherwise. Kierkegaard discovers no positive element at all in the anxiety which is the result of sin. He devotes the three central chapters of *The Concept of Dread* to an account of how this anxiety spreads the baleful effects of sin into every area of life, resulting in the total loss of human freedom and of the knowledge of God. In the first chapter, it is true, anxiety has been shown playing a very different rôle. Here anxiety, as "a qualification of dreaming spirit,"[11] marks man's original innocence and represents the possibility of freedom.[12] Yet this possibility is now no longer a natural possibility, because man has fallen universally into guilt;[13] and it appears on the scene once more only when faith comes and conquers guilt. In his fifth and final chapter, Kierkegaard describes how the advent of faith re-establishes the realm of possible freedom and makes anxiety creative. The condition of anxiety's transformation is unambiguously stated:

> But in order that the individual may thus absolutely and infinitely be educated by possibility, he must be honest toward possibility and must have faith.[14]

So it appears that Berthold has confused the role of anxiety in connection with natural, sinful man with its rôle in connection with redeemed, believing man. For Kierkegaard, anxiety works death in all who have not been rescued out of sin by faith; and it is a dynamic and educative force only for those who have known God's atoning action in Jesus Christ.[15]

Berthold dismisses the traditional doctrine of Original Sin as too simple and undialectical. Yet it is his own notion of anxiety as a positive bond between man and God which misses the dialectic of Kierkegaard's understanding of anxiety and sin. He is therefore led into a curious misreading of Kierkegaard's terminology. He says that Kierkegaard conceives the possibility of going beyond anxiety to the despair which is "sickness unto death"—in which case man has gone so far as to lose the normal human longing for God.[16] But Kierkegaard never teaches that despair is an extreme form of anxiety and thus an exceptional state. Far from being the ward for chronic cases in the hospital of life, despair is the ordinary accommodation for all who are admitted there.

> At any rate there has lived no one and there lives no one outside of Christendom who is not in despair, and no one in Christendom, unless he be a true Christian, and if he is not quite that, he is somewhat in despair after all.[17]

The sole antidote to the common human experience of despair, as Kierkegaard conceives despair, is the courage of faith.[18] Similarly, in his eyes, anxiety is not a stage of experience this side of despair. Rather, it is the indelible mark of man's spirituality; yet it is no necessary proof of human longing for God, since it manifests itself in a sterile "shut-upness" which is a deliberate choice of evil even at the cost of self-destruction.[19] Anxiety, in so far as it is the consequence of sin, does not demonstrate that mankind is threatened with separation from God; for it witnesses to the reality of actual separation. Anxiety reveals the working out of the mechanism of despair.

Berthold misrepresents Kierkegaard because he fails to enter into the Kierkegaardian dialectic of anxiety. Yet the failure of comprehension begins at a much deeper level than that of over-simplified analysis. What is basically wrong with Berthold's approach is his belief that a psychological description can yield the solution needed to resolve a problem belonging to dogmatics. In other words, he imagines that *The Concept of Dread* provides us with valid insights into human nature even if we disregard its orientation in the direction of the doctrine of Original Sin; and, indeed, he assumes that these insights constitute the *real* value of the study. Now, although this viewpoint is one making nonsense of Kierkegaard's teaching, it is sufficiently widespread today to present a religious philosophy to be reckoned with.[20] For this reason, the consequences for Christian faith of the attempt to substitute *anxious* man for *guilty* man must be a matter of concern. These consequences are both negative and positive: negative, because elements in traditional Christian doctrine have been suppressed; and positive, because other elements have been introduced from elsewhere. And, in investigating these consequences, we shall find the doctrinal emphases of Kierkegaard very relevant. For this thinker, believing that Christianity could be interpreted, believed also that the dogmatic basis of Christianity could not be altered without destroying its truth. The ultimate betrayal of Christianity, in his opinion, is to say "that it is to a certain degree true."[21]

The chief negative consequence of adopting a view of man as essentially anxious is the one exemplified in Berthold's contention that it is not correct to say that man is truly separated from God by sin and death. Here the argument is that Original Sin is not a barrier between man and God which can be removed only by God's intervention. Berthold denies that his understanding of man as a being threatened-but-not-separated means taking sin lightly. His defense is that he recognizes that man, if he is to overcome his anxiety and find God, needs help from "outside" (i.e., divine grace). "I am not trying, therefore, just to be optimistic," he explains, "the battle, of which anxiety is the sign, is a mortal combat."[22] Yet the issue is not, in fact, one of deciding whether man is engaged in mortal combat with evil. All shades of religious opinion unite in believing that man's situation is one of spiritual warfare. The issue is not even whether man needs help from "outside" if he is to triumph in the fight. All religions preach the availability of grace in some form or other. The issue is precisely how man's situation in the battle is to be assessed, and what kind of outside help brings about the final overthrow of evil. Christianity was born out of the preaching concerning the grace of Jesus Christ "who was delivered up for our trespasses and was raised for our justification" (Romans 4:25). In such a perspective man needs more than assistance to realize his potentialities. He is not merely weak and threatened by the power of evil, but evil has become lodged in his inmost nature. He carries a load of shame. Therefore, every diagnosis of man's situation takes sin lightly if it assumes that man the sinner genuinely longs for God and actively struggles to attain to righteousness. Salvation in terms of Christian faith means forgiveness most of all. Christ does for us what we are powerless to do for ourselves . . . or even to desire to do. So the Christian confesses that Christ "is our righteousness; in him we are consecrated and set free" (1 Corinthians 1:30).[23] Grace deals with both the power and the guilt of sin.

Being convinced that Christianity "begins with the doctrine of sin,"[24] Kierkegaard argues that whenever sin is discussed apart from dogmatics there is a false *mood* induced, causing the true concept of sin to evaporate.

> As soon therefore as one sees the problem of sin treated, it is possible at once to see from the mood whether the concept is the right one. For example, as soon as sin is talked about as a sickness, an abnormality, a poison, a disharmony, then the concept too is falsified.[25]

Berthold's favorite way of speaking about the effects of sin is to refer to a "threat" or a "blockage."[26] Plainly, Kierkegaard would judge this to be the wrong *mood.* And, as guilt is suppressed in connection with sin, so also neither conversion nor re-birth through the Spirit are allowed to appear. Instead, man is shown to be ever battling on his own account for his true end, displaying the "still living power" of God-desire,[27] and requiring simply an increase of that power. He does not need to be turned around. He needs to be given a good push in the direction he is already facing.

Thus, if the outstanding consequence of the view of man as anxious man is the denial of sin as guilt, its principal positive consequence is the affirmation of man's essentially pure spirituality. This follows from the belief that man spontaneously recognizes his true end, and it entails an implicit doctrine of *eros* as the bond linking the human and the divine. Berthold comes near to giving this doctrine an explicit expression when he writes:

> Throughout my argument, I have tried to show that anxiety is a phenomenon of love. Without love, or *desire for what is felt to be good,* anxiety could not arise.[28]

What is here asserted is that man's innate *feeling* for the divine is the ultimate source of his knowledge of God and the pointer directing him to his true end. The tensions of anxiety are, on this account, to be viewed as proof of the spiritual power of *eros* at work within the soul. Berthold identifies the power with the concept of the "image of God," but, to judge by his description of it, it has much more in common with Plato's *Symposium* than with *Genesis*.

> Something ineradicable in man's nature, the image of God, calls him to that life of love and adoration which he has glimpsed again and again in his religious contemplation, and the glory of which has burst upon him in the person of Christ.[29]

Seemingly, the gateway to salvation is religious contemplation, while Christ comes as the confirmation of the human vision. Atonement does not enter into the picture, but all depends (as in the *Symposium*) upon the strengthening and enlarging of spiritual desire, the *eros* leading the soul from the earthly to the heavenly.

Finally, then, the positive consequence of this view of man as anxious reveals itself to be a doctrine which is not Christian but which instead puts its faith in a general religious or spiritual consciousness. It cannot be Christian in Kierkegaardian terms, certainly, since it turns away from dogmatics and—especially—from the dogmatic understanding of sin as guilt standing in need of atonement. In the present essay I have concentrated upon a single expression of the view. Berthold's exposition is a convenient one to analyze because of its clarity and concentration, but it reflects a development in current thought so widespread as almost to be worthy of the name of "Post-Kierkegaardian *Angst*-Orthodoxy." There is an ironical twist in this development which would have drawn a wry comment from Kierkegaard, that master of irony, had he lived to see it. Modern *Angst*-Orthodoxy finds supreme religious comfort in the thought that man is anxious, arguing that those who know anxiety also know God. Kierkegaard, on the other hand, explains that those who known anxiety most thoroughly are the pagans, and they relate themselves not to God but to fate; for a pagan is precisely he who never goes beyond anxiety to discover the reality of guilt and sin.[30]

Modern *Angst*-Orthodoxy is the result of trying to abstract a self-contained "existential" analysis of human life from Kierkegaard's teaching, while ignoring the specifically Christian orientation of that teaching. Not unnaturally, the end-product has no real relation to the original material—it is rather as though an airplane had been made over into an automobile and then was advertised as supreme in its road-holding qualities! It is possible, of course, to believe that man is anxious rather than guilty and that such a view of man is the proper foundation for a religious anthropology. But those who follow this course have no right to call Kierkegaard their ally. A second look at *The Concept of Dread* must convince us that such a program runs entirely contrary to the author's intention and conflicts with both the spirit and the letter of his work.

REFERENCES

1. *Existence and Being* (Vision Press Ltd., 1949), pp. 366f.
2. *The Courage To Be* (Yale University Press, 1952), p. 40.
3. *The Origin and Goal of History* (Routledge & Kegan Paul, 1953), p. 151.
4. Harper & Brothers, 1959.
5. *Op. cit.*, p. 134 (italics in the original).
6. *Ibid.*, p. 62.
7. *Kierkegaard's The Concept of Dread*, trans. Walter Lowrie (Princeton University Press, 1944), p. 13.
8. *Kierkegaard's Concluding Unscientific Postscript*, trans. David F. Swenson & Walter Lowrie (Princeton University Press, 1944), p. 241.
9. As Berthold uses the word *anxiety* to render the Kierkegaardian *angst*, I shall follow suit, although Kierkegaard's translators use the word *dread*.
10. *Op. cit.*, p. 64.
11. *Op. cit.*, p. 38.
12. *Ibid.*, p. 44.
13. *Ibid.*, p. 32.
14. *Ibid.*, p. 140.
15. As *The Concept of Dread* is a "psychological" work, it cannot enter into a discussion of the content of faith. Therefore Kierkegaard ends the book by saying that the man who is educated by dread will "repose only in atonement," adding: "Here this deliberation ends where it began. So soon as psychology has finished with dread, it has nothing to do but to deliver it over to dogmatics." (p. 145).
16. *Op. cit.*, p. 64.
17. *The Sickness Unto Death*, trans. Walter Lowrie (Princeton University Press, 1941), p. 32.
18. *Ibid.*, p. 14.
19. This is the apex of guiltiness of spirit issuing in the *demonical* or dread of the good (*The Concept of Dread*, pp. 105ff).
20. For example, Tillich writes that Kierkegaard "developed a doctrine of man which describes the estrangement of man from his essential nature in terms of anxiety and despair" (*op. cit.*, p. 119). Here too Kierkegaard's psychological description is wrongly called a doctrine of man, and his appeal to dogmatics is ignored.
21. *Concluding Unscientific Postscript*, p. 209.
22. *Op. cit.*, p. 143.
23. *The New English Bible*, translation.
24. *The Sickness Unto Death*, p. 195.
25. *The Concept of Dread*, p. 14.

CHAPTER ELEVEN

THE RELEVANCE OF KIERKEGAARD
TO THE DEMYTHOLOGISING
CONTROVERSY

by J. Heywood Thomas

The controversy which has this forbidding name arose as a result of Bultmann's essay 'New Testament and Mythology.' The essay appears to have evoked a very loud and fierce criticism in Germany and has become the bone of contention among its theologians. This controversy has spread to America where Bultmann's friend Professor Paul Tillich has put before the theological public not only the issue involved in the debate but also his own unhesitating support of Bultmann's programme. It has also come to us in Britain through the publication of Professor Henderson's *Myth in the New Testament*. First let us see what it is that Bultmann has to say.

Bultmann claims that the New Testament Kerygma is embedded in the definitely mythological setting of ancient cosmology and Jewish and Gnostic redemption stories. For the New Testament writers the universe is a three-storied edifice consisting of heaven, earth and hell. The top of the universe is heaven; beneath it is the earth, and at the bottom is hell *(Sheol)*. The earth is more than the scene of man's natural mundane existence: it is also open to invasion by demons and spirits who may literally take possession of men. 'Man is not in control of his own life. . . . Satan may inspire him with evil thoughts. Alternatively God may inspire his thoughts and guide his purposes. . . . History does not follow a smooth unbroken course; it is set in motion and controlled by these supernatural powers.'[1] The present age is in fact held in bondage by Satan and the 'powers' of sin and death. It is hastening towards its end, which will come very soon in the form of a cosmic catastrophe.

This mythical cosmology is the setting against which the Gospel message of the redeeming act of God is proclaimed. The mythology is not only background, however; it is the presupposition of the message and the very language in which it is spoken. The proclamation is that the last time has now come. Jesus Christ, the pre-existent Son, is sent by God 'in the fulness of time,' and appears on earth as a man. He

Reprinted with permission from J. Heywood Thomas and THE SCOTTISH JOURNAL OF THEOLOGY, September 1957.

dies the death of a sinner on the Cross and makes atonement for the
sins of men; His resurrection means that death has been stripped of
its power. So the beginning of the new age is at hand because the
dominion of demonic powers is at an end. The risen Christ quite literally ascends to heaven to the right hand of God where He is made
'Lord' and 'King.' He will shortly return on the clouds of heaven to
complete His work of redemption and abolish sin, suffering and death
finally and completely. Till this will take place, those who belong to
the Church are joined to Him by means of the sacrament of Baptism
or Communion. Those who believe already enjoy the first fruits of
salvation, for the Spirit, working in them, attests that they are God's
adopted sons and so guarantees their final resurrection.

Bultmann's contention is that all this is plainly mythology and
its sources in contemporary mythology can in fact be traced. 'To this
extent *the Kerygma is incredible to modern man, for he is convinced
that the mythical view of the world is obsolete.*'[2] The problem which
inevitably arises, then, is whether the New Testament contains a
truth which is quite independent of its mythical setting. Clearly, the
answer of any Christian theologian is that it does. Bultmann's point
is that, if we are so convinced, then we must undertake the task of
stripping the Kerygma from its mythical framework, of 'demythologising' it. He makes a somewhat lengthy examination of the inability
of modern man to accept the mythical world-view, and it becomes clear
that he is concerned not only with the question of the conflict between
the myths and our scientific discoveries, but also with the problem of
the conflict between the myth and our contemporary metaphysical
Weltanschauung. There is, he says, no point in asking modern man to
accept the mythical world-view because there is nothing specifically
Christian in it. Moreover, it would be impossible for him to do so—because one does not accept a world-view by making up one's mind to
accept it but rather as a result of inspecting the evidence in its favour.
The New Testament mythology cannot be accepted by modern man for
more than one reason. First, the world-picture it presents was discred-
ited by the fact that the end of the world which the Apocalyptic
claimed to be imminent just did not occur. Secondly, the advance
which has taken place in science and technology with the resulting
advance in man's knowledge and mastery of the world render the New
Testament view of the world meaningless to modern man. 'There is
no longer any heaven in the traditional sense of the world. The same
applies to hell in the sense of a mythical underworld beneath our feet.
And if this is so, we can no longer accept the story of Christ's descent
into hell or his Ascension into heaven as literally true.'[3] Then again,
the New Testament mythology faces the still stronger challenge of
modern man's understanding of himself. Whether he regards himself
as 'pure nature' or as 'pure spirit' he regards himself as essentially a

unity. He is not the dichotomy which the New Testament understands him to be.

Confronted with this mythology which is impossible for him to accept the modern theologian must use drastic measures according to Bultmann. We 'cannot save the Kerygma by selecting some of its features and subtracting others'; the mythical view must either be accepted or rejected *in toto*. Bultmann describes the real purpose of myth as being that of presenting man's understanding of himself in the world. 'Myth should be interpreted not cosmologically but anthropologically, or better still, existentially.'[4] In dealing with a myth then we must ask what the writer is saying about his own existence. 'Hence the importance of the New Testament mythology lies not in its imagery but in the understanding of existence which it enshrines. The real question is whether this understanding of existence is true. Faith claims that it is, and faith ought not to be tied down to the imagery of New Testament mythology.'[5] In his attempt to give us an existentialist interpretation of this mythology Bultmann deals with the contrast between the life of faith and human existence apart from faith. That is, he takes the two sets of stories in the New Testament and recasts them into 'existential' statements. According to the New Testament, he says, the life of the man without Christ is the life of anxiety. This man is at the mercy of certain forces which are indifferent or even hostile to him. He is the slave of the very sphere that he had hoped to master. 'Whereas hitherto he might have enjoyed the world as God's creation, it has now become 'this world,' the world in revolt against God. 'This is the way in which the "powers" which dominate human life, come into being, and as such acquire the character of mythical entities.'[6] The man of faith, on the other hand, finds his security not in things visible but in the invisible world. His confidence is in the grace of God. 'It means faith that the unseen, intangible reality actually confronts us as love, opening up our future, and signifying not death but life.'[7] The grace of God brings forgiveness of sins by which Bultmann means 'deliverance from the bondage of the past.' At the same time faith means obedience, for it involves our turning our back on all attempts to contrive our own security and resolving to trust in God alone. This detachment from the world is eschatological existence.

The New Testament faith is always faith in Christ. Can this be a remnant of mythology that awaits translation? Bultmann admits that it does seem as if the decisive event of Jesus Christ were a relic of mythology. The problem, he says, is that the existentialist philosophers have given us an account of being which is the same as the New Testament and yet independent of it. At the same time these philosophers are convinced that all we need is to be told about the 'nature' of man in order to realise it. The New Testament does not give us a doctrine of man's 'nature' in this way, but rather proclaims the event of redemption in Christ. The existentialist philosophers agree that man is fallen but regard him as able to achieve his real existence by his own decision. For the New Testament the fall is total. 'Man's radical self-assertion blinds him to the fact of sin, and this is the clearest proof that he is a fallen being. Hence it is no good telling man that he is a sinner. He will only dismiss it as mythology. But it does not follow that he is right.'[8] In fact, this is the point where man can do nothing and the very point where God steps in and acts. This affirmation of sin and of what God has done for us cannot be demythologised. The story of the event of Jesus Christ is a combination of myth and history, and Bultmann is led to say that the mythological language is simply an attempt to express the meaning of the history. The remainder of the essay illustrates this conclusion by examining the two crucial incidents in the Christ-story, the Cross and the resurrection.

We have endeavoured to give a clear and impartial account of Bultmann's essay. What we now wish to do is to show how relevant Kierkegaard's understanding of the Christian faith is to this controversy. There is one obvious point which we can mention at once— that one can discern the influence of Kierkegaard in Bultmann's idea that existentialism is the proper method of interpreting mythology. That there lies behind Bultmann's work a definite existentialist philosophy has been admitted by Gotz Harbsmeier, who is one of his warmest supporters. 'Harbsmeier ... has agreed that for Bultmann, Heidegger's analysis of being is the cradle in which the (Christian) message is laid.'[9] Professor Henderson points out that the seriousness with which Bultmann considers the claim that this analysis has superseded the Christian revelation indicates how close to each other these two views are for Bultmann. We have mentioned Heidegger's analysis of being as the presupposition of Bultmann's demythologising programme. We shall now suggest four ways in which Bultmann's essay leads us back through Heidegger to Kierkegaard. The first is by means of this concept of being. Kierkegaard's philosophy was a philosophy of existence, and Heidegger's interest is also in being and existence. As Ruggiero puts it:

> Almost a century later the motives of the Kierkegaardian thought return in the philosophy of Martin Heidegger but they return depersonalised and emptied of their religious content. More closely linked together, they give us a kind of parabola of existence in the act of emerging from nullity when after an ephemeral journey, it relapses into nullity once again.[10]

Heidegger takes over Kierkegaard's special use of 'existence' as something essentially personal. The basic concept in his ontology is the contrast between *Dasein* and *Vorhandenheit*, the being of a person and that of inanimate objects. Heidegger protests against the way in which philosophy has used categories of the former which are really applicable only to the latter. In his analysis of *Dasein*, Heidegger stresses two things as characteristic of it: *Entschlossenheit*, being open to oneself, and *Befindlichkeit*, the sense of fortitude or of being cast into the world. To know our own existence in this way is an essential part of that existence. To understand our being means indeed for Heidegger a real change in our being. It is this which lies behind Bultmann's understanding of Christian faith as a change affected in the Christian—as Thielicke says, nothing happens in Bultmann's interpretation of Christianity except consciousness. The second way in which Bultmann points back to Kierkegaard via Heidegger is in his view that the proper method of interpretation to be used in demythologising is the existentialist. It is clearly a result of his acceptance of Heidegger's views according to which change in my *Dasein* comes about only through a change in my understanding of myself. And this is Heidegger's expression of the Kierkegaardian theme that existence is something that can be understood only as I am concerned with it. Thirdly, Bultmann has suggested that Heidegger's idea of the fallenness of man is the same as the Christian idea. Not to understand one's existence is for Heidegger to live unauthentically, and in unauthentic existence one is in a state of fallenness. This state is characterised by the self's failure to find itself. This failure is revealed in the way I think of myself as one of many, which means that I have lost myself among 'the others' so that I am a *man*. In this we can easily discern the influence of such typically Kierkegaardian ideas as the error of objective existence, the distrust of the crowd, the loneliness of personal existence. The final point is that Bultmann appears to be indebted to Kierkegaard for his basic interpretation of what Christianity is, namely something which the individual must decide for himself. Whether this is evidence of direct influence or not it is impossible to say and is anyhow irrelevant. It is sufficient to note the resemblance which would indicate indebtedness. Professor Henderson says:

> A persistent feature of Bultmann's exposition of Christianity (is) the emphasis which he lays upon decision. Time and again he sets aside doctrines which would protect the Christian from the necessity of coming to a decision. . . .

> And he is at pains to emphasise that even when demythologised the New Testament message will not be something self-evident or provable to the man of today but only a possible way in which he can interpret his own existence. In the last resort modern man will have to decide, whether or not he is to accept that particular interpretation of his life.

> This emphasis on decision will have a familiar ring to those who come to Bultmann via the existentialists. As the late Dr. H. R. Mackintosh has said, to think existentially is to think not as a spectator of the ultimate scenes of life and death; but as one committed to a decision upon them. And indeed a determination that man shall not be spared the toil and sweat of decision accounts for . . . Kierkegaard's dislike of a *Volkskirche* into which a man could be born. . . .[11]

It is thus true to say that Kierkegaard is relevant to the demythologising debate as one of the sources of Bultmann's thinking.

Our main interest, however, is to show how what Kierkegaard
has taught us can be made a criticism of Bultmann's view. This criticism, we would suggest, is threefold.

1. Bultmann makes essentially the same mistake as Hegel in his
   assumption that understanding the truth is a necessary part
   of being in the truth.
2. In his existentialist interpretation of the mythology Bultmann
   seems to be very close to the too empirical understanding of
   faith which Kierkegaard associated with Schleiermacher.
3. The demythologising of the New Testament means a translation of Christianity into a philosophy. This was the error Kierkegaard found in the Hegelian theologians. This can be done
   only at the price of losing certain distinctive elements of the
   Christian faith.

We shall consider these three points in turn.

(1) First, then, one of Bultmann's basic assumptions is that I am
changed only by understanding myself. We have seen how he has
arrived at this position through the influence of Heidegger. How is it
wrong? It may be argued that there is a very real point in such a
statement, and doubtless it does make us more aware of the interplay
of thought and action. Yet in the end it seems indistinguishable from
the Hegelian confusion of understanding Christianity and living
Christianity. Bultmann does insist on the element of decision—one
must decide to accept this view of oneself. This is, nevertheless, only
a pale image of the decision which Kierkegaard described when he
talked of deciding to accept God and of the decision to follow Jesus
Christ. It is thus impossible to agree with Professor Henderson (p. 29)
that the relation between Heidegger and Bultmann in this respect is
'harmless enough.' To accept it is to forget the difference between the
understanding of the truth of Christianity and living that truth. If I
am changed only by understanding myself better, then all religion
would be in the sphere of immanence as Kierkegaard would have
said. However, this is a purely theological difficulty except in so far as
it oversimplifies the logical description of religious faith. We see this
oversimplification better if we compare Bultmann's position with
that of Hegel and also with what is traditionally regarded as the Socratic theory of virtue. Hegel had been so concerned to absorb Christianity into the System that he was oblivious to the dangers to which
this exposed faith. The most important was that the vital distinction
between knowing the faith, that is an intellectual grasp of it, and believing the faith, accepting it as one's way of life and living it, could
no longer be drawn with any certainty. In the same way Bultmann
seems so intent on showing that the existentialist way of interpreting
myth is the proper understanding of myth that he leaves no room for

the distinction between the knowledge of this interpretation and the living commitment to the message thus obtained. We can see how very like Socrates this is. Socrates is reputed to have taught that virtue was knowledge, and that to know the good was to do it. The obvious difference between knowing the good and doing it was no less obvious to Socrates than to anyone else. Despite this, he maintained that there was a necessary connexion between knowledge of the good and its performance. Bultmann's position is slightly different—but not very much different. According to him to understand the mythologically proclaimed Gospel constitutes a necessary part of its living. Thielicke has complained that for Bultmann 'the real event takes place in human self-consciousness,' and whether Bultmann succeeds in answering what Thielicke means by this charge or not, it is difficult to see how he can avoid the criticism which I have sought to express by quoting Thielicke's words. I am well aware that I am concentrating on one item in the long and intricate argument that Bultmann has produced. This does not involve any violence to his meaning, however; and therein lies the difficulty. It seems undeniable that he makes the directive quality of religious belief dependent on our understanding of this interpretation of our existence. It is difficult to bring out this point clearly; but what I have been trying to indicate is a basic confusion, resembling Hegel's confusion of understanding and existence. The confusion is similar to Hegel's, not only because the same things are confused, but also because the confusion results from an abstract metaphysics which is concerned with the question-begging and misleading notion 'Being.' Once we start talking in terms of Being then an existentialist analysis can easily become almost identical with religious living. However attractive this existentialism of Bultmann's may be, it is very suspiciously like a new Gnosticism.

(2) Our second Kierkegaardian criticism of Bultmann is that his interpretation of faith is dangerously like the empirical reduction of the meaning of the word 'faith.' This was the criticism that Kierkegaard made of Schleiermacher and Hegel. We need not consider the latter here, but it is very interesting to notice that Thielicke also compares Bultmann and Schleiermacher. He is quite emphatic in the charge of subjectivism which he makes, and he makes it by referring to Schleiermacher. 'All we have to do is to substitute Schleiermacher's famous "self-consciousness" for Bultmann's term, "understanding of human life" (after all, the two terms are practically synonymous), in order to see this.'[12] He insists that if we are to understand the New Testament message with Bultmann as an 'understanding,' then 'the emphasis lies on the subjective element' with the result that there is 'no room for an historical revelation in time, at least not in the sense of an intervention on the plane of reality.'[13] Thielicke's point seems quite justified, but on the basis of what we have learnt from Kierkegaard's criticism of the empiricism of Schleiermacher we can extend

this argument. That there seems no room for an historical revelation in miracle or the event of Jesus Christ is symptomatic of something deeper. And this is that the danger of such a view as Bultmann's is that it has no need of God. If the end we have in view in our activity as religious men is to derive a mode of understanding oneself, there is no need to have any objective constituent to this experience other than ourselves. It could be argued that this would not be subjectivism —that is where Thielicke fails to grasp the great subtlety of the position Bultmann describes. There is a real difference between Bultmann's 'understanding of human life' and Schleiermacher's 'self-consciousness'—at any rate as Schleiermacher used this phrase. For the latter expression meant nothing more than that we enjoy certain feelings, and this way of talking is dangerous because feeling can always be translated into the language of appearance without making any reality-claim. However, the phrase Bultmann uses is not subjective in the same sense, though it too must be criticised in the same way. Here, however, the error involved is that of failing to make any reality-claim over and above what is implied by talking about myself and other human beings who are all quite real objects. The weakness of Schleiermacher's position was that it 'made faith too inward' so that faith could be translated in terms of 'it seems' without any remainder. Bultmann makes the same mistake in a different way. If what I want is to understand myself then it matters not whether there is a God or not. Indeed all that is required is myth (in the pejorative sense of the word), a story which will evoke in me the necessary attitude towards myself. And if this is so then religious faith has disappeared. I am far from suggesting that religious faith has nothing to do with understanding ourselves. On the contrary, religious faith necessarily moves in this way from the commitment to God towards a unification of our experience in terms of it. But there is a great difference between saying 'We are convinced that there is a murderous lunatic at large and so we are going to avoid the place where we saw a suspicious character yesterday, etc.', and saying, 'Our conviction that there is a murderous lunatic at large *is* that we are going to avoid the place, etc.' In fact, in this case the second sentence is nonsense. The same difference (in logic) is seen in this other analogy, which is perhaps a better case. Take two people listening to the Beethoven *Sonata Pathétique.* They discuss the music after the recital and agree that it was the greatest aesthetic experience they have ever had. 'Somehow,' says one, 'I could see whole vistas of experience being disclosed as I listened.' It would be quite wrong to say that this man's enjoyment of the *Sonata Pathétique* was his new understanding of life. This is not nonsensical, and one can build up a story which would give it meaning. But in our story it is not true to say this. Now this is very close to Bultmann's case and it helps us to see the point that needs to be brought out. This is that the strength of Bultmann's position is that we do tend to make it a test of true religion that it should reveal myself to myself. Thus Jesus Christ says that it is not only adultery that is wrong but those thoughts that a man harbours and cherishes in his heart. It is only as we practise the presence of God that we begin to understand our sinful nature. We cannot and do not deny this. In the same way we do not mean to say that Bultmann in fact does not think that religion is an awareness of an objective fact. Our point is quite simply that he does not succeed in saying this, for his view implies the opposite. When we consider, as Thielicke does, the Christological element of our faith as well as its basic theism, it becomes quite clear that Thielicke is justified in his belief that Bultmann's formulation will not suffice. For at the very heart of the Christian faith is the assertion that a historical person was the perfect revelation of God. Again this does indeed enable me to understand myself and purify my heart as nothing else can, and moreover necessitates my doing so. But this is not what I *mean* when I say that Jesus Christ is God.

(3) Finally, it is by no means clear that Bultmann has avoided the pitfall which was described by Kierkegaard as being the fate of all Hegelian and indeed of all systematic philosophers. We may ask, then, whether Bultmann in his attempt to rid the New Testament of its mythology has not translated the mythology and the message enshrined therein into a philosophy. Clearly some of his critics have no doubt that he has actually done this. Thus, for instance, Thielicke says:

> It is impossible to remove the mythology, as Bultmann tries to do. In other words, it is impossible to substitute the world view of modern science for the biblical mythology by what he calls 'interpretation.' This is because it involves the substitution of an abstract philosophy of existence for a kerygma rooted in history.[14]

One would have liked to see a clear discussion of this by Bultmann, but he never does more than make casual remarks on the topic. Bultmann's only answer seems to be that there is not the contradiction between the philosophy he uses and Christianity that Thielicke claims there is. Thus Schumann says that Bultmann's 'guiding conviction is that it is possible to have a formal analysis of human existence which can be detached from every "existential" attitude, from every actual disposition to one's own existence.'[15] But Bultmann, quoting these very words, agrees with Schumann that this is impossible. This confirms our suspicion that it is not very clear what the argument is about, that neither Bultmann nor Schumann has asked what question each is trying to answer. The question that concerns us is whether Bultmann has, by his demythologising, translated the Gospel into language which inevitably distorts it. And it is irrelevant to this question whether there is in fact the agreement which, according to Schumann, Bultmann finds between 'the Christian understanding and a philosophy of existence not orientated upon the event of Christ (Heidegger and others) on the negative side—*i.e.*, the fallenness *(Verfallenheit)* of human life.'[16] The question is indeed whether you can ever translate Christian statements into other language which is secular in the sense that it is not logically dependent on a Christian framework. The question is not an empirical but a logical one. Is the scheme of assertions which will be the translation of the mythological form of the Christian Gospel logically equivalent to Christian theology or doctrine? When the question is framed thus we see that it is not at all to the point to argue, as Bultmann does on p. 196, that pure analysis of Being without reference to God not only is possible but also makes sense. The confusion in the argument would have been avoided in part at any rate had not Bultmann used this highly ambiguous word the meaningfulness of which is far from certain. It makes no difference to our question whether the analysis he proposes can in fact be carried out. The important point is whether statements which, be they pictorial and mythological or not, are logically dependent on the concept of God can be translated into language which is by definition logically independent of this concept. Clearly the answer is a negative one. It would be a reduction of the religious man's statements. Bultmann does not seem to appreciate the force of this, for he ardently denies that he is claiming for existentialism the position of being the 'right' philosophy. The point is not that we think his method too *a priori* and not sufficiently empirical, that he does not leave room for corrigibility. The error is logical and not empirical, and a logical error cannot be repaired by patchwork. No such language will do.

It is therefore not surprising to find Schumann maintaining that in fact Heidegger's analysis is not identical with the Christian view of the nature of human existence.

> To be fallen to 'nothingness' is quite different from being fallen to sin and guilt and being fallen under the wrath of God. It is simply impossible to agree on a formal understanding of human fallenness, and then to diverge, one side believing that human life is fallen to 'nothingness,' and the other that it is fallen under the wrath of God. The understanding of fallenness in the two cases is not identical.[17]

And if the concept of fallenness is not the same in the two cases then it must follow that the interpretation of sin will be inadequate. Thielicke contrasts the biblical conception of sin with the abstract philosophical conception, and he contends that Bultmann sides with the philosophers.

> Sin is man's consciousness that he is lost, and therefore it is not in any real sense an event. At most it is but the shadow of an event projected on the screen of our understanding of human life.... Sin is thus a phenomenon of the ego on the same level as the philosophical understanding of human life.[18]

The same strain and tension is again seen in the way Bultmann regards Jesus Christ. Schniewind, in discussing Bultmann's description of the paradox of Jesus, brings out Bultmann's anxiety to do justice to the 'ἐφάπαξ of Christ. Yet Schniewind is himself very doubtul whether he maintains 'its full force undiminished.' 'One cannot avoid the impression that he places the event of redemption in some transcendental sphere far beyond the relativities of history.'[19] When he replies to these criticisms Bultmann makes the very puzzling comment (p. 118) that 'an eternal idea is just as discernible in the mythical presentation of the Cross as it is in pagan mythology.' If by this he means to say that this is the meaning of the Cross then he is indeed guilty of an abstraction that leaves us with no distinctively Christian message.

In making these comments on the demythologising debate I have been anxious to see how the lessons we learn from Kierkegaard can be used as criteria. He himself would not have countenanced any dogmatic pronouncements, and to imagine that we either can or should dispose of Bultmann's work by such comments as these is a mistake. If, however, our comments are at all helpful in a negative way, it confirms the view that Kierkegaard is a useful guide.

REFERENCES

1. *Kerygma and Myth* (London, S.P.C.K. 1953), p. 1.
2. *Op. cit.*, p. 3.
3. *Op. cit.*, p. 4.
4. *Op. cit.*, p. 10.
5. *Ibid.*, p. 11.
6. *Op. cit.*, pp. 18-19.
7. *Ibid.*, p. 19.
8. *Ibid.*, p. 31.
9. I. Henderson, *Myth in the New Testament* (London, S.C.M. 1952), p. 21, *Vide Kerygma und Mythos*, p. 59.
10. Ruggiero, *Existentialism*, p. 31.
11. Henderson, *op. cit.*, p. 23. The reference to Mackintosh is to *Types of Modern Theology*, p. 219n.
12. *Kerygma and Myth*, p. 146.
13. *Ibid.*
14. *Kerygma and Myth*, p. 164.
15. *Kerygma and Myth*. p. 185.
16. *Ibid.*, p. 184.
17. *Kerygma and Myth*, p. 185.
18. *Ibid.*, pp. 150-1.
19. *Ibid.*, p. 85.

CHAPTER TWELVE

THEOLOGY AND BELIEF

by Paul L. Holmer

"Religion invites an almost continual effort at reflection. Of course, there are numerous things to know and to think about at length, some of them legitimately theological. But is there not a great deal of theology which is idle reflection and principally because there is so little in being faithful? When there is nothing to be, very little to do, very little to believe that are the ways of a Christian, then the burden has to fall on 'understanding' and its correlative, 'meaning.'"

The issues of this essay are two in number: first, to get at the tangle of themes which make us think that theologies must change, must be made explicit, and must, above all, be the way to, or of, "understanding"; second, to enliven some thoughts about being a believer. This essay is engendered by the discomfort occasioned by hearing that theology leads to something called "theological understanding" without which the ordinary believer is deemed to be bereft.

I

If a student of esthetics or esthetic philosophies should be overheard telling a first-rate artist, "But you must understand the esthetic principles involved," most of us would at least smile. For it is funny and deeply incongruous to hear someone who has no art to his credit insisting upon the necessity of understanding esthetic principles, almost as a condition for artistry. In religious efforts, it is not easy to laugh; in fact, the presence of an interest in very abstruse matters might mark the young man as a possible candidate for the ministry or priesthood and otherwise at least as very serious.

In all areas where the performances are obvious and clear, there does not seem to be quite so much to understand; it is all right there! But in areas where the performance is neither present nor obvious, there we cannot speak so candidly. In the latter instances, "understanding" becomes highly internalized, very complicated, often ter-

Reprinted with permission from Paul Holmer and THEOLOGY TODAY, October 1965.

ribly abstract. Think about art again. It is often noted that esthetics is not a very widely nor deeply cultivated field of philosophy. I suspect that the presence of pictures, poems, compositions, and all the other things said and done, make abstract reflection a little gratuitous. But in areas where the doings and happenings are few or even confused, there all kinds of things must be reflected upon simply to ascertain whether or not anything is there at all. Much of theology certainly must be so relevant, not because it illumines holiness and good news but simply because it provides something, call it "understanding" if you will, when so little else is already there.

Christians are supposed to be faithful. Sometimes "being faithful" is a very vague matter for us. We do not have visible marks, no stripes on our bodies, no hungering and thirsting after righteousness —at least not to speak of it on an ordinary day, very little charity, maybe only a few feelings that look like cultural hangovers. And even subtle performances, private feelings, secret groanings? Where are they? Is there any contrition? guilt? forgiveness? prayer? It is no wonder, then, that there is a continual interest in a kind of reflection, a lot of abstracting, about what in the world being faithful and being a Christian are. Maybe some things in theology are, indeed, "metaphysical," as so many students of both metaphysics and theology have repeatedly said. If that be so, it might also be the case that metaphysical urges are sometimes like the urges to theology.

Religion invites an almost continual effort at reflection. Of course, there are numerous things to know and to think about at length, some of them legitimately theological. But is there not a great deal of theology which is idle reflection and principally because there is so little in being faithful? When there is nothing to be, very little to do, very little to believe that are the ways of a Christian, then the burden has to fall on "understanding" and its correlative, "meaning."

Some students once explained to me that the Peace Corps had replaced the churches' social endeavors, that the government's legislation had now become God's principal action, and that community life was really the divine life. If this is so, one must think very hard indeed; for these things are not obviously one thing or the other— ethical, political, religious. Maybe they have, nonetheless, a divine and theological meaning? Unlike earlier religious men who would dare to believe that God makes even the kingdoms which rise up against him, along with the heavens and the earth, to serve and to praise him, some contemporaries profess not to know any instances at hand of serving and praising him. Therefore, they seek out what serving and praising him mean. They dare not extrapolate from the small to the large, from the seen to the unseen; instead they look for religious "meanings" in current literature, in current social programs, and just everywhere they can manage.

II

Maybe this is what theologians are for—to tell us how we can be religious by doing what we would do anyway and believing what we would believe anyway. There are some theologies about, very new and very relevant, by which we supposedly discover the meanings that are apparently the gist of God and Gospel. They are found in our world where God is not apparent and where even the word "God," if not God himself, is claimed to be dead. This much is now said over and over again. Apparently this is what makes theologians want to do "ontology," where somehow everything can be grounded in "being" with profundity and, hopefully, with some religious pathos. Others want to do linguistic analysis, not because they really have some intellectual snags that need unsnagging, but rather because they do not believe very much and are, instead, rather earnest about "meanings." Maybe the "use" of linguistic analysis will help; and "use" and "meaning," contrary to Wittgenstein's careful and painful investigations, get badly misused.

Recently there have been books, both popular and technical (Bultmann's, Paul van Buren's, Bishop Robinson's, some of the new "ontologists" doing theology, much of Tillich's), wherein it is said that the talk about God's existence is of no point. For better of for worse, this is an attack upon traditional theism, or upon the strange business of supernaturalism, and, according to some, upon that which the ordinary man, mythologist that he is, surely believes—if he believes in God and Jesus Christ and the Holy Spirit. The theologians of this bent are telling us that we can no longer believe in God's existence and all those descriptions of his nature. This is what some people mean when they say that the word "God" is dead, that is has no life apparently in those metaphysical schemes we call theism and supernaturalism and which were once described as "transcendent theology." And if life is gone here, there is no life or meaning at all, so say the critics.

This must be coupled with something else, allegedly more widespread and devastating. "The whole age," "modern society," "contemporary culture" is said to be against belief in God. So there are students of the times, apparently with practised detecting eyes, who tell us that most, if not all men, are no longer pre-scientific. They are not believers, at least, in old myths; they are industrialized, empirical, tentative, skeptical, this-worldly, impressed by evidence, repelled by things heavenly. Fortunately, or unfortunately, depending upon how detached one can be, they are still anxious, dissatisfied, and occasionally fed-up—all of this enough to make "meaning" their goal. "People" cannot believe in gods, sins, God, or the devil, but they still need the "meanings" with which those were linked. So now the theological task, enough to make every Saul into a Paul all over again, is to isolate those meanings and somehow launch them into the sea of men!

Theology is reportedly faced with the fact that the word "God" is dead, at least in the sense that it is no longer a name, no longer a word to be used for that which exists. "Post mortem dei." So, we are told, by so many today, that God does not exist, that "God" is therefore dead almost beyond revivifying. Apparently it is like this. Most people, if not all, were accustomed by Scripture, church, and older theologies, to think that "God" (*i.e.*, the word) named, or at least, went with and referred to something. Now, for very subtle causes, long in the making, we cannot think that way. "God" does not "refer" and "point to" or "name"; for "God" is apparently not like that. God does not exist at all and there is no way to believe in God. But the theme is that "God" (again the word!) after all can still mean a great deal, even if one cannot use it in the old way. Modern theologies, including Tillich's and several others, are ways to show us that the term has meanings galore, if one will only think abstractly and in certain prescribed ways. As almost all readers of modern theology know, we can now do "Christology" in this new way, along with "history," "divine judgment," "sin," and many other of the big topics, besides that of "God." Maybe there is still a *Geistes-kraft* in language and culture, if not in nature, in Hebrews if not in Greeks, in the Bible if not in Cicero; at least this continues to look promising for anxious theologues.

Things have gotten to such a state that sketching out a new scheme of such meanings is thought to be a "positive" offering, essential both to Christianity (for what is theology but the "understanding" of Christianity?) and to modern men (for who can understand without a scheme of meanings?). That historical research should be endless and small qualifications the part of it mattering most, can only be gratefully granted; that conjecture and surmises might be the investment of thought which will lead to intellectual profit, can be manfully conceded; but these freedoms of mind, guarantors indeed of objectivity, integrity, and criticism, ought not to be also the cause of confusions, however learned. For the temptation of the intelligent is to make everything count for everything, and consequently to lose sight of the precise and limited role of most if not all that we know and do in our genuine researches. In one sense of the word "theology" there is no excuse for not relating it also to the business of living faithfully. If there is any merit to what is here said, it might be hoped that a penetrating simplicity and candidness, open to most men and not always a function of vast learning, can be encouraged, whereby an individual can also become his own theologian and mentor in faith. Otherwise how can we explain the profundities of even the scriptural authors?

"Was Christ really born of a virgin?" asks the wife of her pastor-husband, after hearing his sermon on the Third Sunday in Lent (in

Olav Hartmann's extraordinary novel, *The Holy Masquerade*).[1] Her theologically modern husband, reminding her that she is ignorant of recent theology and too much a literalist anyway, tries to explain:

> God has indeed revealed Himself in the man Christ. . . . It is the whole life of Christ that is the miracle and the miracle is not made any greater because one tries as formerly to explain how it happened. Furthermore, the explanation is only a literary form for the truth of the incarnation. For that reason one can use the archaic words without lying. One really means the same as the old biblical authors.

The wife is very much like most of us most of the time. We are "literalists" by which is usually meant that we want to translate everything into something like that medieval world-view of which Santayana spoke so eloquently, making every biblical literary piece a part of a very big picture. The husband-minister has had this picture disturbed, and something very subtle and adaptive, namely a new set of meanings, substituted. So, now he talks about the whole teaching and the main themes, and he refers his specific difficulties to this more evanescent and somewhat abstruse backdrop of meanings. This much theology has done for him.

The fault here is not only intellectual and formal, though there is plenty of that. But there is something terribly wrong with thinking that every linguistic assertion needs explaining and unpacking, as if it were incomplete and partial, until placed in a mutually enriching and artificial context of theological or metaphysical discourse. The matter is also painfully religious and affects everyone in turn. For is it true that no one understands religious matters except the one who has a scheme, be it transcendent metaphysics or another meaning scheme? Think of the effrontery too of insisting that the teachings of the Bible and the church must be considered as a whole in order to be given their life and meaning. For it makes the conversational and almost anecdotal character of much of the Scriptures either almost a deception or otherwise well-nigh pointless until more properly reconstructed.

But the terms are now rather clearly drawn. And in a time when we have revolutions of thought almost quarterly, there cannot be very much harm in just one more. For against the theologians who evolved a skein of discourse, almost a theory, which was said to be the theory embedded in the discourse of apostles and all Christians, we are reading today the criticisms of that theory. Because "God" is dead, we are being urged to another theory, one less antiquated, pictorial, and transcendent; but one still said to be relevant, in its way somewhat metaphysical, but above all a veritable nest of meanings.

III

Our point is not to flail all the special issues involved, though there are plenty of these. For example, Canon Alan Richardson thinks that the scientific study of biblical language, which he very rightly believes is quite new and a startling development, also is the way to "... discovering what such words as 'God' really mean."[2] Thus his argument is that the new theology of meanings, contrary to the older supernaturalism that continues to bother so many people, is really a kind of product of, not just a concession to, the age of science. In ways a little hard to trace (and which must make the non-religious textual and philological students wince to read), a very modern biblical theology, claiming to share in the age of science, purports to have derived in elaborate scholarly ways from earlier and non-scientific uses of words. The fact that earlier users never quite described or used these meanings themselves is, apparently, beside the point. The thousand and one informal associations of words, concepts, and ideas with the uncharted course of human life that Scripture documents is now fixed by the narrowing and prescribing "meanings" of the theologian. Our issue is still, though, not these contentions, hard as they are to understand, as much as it is the odd logic that makes it all so plausible.

Is it really because there is so little to most men's religious lives that something intellectual and explanatory has to be there to give even some substance, abstract as it might be? Or is it because even the language of the Scripture and the churches, along with everyday speech, is after all already theory-laden? When one author tells us that the language of the past, though mythological, was "only a medium for conveying the meaning of the past event," is this to say that every event had to have another medium declaring its meaning? Is this what theology is finally for? Does it only release and state the theory already contained in the simpler discourse?

Perhaps we are coming to a kind of summarizing point of the changes begun in the nineteenth century. There are any number of scholars who say that the new critical and historical methods which have made for finer discrimination and more accuracy also have made more sense of the Bible than did the old supernaturalistic and non-historical convictions about static revelation. But in some ways this is still a negative point, even rather old now. The new theme, not altogether done up yet, is that biblical scholars (mind you! textual and critical students) can also create a kind of biblical theology, in virtue of affirmative generalizations, holding the parts together in a variety of sub-themes about symbolism, myth, history. Perhaps this gives illustration to Canon Richardson's polemical historical claim, "... In the twentieth century the last lingering vestiges of the nineteenth-century positivistic outlook have been transcended."[3]

So whether every man holds metaphysical beliefs may be a question; but the above noted argument assumes that there is a kind of elucidating of what biblical authors held, which elucidation is not simply reiteration nor is it simply discerning the outlines of transcendent metaphysics, but it is, instead, the matter of explicating the meanings. Needless to say, this kind of thing has not impressed everyone, but there are signs now that this kind of elucidation, seemingly scholarly, historical, and philological, can be successfully blended with more typically philosophical and free-wheeling kinds of efforts. Maybe some such synthesis will be the next theological "ism."

Perhaps it has been made clear enough already, but nothing said here has made light of many kinds of historical, philological, textual inquiries. The difference, the quarrel, is not with research *qua* research, whatever the subject matter. If men are ignorant, it seems most plausible and most worthy to become knowledgeable, however small the topic and however trivial it might seem to others. Our point is a different one altogether. For a great deal of theology, old and new, has not been as much a matter of vanquishing ignorance and supplying knowledge as it has been a matter of speculative ardor and lately a fashioning of some extraordinary meanings. Our case is not against learning as much as it is against some conventions, old and new, by which that learning is used and most often misused. In conclusion, therefore, we sketch a couple of points that might remind us of proprieties and improprieties of so much theology.

IV

Concerning respect for the Bible, maybe it is true that people have read it using pre-scientific concepts to hang it together, or Greek philosophy, or this, that, and the other. Tyndale's insistence that the Bible must not be read always to document the medieval distinction between the religious and the secular is a case in point. Household tasks, he says, are as good works in the Bible as the ascetic life. But, let it here be said that surely there are all kinds of misunderstandings of Christianity, of the Bible's teachings, of creeds, and of many other concepts, words, and parables associated with Jesus of Nazareth. So, there are tasks for students of the Scriptures, all kinds of them, for which every kind of exacting study might be useful.

But to assume that there is "an understanding" or "several understandings," still waiting to be expressed, lying, as it were in front of the texts (like Plato's ideas in that famous story of the cave), still to be apprehended by great efforts—this surely is a mistake. Theologians then rush to this front—some from linguistic studies, some from historical, some from the no-man's-land of philosophy—intent upon the meaning. Maybe the text of the Bible allows this and that kind of study, so let it be done, by all means; but can we be sure that its meanings are missing? Of course, if the world, including the Bible, is like Plato's cave, then we certainly need all kinds of things, even meanings. Actually, though, is the text really so badly off? Its meanings very likely are not going to be found "in front of" or "above" the text, even in that other realm.

The trouble has been that once bereft of one system of artifices of thought, now we have all been led to think we can not do anything unless we have another. So, having gotten rid of "divine meanings" we now gaze longingly at "secular meanings," or having been deprived of scholasticisms we now want ontologies. The man who says away with those "isms" looks like a "positivist" (oh cursed fate!), only fit for words without thoughts and the Bible without meaning. But so misled are we! For the situation is not like that at all. Even the Bible can probably be "understood" (in a certain manner of speaking) not by extending its language into other media as making it very clear to oneself how completely different it is, just as it stands. Instead of assuming that there are thoughts, deep and rich, for which the biblical text is but an approximate and local expression and the theologian the one qualified to unearth, let us really give honor to the text once more! For it might well be that we have to learn how to make the text become our very life-enthusiasm.

Surely people misunderstand the Bible. But "to understand the Bible"—does that imply that one must write out a scheme of understanding, something called a theology? No, the purposes of theology are to help one to understand but not to be the understanding. Everyone knows, furthermore, how easy it is to misunderstand. For example, the word "grace" occurs in many places, including Scripture. So, too, do "world," "God," "truth," "faith," "teacher," "sin," "creation," "good," "love," "righteous," and many others. Many difficulties arise from the fact that words like these are often known to us in quite different contexts, and we misunderstand very often by not seeing and using the word in the right context. Now, there is good cause for thinking that the Bible is quite distinctive and that getting at the way of big words like those above is to see that they do all fall in place, belong together, and make for a distinctive perspective. The role of theological teaching is to help one to see this or to do this but not necessarily to be "an understanding" by itself.

Perhaps we can now see how deceptively simple it is to believe that there is a level of meanings, more refined, clear, distinct, and transcendent, for which scriptural words are only temporary media of expression. Then the temptation is to look in Scripture for clues to the overarching meanings, instead of pushing hard into the respective contexts and reduplicating for oneself the more homely ways of handling them. Theological training can well afford to force us to the differences that even biblical language makes (though one has also to be careful lest those differences be too easily summarized and written down once again as the essence of the Bible!).

It is unfortunate that the so-called theological revival in our time, biblical theology included, has been primarily one more way to attract the talkative bright college set. All over the land these past few decades it has been very easy to get audiences on behalf of theology. Much of it seems to me to have been because, indeed, the students and bright people were sick of naturalism, positivism, and all these other sparse and frugal convictions. Along came theologians. Totally unexpected in such an age as ours, were they preaching Christ? Well, yes, some of them were indeed doing so; but most often the appeal was not here. Rather it was the meanings, the generalized views, the invitation to having terribly big views that was so thrilling. Instead of the Bible coming in for either sober analytic and scholarly study, hard-nosed and objective, or for the painful reading by a man who was convinced that it might be bread for his hunger or a lamp for his feet, it became a matter of biblical views of history, of man, and goodness knows what else. More views; and bigger than the psychologists', historians', and the new breed of philosophers'.

Is it not time that we think hard about these matters once again? And if our lives have been made anew by Jesus Christ and we want to wax earnest for him among others, then the Scriptures are still our tools as well as his cradle. Then the task is to help others to understand, but not by always substituting general views, supernaturalistic, scholastic, ontological, or secular, for the specific sentences and passages, but rather by using every means (including *views*), to get men familiar and intimate with the differences those texts require.

V

We need more theology rather than less. But theology does not have to be secular because men are thay way, nor does it have to trade in some current coin of the realm. There is an oddness in the fact that so much of the thought of so many talented thinkers, not least theologians, in our day issues in nothing more than an idle set of speculations, quite devoid of the pulse-beat of personal assimilation, despite its evangelical aim. Surely this is the place to reiterate that learning for its own sake is in order, even about the Bible, Jesus, and Jews; and one would be a fool to complain over worthy intellectual and disinterested accomplishment (of which there is a great deal!). But if theology is going to be done also for others, with the express purpose of making Christianity the evangel for the age and the news very good, then let it be done; but honestly and well! Now it seems to be done by a kind of nondescript speculative philosophizing, crude and intrinsically dubious, save to the naive. Otherwise it is done by what often seems to be an almost reckless use of expressions like "meaning," "mythology," "symbol," and "history" (and there are more), so that neutral researches will somehow yield religious results.

    More than this, the text surely must be taken seriously, but also
it must be stressed by the theologian (with the evangelical intent)
how important it is to use that text, and other things too, in order to
learn all the Christian virtues. For example, it is eminently significant to learn to be patient and long-suffering, to learn to be courageous and bold, to be hopeful and faithful to the end of one's life.
These things are not simply by-products of something else, even
beliefs or convictions. For we have over-intellectualized the matter,
almost as if everyone, all of the time, must first have the beliefs of a
transcendent sort in order to have these virtues. Therefore the hue
and the cry when the beliefs, or what we think have been the beliefs,
are criticized; for then the virtues seem irresponsible and rootless,
almost without reason or just cause. Here again, we have thought too
quickly about the text and not enough with it, for it gives plenty of
instances where these things are simply enjoined and not invariably
as though they were necessarily consequent to very complex acts
of belief.

    One of the aims, then, of theology should be precisely to root
believers firmly in the Christian life. But this does not mean that the
beliefs are of no significance. For one of the features of much of modern theology, "post mortem dei," and in the post-Christian era (that
so many think already obtains) is that it indeed helps to liquidate
whole sets of beliefs. It suggests that we can have the virtues and the
way of life without the beliefs and the view of life. Insofar as Christians are now suffering the blistering effect of severe criticism of odd
philosophical components, theories about reality, stray bits of metaphysics, it seems to me all to the good. Maybe it's very healthy, at
least for some people. But the alternatives provided—no myths, no
views, no beliefs, no God, but a host of meanings plus a little vague
ontology and slippery philosophy, is much worse.

    Perhaps it is the task of theology not to be God's revelation but
only to help people again to believe in God. Surely there are ways to
come to this, but none of them is easy. The world has never made God
obvious, and there is precedent for thinking that it is fairly well organized to keep most of us from acknowledging him. But theology can
surely again show us how men come to believe in him and believe too
that everything was made by him. It seems a little doubtful that the
world around us is ever going to yield up some secret that will show
everybody at a stroke that he is really the maker of everything. Maybe
there is still a crack or two that men have not looked through to spy
him out, and if so, by all means, let them peer all they wish.

    Meanwhile, there is still the matter of men themselves. For the
issues of belief are, it appears at least, not strictly a matter of the
quantity of learning one has, nor the talent one possesses, not the
extent of one's acquaintance with historical things (even others'
thoughts), as much as it is the way in which one comports oneself.

Therefore, the theologian has to be concerned with "how," for it is in the "how" that one comes to the "what." And the Scripture is full of the "how" along with the "what." Seeking God with one's whole heart is no joke, especially if it might be the only way to find him. More pedantically it might be said that even gaining the confidence that the word "God" can be used for something besides a meaning, might be not just a matter of ontology or a clever move; it might be of a piece with the other Christian virtues and indeed so different that it might look like a major accomplishment if not a real miracle.

In fact much of the Christian's confidence that there is a God who cares and loves him comes, not from metaphysics, but from such odd things as the sense of guilt and the personal vicissitudes that guilt involves. And the concept of God, so rich and manysided, indeed does belong within something one might call a kind of Christian perspective or outlook. Maybe one can separate the concept of God out of its tangled place in this perspective in order to examine it alone, maybe to compare it with other concepts, and so on. But if one were going to say it were meaningful, one could only then be commenting upon what the word "God" did for people when they believed, prayed, worshipped, and perhaps tried to love Him with all their heart, soul, mind, and strength.

If one wanted to make it meaningful to others, one would have to undertake some of the labor involved in showing what it was that allowed it to work that way. It seems unlikely that that word "God" will ever work any other way, for that's the way it gets its meaning. If Kant or Plato, Huxley or your neighbor uses "God" to explain some physics, or fill a need for an idea, or just plainly in vain, it surely is the task of a theologian to show that this is not the Christian word "God." Certainly this is a task for a lifetime, if one chooses it! Isn't it a little too early, therefore, to give up on God?

VI

We began with the question whether much of this skeptical "meaning" theology is not finally the way it is because of a lack of religious stuff to deal with. More than this, we might conclude that the reasons for the meaninglessness of much of the metaphysical theology might indeed be better scruples, clearer logic, more science, and the like. That is certainly what is widely said, and it can be guardedly granted. But it only explains some things, superfluous at that, which some Christians have believed. There is, after all, the whole range of convictions that the Apostles' Creed and the pages of Paul and the Psalmist also state for us. We are fools if we think that those are only bad metaphysics (of which there is plenty elsewhere). Much even of that will perhaps spring to life for us if we recover much else that went with those views. Everyone seems to have forgotten, in the enthusiasm for finding the myths and superstitions, bad metaphysics and pre-scientific cosmology that were probably contemporaneous, the fear of the Lord, the contriteness of spirit, the broken hearts, the pathos and need that were also there.

The important point to remember is that these may well be the religious stuff by which meaning will be once more brought to old words. And if the whole age refuses to move at once, is it not enough to do it for oneself? Besides it will be altogether salutary to remember that words, even the biblical and the Christian's words, do many things besides "communicate." Once one trains oneself—and then perhaps teaches others—to be open to the multitude of purposes served by that language (some conveys, some commands, some pleases, some stirs emotion, some entices thoughts) then and only then will adequacy be done both to the religious life and, simultaneously, to theology itself.

REFERENCES

1. These passages are taken from the text as translated from the Swedish by Karl A. Olsson. Grand Rapids, Eerdmanns Publishing Co., 1963. Cf., pp. 45-46.

2. *The Bible in the Age of Science*. London, 1961, p. 149.

3. *Ibid.*, p. 135.